Earth's Song

Leonard Hall on Saline Creek.

Earth's Song

"What makes the crops rejoice,
beneath what star to plow,
of these I sing"

Leonard Hall

Foreword by Howard F. Baer

University of Missouri Press

Columbia & London, 1981

Copyright © 1981 by The Curators of the University of Missouri
University of Missouri Press, Columbia, Missouri 65211
Library of Congress Catalog Card Number 81–50529
Printed and bound in the United States of America

Library of Congress Cataloging in Publication Data

Hall, Leonard, 1899–
    Earth's Song.

    Includes index.
    1. Nature conservation. 2. Nature. I. Title.
QH75.H35   333.95   81–50529
ISBN 0–8262–0323–X   AACR2

The illustrations on the following pages are reproduced
through the courtesy of the following photographers:

Leonard Hall: ii, 2, 13, 19, 31, 43, 44, 54, 61, 62, 67, 73,
76, 83, 87, 91, 94, 97, 98, 103, 105, 122, 137, 143, 266
Don Wooldridge of the Missouri Conservation
Department: 7, 65, 188, 217, 246, 248, 253, 262, 265
Charles Schwartz: 115, 132, 138, 142, 157, 159, 160, 163,
164, 166, 169, 171, 172, 173, 178, 180, 190
Bill Palmer: 120, 134, 207, 236
Ed King: 84
Photo on p. 23 by Kosti Ruohomaa for *Life* magazine,
courtesy of Leonard Hall.

For Virginia, good companion on
this long and happy road—and with
a word of thanks to two physicians,
my father and grandfather, whose love
of the country inspired my own

Contents

Foreword

by Howard F. Baer

Both Leonard Hall and I are now what Somerset Maugham used to call "old parties." We have seen a myriad of seasons pass, and with them the rains and the snows, the uncounted—and too often unseen—flaming sunsets, the thunderous electrical displays, the spring crocus and the fall chrysanthemum, the thrusting asparagus spear, and the milky ear of corn, the strong *V* of the migrating Canada geese, the gentle quail, the silver splashing of Missouri smallmouth, and the swoop of the osprey who preys upon him.

And much more—so much more, indeed, that Len has spent a lifetime taking it all in, looking at it, immersing himself in it, loving it, and sharing it through his writing and lecturing.

He has seen far more than I, who did not early understand the complete interdependence of man and his environment. I am fortunate in that our paths, divergent as they were, have always come together, crossed and recrossed. Along with many thousands of others, I have received an added measure of fulfillment because of him.

Len began his true career when we were young men—he with a printing house that, through his efforts, manufactured the large surgical-instrument catalogs for the firm where I worked. But though he was good at his job, he knew then that he wanted and needed something more. He was determined to live his life on the land where he could experience a satisfaction that would come to him only from working his own soil. Len's affectionate curiosity has given him a superb life, lived lovingly with his companion, Ginnie.

How he and Ginnie did it, how he came to write about their experiences, how they traveled to tell about them—all this is contained in his nearly eight hundred columns and his four published books, written over a period of seventeen years. To read his thoughts on country living, wildlife, the Ozark forests, the pleasures of the garden, fly fishing, quail hunting, and to feel his affection for his friends and neighbors is to see that he is essentially a simple man. So were Sophocles, Thoreau, Lincoln, and Einstein in that they saw clearly how man ought to live in this marvelous world; how if he but would, man can realize himself and dwell in peace with his fellows in that vast complex we call nature.

My admiration for Len Hall began quite early. I had hitherto met no other contemporary who would resolutely turn away from the occupations of the marketplace to live in pursuit of a happiness that consisted largely of hard work. I don't know whether Len had read Thomas Carlyle, but he was in perfect tune with his opinion: "Blessed is he who has found his work; let him ask no other blessedness." He sensed both what his work would be and the satisfactions it would bring.

How he came to write so well is not hard to fathom. His family background provided a sound base. For three generations his direct ancestors (father, grandfather, great-grandfather) had been doctors, and throughout his reminiscences their influence appears with a pleasant nostalgia. His grandfather, Lem, rode on horseback to see his patients, and if the science he offered was by today's standards primitive, his concern for their welfare was great. For the benefit of the young in the family, the values of education were insisted upon.

Len's writing quickly acquired that quality of smooth clarity inherent in the best of bucolic writing. Thirty years ago, Harry Owens, in his introduction to Len's *Possum Trot Farm*, attributed his warm, easy style to his enthusiastic love of his subject and to his copious knowledge of it. I agree.

But there is also an angry facet to it, a note of alarm. For, as the years passed, he became a follower of Aldo Leopold, the conservationist, and he began to see and despair of what man was doing to the magnificent world he had inherited. As with poets and philosophers who see farther ahead and more clearly than economists, politicians, or "think-tank intellectuals," so too have those who identify with nature seen the dangers of neglecting its protection.

Leopold, Leonard Hall, and men like them, did not need the upheavals of the sixties and the concern with the pollution of

streams and air, the ravaging of soil and forest, and the extermination of wildlife to make them cry out at those destructions.
Len, like Leopold, had been quietly warning of the evils in
book, column, and lecture for thirty years. We cannot measure
the effectiveness of their voices, but certainly the messages were
received and widely understood.

What Leonard Hall has done with his life, and for his world,
our world, is no small thing. And the happiness that came to
him in the doing of it has spilled over in good measure to those
who have read him or heard his lectures. Here then in this volume is a rich selection from the last ten years of his writing—
witness of his work in full maturity.

Howard F. Baer
April 10, 1981

Prologue

We watched the last harvest moon climb up over our mountain and decided it was the biggest and brightest in memory. The smoky glow along the crest lingered for moments before the great orb became visible—and then the trees were silhouetted in sharp relief.

We are old-fashioned, I will confess. Yet we never watch a moonrise nowadays without hoping man will somehow learn that his true home is here on earth—and so will stop scattering his litter out in space before our moon has become as polluted as our earth.

Many autumn moons have climbed above that horizon since we came to live at Possum Trot forty years ago. Our objective then was a highly speculative one—to prove that man can live at peace with Nature through cooperation rather than exploitation and that this is a necessary prelude to living at peace with his fellowmen.

We have proved neither of these things except in our small corner of the universe. Yet the years have been good; rich in values that make life worthwhile. Values like the recurring swing of the seasons and a growing circle of good friends. Long ago we decided that—success or not—"country living was our business." Today we can hope that regardless of success, we have made some small contribution in a world that needs all the help it can get if it is to survive.

For twenty years farming occupied our days. We tended our cattle, built the fertility of our fields, harvested crops to feed our animals, planted our garden, and stored away its produce. There were four seasons, each as busy as the last. Then gradually the "fields" widened. More writing, more visitors, correspondence with farmers and wildlife folk in many lands. Cameras were added to farm tools, and we spent more time photographing, canoeing, camping, traveling. Soon we were showing our wildlife films to audiences from Maine to California and from British Columbia to the Caribbean.

This took us away from Possum Trot—but when has travel been dull or valueless? Moreover, we found ourselves serving on the boards of the National Parks Association, the Defenders of Wildlife, and the Humane Society of the United States. All work for the preservation of natural resources, scenic beauty, and the creatures that today are too often a vanishing part of our priceless heritage.

Working with these groups whose effort has been for the preservation of life has been a fine experience. And the work with others—Audubon, Wilderness Society, The Nature Conservancy, Sierra Club, often in coalition—must continue as a dominant force in America for preservation of the life environment.

What follows is largely a record of our small contribution toward these ends. Much material for the book had its origin in columns that appeared for thirty-six years in the *St. Louis Post-Dispatch* and *St. Louis Globe-Democrat*, here presented in different form; thus to them our thanks. So many individuals who made contributions are named in the text that these names need not be repeated.

Since her contributions are apparent on every page, I need hardly name my wife and comrade, Virginia.

Leonard Hall
Possum Trot Farm
March 1981

1

At Home in the Ozarks

Once we had a friend down in the Ozark country who would drive our car with the canoe and our gear out to the Current River at Owl's Bend when we were going float fishing. Then three days later he'd bring it down to Van Buren to pick us up for the drive home. This friend has long since gone to his reward—we hope to a heaven where the hounds run the fox on moonlit nights and a fellow can sit atop the mountain beside a small fire and listen to the music of the pack.

It was a good kind of hunting with no killing, and our friend had many a story we'll remember. Back in the thirties he moved to the city and got a job in the steel mill. It was good pay, especially for those times.

Our friend held out in the city for a year or two, then went back to his hills. To anyone who asked why, he would answer simply: "A man could live for years up in that city and never see a sunrise." Several times, on those drives to the river, he would ask when we intended to get out of the city, and finally on one drive he said: "Don't wait too long, Len. It's gettin' late." That was forty years ago, and we didn't wait too long, considering we've been more than thirty years at Possum Trot.

It has been our fortune, through the years, to have traveled well toward a million miles along America's highways. Nor would we have missed for a moment the side excursions into Canada, the Caribbean, and our sister nations to the South. Yet in the end we come back to our Ozarks.

This doesn't mean that when the icy winds blow one may not seek a warmer clime for a spell. It does not mean that on occasion we cannot seek new sights, sounds, or people. But we believe the truly happy individual comes back to the place where he has put down his roots, and that in this place his true destiny lies.

1

Not long ago in discussing the matter of retirement, a friend said to us: "If I could just have a bit of Missouri countryside of my own, to which I might retreat for a break in life's routine and a renewal of the spirit—nothing could make me consider ending my days in some distant and unknown Utopia." Having our "bit of Ozark countryside," we quite agree with him. We try to be, in fact, like Henry Thoreau's farmer friend Minott. "He does nothing with haste or drudgery," said Henry, "but as if he loved it. He makes the most of his labor, and takes infinite satisfaction in every part of it. He is not looking forward to the sale of his crops, or any pecuniary profit, but is paid by the constant satisfaction which his labor yields him. He has not too much land to trouble him,—too much work to do,—no hired man nor boy; but simply to amuse himself and live."

Thoreau complained more than a hundred years ago that most people are too easily transplanted, for they have too few roots—a fair analysis of our way of life today. Americans are a

"A bit of Ozark countryside."

people on the move. And in our rootlessness may lie one primary cause of the problems that beset us. Searching out your bit of land may be no easy task, yet it is a task in which will lie much pleasure.

Possum Trot in the Ozarks

This Ozark Highland is, as we have often stated, unique in many ways. The range runs more or less from east to west and, unlike much of the rest of America, is unglaciated. Although its highest peak, Taum Sauk, reaches an altitude of only 1,770 feet, it is the highest land feature between the Appalachians and the cordilleras of the west, which include the Rockies, Cascades, Sierras, and Pacific coastal ranges.

The word *cordillera*, which can be applied to any mountain range, is Spanish and translates into "a little string." This is an odd term to describe the western giants that stretch from Alaska almost to the tip of South America. The origin of *Ozark* is obscure, but we like best the speculation of Ward Dorrance, whose book *We're from Missouri* is a longtime favorite of ours.

Dorrance concluded from certain logical facts that in the early days of the St. Louis fur trade not all the trappers and woodsmen headed into the northwest. There were many fine spring-fed streams to the south in the territory known as the land of the Arkansas Indians. So when you found a French trapper heading out and asked his destination, he might well say "Aux Arkansas," or to the land of the Arkansas. This was abbreviated to "Aux Arks," which the English settlers soon changed to "Ozarks."

For any lover of blossoming trees and wildflowers, the Ozark Highland is a jewel. It presents to the plant explorer a wealth of flora almost unmatched within a thousand miles to east or west; a flora based on topography, drainage, climate, age, and location. Ozark rock formations date back a billion years to the Precambrian and to formations laid down during a dozen ocean inundations. Thus we find granite and porphyry, igneous rocks fired by the earth's internal heat; and with these the flints, sandstones, and limestones of the ancient seabeds.

The Ozark climate is kind to growing plants, for annual rainfall averages forty inches. The central location of the area has allowed plants to move in and establish themselves from north, south, east, and west. On the other hand, the extreme age of the area has encouraged development of many endemic species—plants that originated and have flourished within the area. At the same time, because of the wide variety of habitats within the highland, many areas have developed their own flora.

Missouri embraces several biotic regions: glaciated and unglaciated prairies, river-valley lowlands, sunny glades, and the Ozark Highland comprising about half of our seventy thousand square miles. This region is among the most ancient lands on the continent, with the St. Francois mountains being part of the original land axis of North America, having been above sea level for 250 to 500 million years. Alongside the billion-plus age of the St. Francois range, the Rockies and Appalachians are merely middle-aged, while the Sierras are still growing.

Thus it is little wonder that the Ozarks possess a highly diversified flora with the largest number of plant species in Missouri. Here limestones laid down on ancient ocean floors build soils that favor alkaline-loving plants. But here also are sandstones and igneous rocks such as granite that build soils best suited to acid-tolerant plants. Also throughout the Ozarks are rocky outcrops that may be either alkaline or acid. Here little soil is built so that we find few trees or shrubs, although each glade has its own specialized herbaceous plants.

Missouri's Big Springs

Few of Missouri's natural wonders have inspired more interest than her great springs. Most of these rise in the Ozark Highland south of the Missouri River; a majority in what we call the Salem Plateau and a smaller number in the Springfield Plateau. In addition to these are hundreds of small springs scattered across the state. For many years the standard work on the subject was *The Large Springs of Missouri*, published in 1944 and written by Henry Beckman and Norman Hinchey of the Missouri Geological Survey and Water Resources.

In 1974 an exciting new work was brought out as a cooperative effort of the Missouri Geological Survey, the Missouri Department of Conservation, and the U.S. Geological Survey, under the direction of State Geologist Dr. Wallace Howe. The book is titled simply *Springs of Missouri*. But it is rich in new material, with over a hundred illustrations, maps, and charts, many of these in color. The book contains three sections—the main body giving data on 585 primary springs, with smaller sections on fauna and flora. Geologist Jerry Vineyard, together with Gerald Feder of the U.S. Geological Survey, is primarily responsible for *Springs of Missouri*. William Pflieger, who is a fisheries biologist for the Conservation Department, and Robert Lipscomb, who is botanist for the U.S. Geological Survey, produced the sections on fauna and flora of the Missouri springs.

The Missouri Ozarks comprise one of the nation's greatest concentrations of springs, and these have played an important part in the settlement and development of the state. The size and beauty of the springs along Current River and Jacks Fork, and the desire to protect them from eventual commercialization, were the primary factors in the creation of America's first national river, the Ozark National Scenic Riverways. Some idea of the magnitude of these springs on the Riverways is gained by knowing that the seven largest produce an average daily flow in excess of 600 million gallons.

The fact that most of our big springs rise in pools or come gushing out from openings in wooded limestone bluffs adds much to their attraction. But in pioneer days it was utility that counted. Springs furnished water for livestock and household use. Many became sites for mills that ground cornmeal and flour for the community and often sawed lumber as well. Only a few of these are left today, like the mill at Alley Spring on Jacks Fork in the Ozark Riverways and Hodgson's Mill at Sycamore on Bryant Creek, which still advertises "Stone Buhr Ground Cornmeal since 1885."

Mineral springs were found in Saline and Howard counties along the Missouri River and in Perry County in the Bootheel. These provided pioneer settlements with salt, as they had for the Indians since time immemorial. Several were developed during the late 1800s as health spas advertising their beneficial medicinal qualities. Also on the Salem Plateau were no less than twenty-four ebb-and-flow springs with periodic discharge, a phenomenon that is still not fully understood.

Julian Steyermark was one of the first to explore the rare plant species of the spring areas. Best known is the water cress (*Nasturtium officinale*), although others like water milfoil (*Myriophyllum heterophyllum*), water starwort (*Callitriche heterophylla*), liverleaf (*Hepatica nobilis*), and some mosses are common. As for fauna, we would include many species of amphibians, blind crayfish in cave springs, salamanders, and several species of fish.

Too much credit cannot be given the St. Louis Underwater Recovery Team for its underwater work in exploring the depths of the springs and supplying valuable knowledge as to water sources and structure of the orifices. Their data make one of the most interesting features of *Springs of Missouri*.

Prairies

We talk of our rugged, wooded Ozark Mountains, yet in odd corners here and there we can find preserved small bits of prairie. Thus we have always kept an interest in the giant grass called big bluestem or bluejoint turkeyfoot (*Andropogon Gerardi*) that once grew here. This is the grass our pioneer forefathers talked of as growing "higher than the shoulder of a horse."

Today there are a few sizable remnants of tallgrass prairie in Kansas and Oklahoma, with smaller bits in Illinois and Missouri. Even here in the heart of the St. Francois range of the Ozarks, we find big bluestem and many of the prairie flowers growing on limestone glades, in natural forest openings, and along back-country roads.

Possum Trot is actually located in an upland valley, surrounded by forested hills and watered by small spring-fed creeks that are also bordered by timber. When the first white settlers came here in the late 1700s, much of the valley itself was not timbered. It was, instead, a tallgrass prairie of perhaps two hundred thousand acres, where buffalo came to graze every four or five years and where deer and elk were resident. The prairie in that time was crossed by war trails of the Osage and Shawnee Indians.

A visiting Frenchman, writing in 1750, noted the scarcity of forest. This was due, he believed, to prairie fires set each autumn by Indians when the grass was dry, thus destroying the young trees. Even today the forest hugs the creek banks and

Falls of Rocky Creek, in the Ozarks where the granite and rhyolite-porphyry crests of the mountains date from the Precambrian.

climbs the granite mountains. In our valley itself are tame grasses and a variety of limestone-loving legumes that feed beef cattle.

Our land lies on a deep bed of one of the oldest limestones, with soils that produce an especially rich variety of plant life. Yet when Saline Creek crosses our northern boundary, it plunges at once into a granite "shut-in." Here there is a distinct change in the flora, and while some of the limestone-loving plants can be found downstream in the granitic soils, few of the acid-soil natives can be found upstream on the limestone. As for blossoming species, we are far from having cataloged all of them but have managed to list more than two hundred that bloom between early spring and frost.

On certain ridges, however, we find rocky glades and barrens where the prairie flora persists. Some of these openings are of chert and flint, some of granite, and some of limestone. Plant life varies, depending on the soil. Yet the grasses are big and little bluestem (*Andropogon scoparius*), Indian grass (*Sorghastrum nutans*), and other prairie species. Tree growth on the glades consists largely of gnarled cedar, chestnut oak, winged elm, ninebark, dogwood, and wild plum. During the flowering season we find Missouri primrose (*Oenothera missouriensis*), Indian paint brush (*Castilleja coccinea*), yellow star grass (*Hypoxis hirsuta*), shooting stars (*Dodecatheon meadia*), and many varieties of coneflowers, silphiums, sunflowers, and goldenrods. Throughout the area that once supported the tallgrass or big bluestem, there are people who are interested in its preservation. They are conscious of both its rarity and its beauty. They believe, as did the great ecologist Aldo Leopold, that while wilderness may have been the adversary of the pioneer, it is today a thing that must be cherished for the meaning and definition it gives our lives.

Buford Mountain

Our mountain is an important part of the life of Possum Trot Farm, forming as it does the eastern boundary of our world. Each morning throughout the year we watch the sun rise over its crest, moving southward in autumn and into cold weather until the winter solstice, then starting its slow northward journey again. Twelve times each year for more than a quarter-century we have watched the full moon top the mountain to travel westward across the starlit sky.

The dominant mantle of oak timber on the mountain doesn't color up as brilliantly in October as do the sugar maples, sassafras, and sour gums in our valley. Yet when the oaks turn, the color lasts longer, for the leaves cling until after Christmas. On certain days in winter, white frost covers the timber along the ridge tops, and there are rainy mornings when the crest disappears entirely behind its bank of clouds. In spring the color comes a bit later than in the valley, yet we can see here and there the white of the shadbush, or *Amelancier arborea*, which Ozark folk call "sarvis berry."

There are, actually, five gently sloping crests along the four miles of our mountain. The tallest reaches 1,742 feet, which is the second highest elevation in the Missouri Ozarks. Here and there along the flanks are granite outcrops called glades or "balds."

Long ago on the northernmost slope of this mountain, some hardworking pioneer cleared a small farm with a dug well, a cabin, and fields fenced by stone walls. Although it has been deserted for more than a half-century, we can still find a trace of the old wagon road that led upward along a rocky ravine, where water runs in a series of small waterfalls during heavy rains.

Today the road has gone back to wilderness, but when we came to Possum Trot, we used to ride horseback up to the "Old Bode Place." Now it is a good stiff hike, even when we start from the Turner farm, which lies close against the mountain. But the hike is worthwhile, for here we find not only the wildflowers that flourish on our limestone soils, but also others like the little sundrops of the evening primrose family *(Oenothera linifolia)*, the tiny rock pink related to spring beauty *(Talinum calycinum)*, and the blue curls that are a small mint sometimes called bastard or false pennyroyal *(Isanthus brachiatus)*.

Our mountain is unique in many ways. Never a producer of big timber because of granitic soils, it was nevertheless logged heavily in the past. Open-range cattle still grazed the rocky slopes when we came here. Today several species of oak produce browse and acorns for deer, turkeys, raccoons, and fox squirrels. Wild plum, sassafras, huckleberry, persimmon, several dogwoods, and the viburnums all serve as food for wildlife. Bird species abound, and we often find flocks of hundreds of robins wintering on the mountain.

Perhaps most unusual is that, to this day, no usable roads penetrate the area except for old, forgotten logging trials, nor does any power line cut through its wilderness. Thus it may well be the largest wild land area left in private hands in the state. The Nature Conservancy, a nationally known conservation organization devoted to the preservation of unspoiled wild areas, has acquired twenty-two hundred acres and is working to secure more. When asked for its reasons, the Nature Conservancy need only quote Aldo Leopold: "When we see land as a community to which we belong, we may begin to use it with love and respect. There is no other way for land to survive the impact of mechanized man, nor for us to reap from it the esthetic harvest it is capable, under science, of contributing to culture." The land secured to date has been taken over by the Missouri Conservation Department for preservation as a recreation area.

Genealogy

Often we are asked how we happened to settle in Bellevue Valley, and somehow, to find an answer, we always end up by starting down on the Maryland East Shore with William H. Hall, who was born there in 1736. His son Lemuel A. Hall, born in 1776, was also a Marylander. But when James H. Hall came along in 1808, he eventually decided to migrate westward.

James arrived in Missouri in 1838 by way of Virginia and Tennessee and settled in St. Louis with his wife, Sarah. Here, like his father and grandfather, he practiced medicine; and, as his family increased, he found more living space in suburban Chesterfield and then Manchester. At least eleven offspring of this union survived to adulthood, and we recall a reunion when nine were present—the youngest being sixty-five.

Madame Defoe, whose restaurant near Manchester was famous, once recalled a day when she was four years old and the Hall boys came home from the Civil War. They disembarked from a horse-drawn hack near the Defoe farm and were, she said, worn and ragged—doubtless because they had fought on the Confederate side. She was a staunch Union supporter and a power in the local Republican party.

Most of the Halls in this family moved west to California, but three remained to study medicine and practice in Missouri. Most unusual was that all three chose the Ozarks, so that Doctors Lem and Jimmy landed in Potosi, while Doctor Will hung out his shingle in the nearby town of Belleview. The little house where Doctor Will lived had bedroom recesses in the walls with curtains separating them from the main room so the youngsters could retire while their elders talked by the fireplace. When the house was demolished in 1973, we salvaged some eighteen-foot two-by-eight pine timbers that made joists for the new horse barn we built after our fire.

Doctor Jimmy's house was one of the oldest in Potosi, Missouri's second-oldest town, and was built of logs that are still sound. He smoked a small briar pipe that he lighted with tightly rolled paper "spills" that were kept stuck in the mantel. It was an honor to help roll the spills when we went for dinner and were vastly overfed by Aunt Mame, his wife.

Doctor Lem, our grandfather, married in Mobile in 1865, his wife being Anne Bagby, daughter of Arthur Bagby, the Confederate governor of Alabama. Sadly, as so often happened, her life was short. Although her two sons Lemuel and Frederick lived, she died in 1873 and the grandmother we remember was Doctor Lem's second wife, Margaret Bell McGready of an old Potosi family.

Doctor Lem was a true horseback doctor who mixed his own prescriptions from small glass vials containing the pharmaceuticals of that day. His pocketknife sufficed for a spatula, and the powders were neatly wrapped in small squares of white paper. But though he put in long hours for his patients, his first love was his small farm on the edge of town. Today the highway bisects it and most of it is the town park.

Doctor Lem's son—and our father—was Frederick Hall—and the fifth generation to follow the medical profession. He practiced in St. Louis and, with our mother, Corinne, raised a family of eight youngsters there. But he also loved the country, a weakness that at least one son inherited. Thus this one spent much time with his grandparents and, when quite small, rode behind Doc Lem on his mare Sally on his rounds of his patients or out to the farm. The boy came to know the hills and woods and traveled as far south as Caledonia. Here he came to appreciate the beauty of the valley known as Bellevue. Thus it is small wonder that this was the area Virginia and I searched when we came to choose our home.

Because it was our good fortune to spend half our childhood in the country and half in the city, the memories of sights and sounds and smells are doubled. What youngster today has ever heard, for example, the "clang, clang, clang" of an old-fashioned trolley car—unless he happens to have visited San Francisco and has ridden up the steep hills. Or can remember the clashing sparks that flew when the trolley jumped off its overhead wire when going round a curve, or when some mischievous youngster managed to pull it off when the car stopped at a crowded corner.

Horses provided most of the power in those days, even in the city, and each vehicle had its characteristic rhythms. There was the ragman, an immigrant not long from Lebanon or the ghettos of middle Europe. He drove the alleys, and his voice was not musical as he solicited old rags and iron. His horse was thin and his wagon was rickety and, for some unknown reason, he was fair game for teasing by all the boys who lived in the block. Vegetable hucksters had neater wagons and fatter steeds and more melodious voices. They picked up their wares long before daylight, down at markets on the Mississippi levee. Most of them were Italian and, in memory, they always offered "Nize frash STRAW-be-r-r-EES."

The milkman was unknown to us, for his horse went "clop, clop, clop" down the street in earliest dawn. But the iceman was husky and Irish, with two horses to his wagon and a pair of bright iron tongs with which he swung the big ice cakes to his padded shoulder. He had a way with every cook along his route and was often good-natured enough to furnish ice chips to the queue of kids who hopefully followed his wagon down the street. And what youngster will ever know again the cheerful whistle of the little gas flame in the popcorn wagon, or the melodious cry of the "hot tamale man."

Country sights, sounds, and smells come back to us even oftener than those of the city because there are many things to remind us of them. When you sit beside the fireplace, for example, you don't notice the smell of wood smoke. But bank the fire, head for bed, and open the window a crack on even the coldest night, and when you wake in the small hours the smell of the good oak comes drifting in to awaken memories.

I recall a day, a winter or two ago, when we were cutting brush and had a huge fire going, down by the Big Pond. Suddenly, there was a sharp booming as Jack Frost shifted his weight and a crack ran clear across the thick ice that covered the pond. Then for a moment I was back playing crack-the-whip on Sylvan Lake, or maybe it was the Lagoon at Forest Park, and heading for the log fire where a hundred kids were warming their frozen toes. And there was the same sharp boom of the ice as a crack ran across it, and the same good smell of wood smoke.

As for Virginia, she spent some of those same years on a seven-acre country place on the city's edge, adjoining Carondolet Park in what was then entirely a market-gardening and farming community. Although she finished high school in the city, went on to Northwestern, and from there to a distinguished career in the theater in New York, the country had marked her for one of its own. It was "home that our feet may leave, but not our hearts."

Nothing awakens nostalgia like an old photograph album. The one at hand dates from 1906 and its pictures match the al-

Virginia and Leonard Hall.

bum title. They are snapshots made with early Brownies or with a big wooden box camera draped with a black cloth. This belonged to our father who, as St. Louis's earliest roentgenologist, was a good photographer as well as a good physician.

There are pictures of the Hall family when it contained only a handful of children instead of the eventual eight. One shows a mixed group of four sitting in a pool in Breton Creek, completely innocent of any sign of a swimsuit. This was, in fact, our regular Saturday bathtub on Grandpa Hall's farm. After noonday dinner he'd hitch old Sally to the surrey, pile in the kids and a supply of homemade soap and a scrub brush, and away we'd go. Bath over, we'd head for home again, stopping at the orchard for a basket of peaches or apples.

Next photograph recalls that at this point I'd leave the surrey to drive the Jersey milk cows to the milking barn in town. Traffic on the mile of road consisted of an occasional farm wagon, and the summer dust lay deep and warm so that, if a fellow was expert, he could squirt small dust fountains up between his bare toes.

This picture shows a milk cow with her calf, this family being my special charge that summer. She was the cow that got into her feed barrel of bran one night and nearly finished off both it and herself. When I went out to milk next morning, I found her stretched on the ground by the milking shed, blown up like a balloon. I lit out for Grandpa Hall's house, a half-mile down the road, and made it in four minutes flat. Doc Lem had already saddled old Sally for his day's round of calls. He grabbed his surgical kit, mounted, I scrambled up behind, and we tore up the road at a gallop. There is a point in the triangle between a cow's hipbone and ribs that centers on one of the stomachs. A quick incision here with a thin-bladed knife soon relieved the pressure and old Bossy's life was saved.

Next picture shows a typical holiday feast at our home in Potosi. The year was 1907 or thereabouts. Along one side of the table are Grandpa Hall, then Ralph, our oldest, and so on down the line to Mother at the far end of the groaning board. The turkey was no pale, all-breast creature raised on wire, but a big, flavorful, deep-bronzed gobbler that had grown fat on grasshoppers and other natural provender. At the table's other end was the traditional tureen of oyster stew, and between these two, bowls of fresh fruit and raisins and nuts—real treats in those days.

Then comes a picture of Grandpa Hall dressed in his Sunday best and mounted on old Sally, evidently on his way to make a call on a patient before church. Until his last year he spent hours each day in the saddle and sat his horse like the Civil War cavalryman he had been.

Thinking back on that long, full, and useful life, I recalled a talk given by the president of the American Academy of Family Physicians to the medical students at St. Louis and Washington universities. He urged the importance of family practice and stated that the shortage in medical manpower was not in the specialties or in the big hospital staffs, but in primary preventive medical care. This is the family doctor's province, and certainly life in a small community has compensations not known yesterday and not offered by city living. This is especially true since so many small communities today have adequate hospital facilities. I'm sure Doc Lem wouldn't have traded Massachusetts General or the great Barnes group in St. Louis for his life or his occasional leisure to enjoy his grandchildren and his farm.

Those were simple times, and it seems to me that their essence was individual self-sufficiency. Our grandfather is an example of the era. He practiced medicine on horseback over a wide rural territory for fifty years. Otherwise, like his neighbors, he lived a remarkably uncomplicated life.

Although Doc Lem's home was in the center of town, he maintained his farm on the outskirts just a half-mile away. Here in addition to field crops was an orchard and a herd of Jersey cows that were driven to town each evening to be milked, and back to pasture next morning. The home place embraced five acres, enough to pasture Doc Lem's saddle mares and make room for chicken house, smokehouse, vegetable garden, and small vineyard. These, with the products of the orchard, filled the cool brick-floored cellar with a great store of food. Whole-wheat flour and cornmeal were ground from our own grain at the local mill.

Two cisterns supplied water, and the original plumbing was outdoors. The house did boast the first running water in town, which each day had to be hoisted to a zinc-lined oak tank in the attic with a hand pump. Fresh garbage, along with grain, went to pigs that furnished much of the winter's meat, since lack of refrigeration made beef only an occasional treat. Trash was at a minimum since there were few tin cans and the mason jars were used year after year. Moreover, packaging was unknown and the newspaper came once a week. Eggs, milk, cream, and home-churned butter were taken for granted.

In our town, everyone was almost equally self-sufficient. We knew every neighbor as well as the farmers out in the countryside. We walked to the post office, church, and school, and to our social events. Homes were heated with fuel from our own woodlots or the nearby forest. Neither heat nor lighting nor water depended on a distant power plant or a fuse box in the basement. Problems were worked out family by family; public and outside services were few; and in that life we found a maximum of simple comfort and security.

Back in those boyhood times, all of my holidays were spent down at Grandpa Hall's house in the Ozarks. There in winter the day's menus were ample but somewhat limited in scope. Thus breakfast was home-cured bacon, fried apples, and buttermilk biscuits so light you didn't dare let go of them for fear they'd float up to the ceiling.

Dinner at noon would be vegetable soup, a slice of ham, grits with redeye gravy, cornbread, and sweet-potato pie for dessert. Supper was cinnamon toast made from leftover breakfast biscuits, plenty of milk, and any odds and ends left over from noontime. Our Great-aunt Lucy, who managed the household, favored a dish of clabber for supper with cream and sugar.

Now and then, when this sort of nostalgia overtakes us and we get to thinking of boyhood days, we whip up a batch of corn muffins to go with country sausage and sorghum for supper. The recipe isn't complicated, and my good spouse can turn it out better than I can, but it is a matter of ritual. And sometimes the ritual can bring on other memories—this time of a Saturday morning in the early 1940s. The place was the courthouse square in an Ozark county near the head of Current River. Our car carried the canoe on top and was stuffed full of camp gear, for we were on our way to the first Current River float of the season. We had stopped at the courthouse to pick up our fishing licenses for the year.

Always on Saturday in those towns, folks came from the

country to visit and do their week's shopping. A coop of hens or load of stove wood might be swapped for staple groceries or yard goods or a new chopping ax. After the trading was finished, everybody lingered awhile in the courthouse square to gossip and gather the latest news. Our courthouse business was soon done, but as we came out, we couldn't help overhearing part of a conversation between two elderly farmwives dressed in gingham and old-fashioned sunbonnets.

The burden of the conversation seemed to center on the culinary arts and, as we went by, one of the women was just finishing up on a new cornbread recipe. Her closing remark described the dish so wonderfully that we've remembered it to this day, "Now—hit'll be coarse," she said, "and hit'll be gritty. But hit'll be good."

That's the way it is with cornbread when it's made just right. Some folks nowadays prefer it not quite so "coarse and gritty" and get around this by using fine-ground meal and some white flour in the mixture, but always use yellow meal if you can get it. Our muffin recipe goes like this:

1 cup yellow cornmeal, ½ teaspoon salt, ½ cup white flour, ¼ cup sugar. Mix 2 eggs, well beaten, with 1 cup milk, 4 tablespoons melted butter, 4 level teaspoons baking powder, and add to cornmeal mix. Put dab of butter in each muffin tin, preheat oven to 425°, and bake until brown.

Johnnycake is another old-time favorite, generally made without white flour and cooked atop the stove on a skillet:

1 cup yellow cornmeal, ½ teaspoon salt, 1 tablespoon butter. Mix well and add 1 cup boiling water. Add ½ cup milk, 2 tablespoons sausage fat, and stir well. Drop onto hot skillet with hot fat. When cakes are bubbling, place skillet in 475-degree oven until brown. Serve with sorghum, honey, maple syrup, or good molasses.

Thus ends the cooking lesson.

*   *   *   *

Have you ever stopped to think that while we may live for today and plan for tomorrow, we can never actually go back to yesterday? All we can do is remember the old days and try to retain values that we still know to be worthwhile. This thought came to us recently when we left Possum Trot at seven one morning to drive to the city. Already at this hour, every few hundred yards along the highway, we would see small groups of youngsters with their books and lunch boxes, waiting for the school bus.

We came to the French village of Old Mines where the parochial school stands next to the historic Catholic church, but where also there is a large elementary public school a few miles north up the highway. The large consolidated public high school, however, is in Potosi, a dozen miles to the south. At this point we were meeting an endless line of buses, hurrying and scurrying in every direction. We felt that these young people, starting out at seven o'clock, were putting in a long day.

All this is quite different from when we came to Possum Trot and is even further removed from our own school days, back before the First World War. When we came here in the mid-1940s, neighborhood youngsters hiked to the little Elm Grove School, a mile down the back road that was once the main Potosi to Ironton highway. Elm Grove School had one room, one teacher, a potbellied stove for heating, a water well and long-handled pump outside the door, and primitive sanitary facilities at the edge of the wild land behind the building. We can never go back to the one-room school, though it often did a remarkable job. And we miss the pie suppers and spelling bees that made the school an intimate part of community social life.

Likewise, the farm life was quite different from the subsistence farming practiced in the Ozarks during our boyhood, and almost equally different from what it is today. Before World War I, the tractor was unknown and horse and mule were the primary power source. Farm tools were still quite primitive. The binder cut the wheat and tied the bundles, but wheat was shocked by hand and hauled on wagons to the steam-powered threshing machines. Small fields were still harvested with scythe and cradle. Diversification was the order of the day.

Much of this had changed by the 1940s. Horses were on the decline and tractors were recognized as the source of farm power. New tools were designed for this power machinery. Yet there were still elements of the subsistence farm. At Possum Trot we kept a dozen hens to supply eggs and bought broilers from the neighbors. A good Guernsey cow, which I milked, pro-

Before World War I, farmers banded together to get big jobs done. This particular sorghum mill stayed in operation even after World War II.

vided milk and cream. Two porkers were fattened, and at hog butchering time in December the neighbors rallied round to help. Everybody banded together for the threshing, moving from farm to farm. And we gathered once a week at the Methodist Church for a Ladies' Day luncheon.

Today in our Ozark hills, time has moved on. Most young farmers have increased their acreage so that mechanization proceeds swiftly. There are few small poultry flocks, and butchering and meat curing are done at the local locker plant. Fewer jobs require a banding together of neighbors, although help is there when you need it. Here at Possum Trot we do try to retain some of the good things from the old days. Yet even we confess that time moves on; that we can plan for tomorrow but can never go back to yesterday. That is, except in memory.

Potosi

The Potosi where we spent so much time during our boyhood has changed considerably. It has expanded to meet the highway originally constructed to bypass the town. But the main street downtown is still narrow and often crowded. And since the highway, which now skirts the eastern boundary of the town, proceeds south, it parallels the headwaters of historic Breton Creek, which seems to have shrunk strangely from the boyhood stream we remember.

Breton Creek still runs down along Bearfoot Street through the thriving town, as it has since the first settler built his cabin there in 1775. The settlement that grew up was called Mine à Breton and got its name in an interesting way. A French cannoneer from Napoleon's army named Francois Azor and nicknamed "Breton" after his birthplace came to America after surviving the Napoleonic Wars. At some point he arrived at Kaskaskia in Illinois, but being an adventurous fellow, he crossed the Mississippi River to hunt in the mountainous country to the west.

It was here, so the story goes, that while tracking a bear down a small creek, Francois stumbled upon a rich lead-ore pocket. Other settlers soon came to exploit the new lead mines, and the village that grew along the creek became known as Mine à Breton, after its discoverer. Years later, Moses Austin came here to open his own mines after receiving a land grant from the Spanish official who still governed the area. Austin was successful in his operations and built his home, Durham Hall, on the banks of Breton Creek.

The name of the settlement was, in due course, changed from Mine à Breton to Potosi after the mining towns in Mexico and Central America. Certainly Potosi was one of the oldest and most important towns in Upper Louisiana. Austin employed a work force of fifty men, built a sawmill and gristmill in addition to his smelting furnace, and became the leading citizen of the area. His son Stephen founded Austin, Texas, while Moses himself lies buried in the old Presbyterian cemetery in Potosi, which had also been an Indian burying ground.

Breton Creek had its primary source in a big spring that rose in the midst of a meadow on Grandpa Hall's farm, out east of

Potosi. What its flow might have been, I could not say. But it was surrounded by an acre of spring-water marsh where water cress grew prolifically and a log bridge led to the spring. Our swimming hole in the creek nearby must have been about the size of four bathtubs, but it was clear and cold and shaded by giant sycamore trees, sufficient for ten-year-olds. When it reached the town, the stream eventually became thoroughly polluted, since sewage treatment was unknown. Yet I recall one family before that time who built a small dam with enough fall to operate a ram that pushed water up to their house. Farther down the stream had been diverted into a millrace, but this had ceased operating before my day.

We have noticed lately that Potosi, to her credit, is cleaning up her Breton Creek where it traverses the town, a sure sign of preservationists at work.

There can be no doubt that long days spent by a youngster along this little stream, and long hours riding country roads behind Doc Lem, had much to do with the point at which we have arrived today. First a hunter, as all youngsters are hunters by nature. Then a conservationist, thoroughly believing in the exaggerated idea that the big task was to supply plenty of game for the bag. Then what hunters often sneeringly call a preservationist, with less interest in the kill but a greater interest in beavers and bumblebees, deer and dragonflies, and blue whales as well as black bass.

Friends

Our love affair with the Ozarks and the tales we've written about our hills have brought a host of friends through the years, including farmers and photographers, authors and artists, naturalists, foresters, and scientists in many fields. Some have been like ships passing in the night, seen once for a few hours. Others have become fast friends; some seen often, others at rare intervals.

In the spring of 1946 a telegram came from *Life* magazine, asking if they could send a photographer to our first Possum Trot to get some pictures of "the plain folks and familiar things we wrote about." Who could say no to such a request, and in a few days arrived Kosti Ruohomaa, *Life* photographer, with an array of cameras and film.

Kosti had started life on a dairy farm in Maine and so fitted himself easily into our country routine, asking only that his coffee cup never be empty. Then for a full week across the Ozarks his camera never stopped, and even today an hour with that 1946 issue of *Life* brings pleasant memories. On the cover is old Tom Moss, our friend and guide on the Current River. Inside we meet our former neighbor and great friend Gerti Ploesser leading her old mule up from her vegetable garden. Smiling storekeeper George Wallace of Old Mines, long gone to his reward, recalls the time he rescued us from a flooded Ozark creek.

A few years went by and we had moved to Possum Trot in Bellevue Valley when our next communication from *Life* arrived, asking if spring had come to the Ozarks and could we find wildflowers for Andreas Feininger to capture on color film. We could and he came—and a friendship has formed, as warm today as twenty years ago. "Ozark Spring" ran to eight full-color pages, and with Andreas we did one more *Life* story, this time on Current River as one of America's famous fishing streams. Andreas was born in Paris, son of noted watercolorist, Lyonel Feininger. He studied architecture under Walter Gropius at the Bauhaus in Weimar and under Le Corbusier in Paris, then turned to photography and came to America. Here he joined the *Life* staff, where he spent twenty years or more. He also produced magnificent books: *Trees, Shells, The Mountains of the Mind,* and a half-dozen more.

The next telegram from *Life* was typical. "We are doing a story on the American family," it said, "including worker, executive, city dweller, countryman. Can you find for us where this all began?" Our answer was a short "Yes," and soon arrived Nina Leen, a young woman of European ancestry who had made her start photographing animals.

We had found the family she needed, our good farm neighbors the Hubert Russells, with grandmother, dad and mother, eight youngsters, and a grandchild. Here were four generations living in our valley, preceded by others who had arrived here in 1810 or thereabouts. (In fact, an early deed to our own farm shows it was part of the original Russell survey, made not long

Ozarkians Tom Moss and his son Ira have manned our johnboats during trips on the Current for many years.

after the Louisiana Purchase in 1804.) The Russells enjoyed working with Nina and she with them. A final shot included all the family posed beneath an ancient daguerreotype of the great-grandparents. We've never seen Nina again. Two years later when in New York for an Audubon lecture, however, we visited the Modern Museum. There in the lobby hung a giant photo-mural of our friends and neighbors the Russells, featured in an exhibit from Edward Steichen's just-published *Family of Man*.

Our own arrival in Bellevue valley wasn't quite as early as that of the Russells, but it was the Russells who helped put our first hay crop under roof in 1946, saving it from a gully washer.

There were opportunities through the years to pay back the help we had received, not only from the Russells but also from other neighbors. Ted Douglas, the McClarys, Joe Ricketts, Otho Sutton, Bryan Moore, Jay McColl—the list is long and we were glad to do part of our share, which included the wheat harvest and threshing, days for vaccinating the calves, hog butchering in November, teaming up to get a crop in; we have enjoyed it all.

Not long after the story on the American family in *Life*, we got a call from Frank Mayfield, then head of a leading depart-ment store in St. Louis. They were, he said, bringing fourteen talented artists out to paint "Missouri, Heart of the Nation." The names read like a *Who's Who in American Art* and included Wally Smith and Fred Conway of St. Louis. Among others were Peter Hurd and Aaron Bohrod.

They had chosen for our Ozarks a young fellow named How-ard Baer, who had marched with our troops across India-Burma-China to record in paintings the work of our medical corps. Would I, asked Mayfield, be Baer's guide to the Ozark country? So we traveled with Howard, a delightful companion, while he sketched and painted the livestock auction at Potosi, a country sawmill, Uncle Paul and Aunt Luce in their little cabin at Old Mines, gigging fish at night on Current River, the pros-perous farm of our neighbors, the McColls.

While many old friends who have shared our Ozark experi-ences are no longer here to enjoy them with us, we still have opportunity to see our biologist friends in Jefferson City. Charles and Libby Schwartz have a home just beyond the city, not far from the Department of Conservation headquarters where they are both employed. Two busier people we've never known, although it is a quieter household now than when their three youngsters were at home. Still, four retrievers of various ages and colors do provide company, as does the flock of wild geese that lives on the pond some two hundred yards from the picture windows.

The Schwartz home stands on a rise sloping down to a large pond. This side of the house is entirely of glass, ideal for observing the resident waterfowl. Best description is that it is one large workshop. The living room with its fireplace is filled with books and magazines relating to natural history. Paintings done by Charles and his daughter Barbara cover the walls, while every corner is crowded with cameras and recording equipment. Open any closet and out will fall photography blinds, sleeping bags, guns, and other gear.

Charlie's studio occupies the next room, where a dozen projects are under way. In a small cage a woodcock is recovering from a broken wing. Paintings and drawings are in process everywhere. From the terrace, you can see the geese on the pond: Canadas, blues, and snows.

Some years ago, Charlie and Libby spent part of a summer in Canada's Northwest Territories on Hudson Bay, up near the Arctic Circle. Their purpose was to study and photograph the great nesting flocks of geese that use the Mississippi flyway and fill our wildlife refuges each year. Here are the same Canadas, snows, and blues that we know.

The Schwartzes were making ready to fly home at the same time that the geese were heading south, when they discovered a nest or two in which single goslings not ready to fly had been left behind. So Charlie and Lib, knowing these youngsters would die, rescued two and fed and kept them in their sleeping bags through the long trip home by plane.

Back at the Schwartz pond, the goslings grew to adulthood. One was a snow goose and, never having seen any but dark-colored geese, he decided he was a Canada and eventually mated with a dark hen and raised a family of hybrids. The other baby, a Canada gosling, became Charlie's constant companion. By the strange process of imprinting, he decided Charlie was his family and paid little attention to the rest of the flock.

As we sat on the terrace one day, Charlie started making

goose talk. All the geese answered, but soon we saw one move out from the flock and start up the hill toward us. The nearer he came, the more excited he was to see his friend. Charlie crooked his arm and hand to make a goose head and continued talking. The rest of the flock moved toward us, grazing as they came. Finally the imprinted Canada stretched out his wings, gave a few loud honks, and came on the run. His idea of affection was to grab Charlie's hand in his powerful bill, a process that left serious bruises. Finally he became a bit jealous of my sitting next to his friend and took a couple of nips. It made me think again about the little Mexican burro that Ginnie wanted to bring to Possum Trot on our last trip—and whether it would have decided to become a member of the family and have moved into the house.

As we travel around the state, there are many places that bring memories of old friends, places that probably wouldn't be in the condition they are today if it hadn't been for those friends. Carman Spring Wildlife Refuge near Willow Springs in the Mark Twain National Forest is one of those places and may well be one of the best examples of ecological land management in our state. It has been closed against livestock grazing since its establishment in the 1930s. The heavy undergrowth and ground cover create a microclimate that has discouraged forest fires. Timber harvest has been selective, while improvement of the stand by deadening the old cull timber and letting it return to the soil has resulted in a constant enrichment of the land.

Here our friend Leon Hornkohl showed us an interesting fact. Almost anywhere in this forest you can dig down into the humus-rich soil with your bare hands to a six-inch depth. Here in the deep litter you realize the tremendous life processes that are taking place, in comparison with the average Missouri forest soil.

At once apparent are the underground tunnels of moles, mice, and the fierce little shrews that feed on them. But moles and mice have their food supply in earthworms and grubs and tender plant roots. And always at work are the decomposers; the mycelium and other fungi that break down the forest litter into usable organic matter. In this humus are dead leaves and twigs, droppings of deer and wild turkeys, and hundreds of other substances.

Wildlife is everywhere evident in this forest. Favorite food plants and shrubs are browsed by the deer. Bare places show where wild turkeys have scratched. Cuttings under every oak and hickory give ample evidence of the squirrel population. In the creeks are tadpoles, crayfish, grass pike, bluegills, and bass.

As we stopped at the Willow Springs Ranger Station one day in 1974 we learned that refuge manager and our good and long-time friend Herb Davis had succumbed to a heart attack a few days before our visit. As we ate our lunch near the old CCC camp, a pickup truck came down the dirt road. Its occupants turned out to be Herb's son, whom we hadn't seen for nearly twenty years, and Mr. Woodring, who had been refuge manager before he retired and Herb came over from the Peck Ranch Wildlife Area.

Later, as we started home, we stopped to visit Dorothy Davis and couldn't help reminiscing about old times when Ginnie and I used to stop by Peck Ranch headquarters to visit as we drove down Mill Creek to camp by the big spring on our Possum Holler property. The Davis sons were youngsters then, and Herb used to run his road grader down past the Peck Ranch gate so we could use our woods road.

In those days Herb Davis, a top woodsman and game manager, was building the state's deer herd and wild turkey flock that were the main reasons for purchase of the area by our Conservation Department. Naturally some animals spilled over onto our land. Thus when we pitched our tent there, we were apt to be awakened at dawn by the talking of the big gobblers. And often at night we'd go to sleep to the music of the "song dogs," as the southwestern Indians call the coyote.

We recall one night, it must have been in the mid-fifties, when we were camped in an old "thrown-out" field near the spring. Old Mac, first of our long line of Irish setters, dozed by the fire as we washed up the dishes. We heard a motor and saw the lights of Herb's Jeep coming down the trail, and soon he and his boy climbed out to sit with us beside the fire. We heard tales of the old Wilderness Refuge on Eleven Point River and of the problems of running Peck Ranch. The boy sat and scratched the old setter's head. Whip-poor-wills called back and forth from hill to hill. A great horned owl boomed, far down the creek.

Then came the coyote chorus of yips, yaps, and doleful howls. The ancient Indian tribe used to say that "brother coyote would be earth's last animal." Herb and I agreed they were right.

2

And the Earth Brings Forth

We started farming in the Bellevue Valley a quarter-century ago with certain beliefs and convictions that sometimes seem pretty far removed from today's objectives in American agriculture. One conviction was that the land owed us nothing and that nature would respond richly to our efforts at cooperation.

We were equally convinced that she would demand, in the end, a high price from those who exploit and waste her resources. Our belief was that man can live at peace with nature and that this is a necessary prelude to living at peace with his fellowmen.

During the years we have seen the first proposition proved countless times in many parts of our continent, and nowhere more convincingly than in our own Missouri. As to the second proposition, it is in the balance. The instances of man living at peace with either nature or his fellowmen are so few that we cannot draw conclusions. Yet we persist in the belief that peace may be possible.

It was our fortune, in those early days at Possum Trot, to associate with men who were revolutionizing agriculture and wildlife conservation. They fought the Dust Bowl that many today have forgotten. They fought the erosion of our topsoil, which we are still losing at the rate of millions of tons each year. They fought the destruction of wildlife habitat and the overkill that was endangering many species.

They convinced us that to work intelligently with the land we must learn all we could about it. Thus we persuaded the Soil Conservation Service to help us survey and map our farm as to soil types. We determined the potential productivity of each field, the treatments such as terracing that were necessary, and the crops best suited to the land.

With district conservationist Bill Colman and others we made big blowups of the aerial maps of the farm. These showed the physical layout of fields, streams, and woodland, together with the acreage. Each was then inventoried as to soil type, slope, and past erosion. From this analysis we found we had seven kinds of land, five degrees of slope, and three erosion factors.

This knowledge helped us, with the assistance of our Extension Service, to build high fertility pastures that farm expert Howard Doane characterized as equal to any in the Midwest. These fields this summer are producing one of the best hay harvests of recent years—with orchard grass, smooth brome, red and sweet clover, lespedeza, and remnants of alfalfa seeded fifteen years ago.

The knowledge of land and its capability for crop production gained through the years has enabled us as we have traveled in Missouri and throughout our continent to trace the relationships between men and animals and farms. We have seen mountainsides turned into deserts in Latin America and our western grazing lands destroyed through overuse. In Missouri we see steep-sloping, gravelly hillsides where scrub timber is poisoned, bulldozed, windrowed for burning, and the land seeded to pasture grasses that can only be maintained through heavy annual fertilization. We have also seen such lands worn out in past years and finally deserted and abandoned to their original scrub timber. This is the opposite of cooperation with nature.

The Family Farm

People now and then still ask us what charm—what special satisfaction—we find in country living. In this day of the three-hundred-horsepower monster car, the superhighway, and a thousand gadgets as the criteria of the good life, perhaps the question is not as strange as it might seem. Thus at the very beginning I think we may as well accept the fact that unless we start with a backlog of capital and knowledge not acquired from the land, the family farm is no place to grow rich. Or, at least, that we must find our riches in other areas than bank notes.

Not long ago we read that today less than one-fourth as many farmers live on the land in America as in 1920—although the population has grown from 50 million to more than 200 million.

When we started farming, it was our conviction that the land owed us nothing and that nature would respond richly to our efforts at cooperation.

One reason we have enjoyed life in Bellevue Valley is that farming here has not yet graduated into what is called "agribusiness." Not all of us still do our own hog killing or cure and smoke our own hams, but neither do we farm by computer. When a chore comes along that needs several hands, we get together and do it.

Our own Ozark farm is small by today's standards, and certainly during a goodly portion of our years we have not hesitated to take part of our small harvest in other endeavors connected with agriculture. But we also know there are certain forms of capital that belong to working farmers and to no one else. One of these lies in the opportunity for growth that comes from constant contact with the earth; from joy in a life that can be rich in friendships and associations, yet can maintain a very precious "separateness" that is impossible elsewhere; from a growing appreciation of nature's surroundings—of crops and wild plants, of trees and streams, of birds and animals, wild and tame. We suppose that without an appreciation of these things, there would be little incentive to live the country life—especially considering that some material sacrifices are inevitable.

It has been pointed out by many that to be satisfying every project must achieve something more than cash in hand. Yet in few places and few callings is this as true as in farming. Fields built to higher fertility through one's own effort; a garden well tended and yielding produce no city market can duplicate; a household well managed and smoothly run—in all these exist satisfaction and even leisure that has been earned through hard and effective physical effort which brings pleasure that warms the heart.

Not long ago a young couple told us they had bought a bit of land on which to build their home. The former owner, a great gardener, had told them, "The deeper you dig, the closer you get to heaven." They said they were finding this to be true. Another new landowner boasted about his acre. "It's a wonderful acre," he said. "It reaches down to the center of the earth in one direction and takes you clear up to the stars in the other." Somehow we believe that landowner will make a success of his landowning project.

But in spite of our own commitment, the question still arises: Can the American family farm survive? When we look at the tremendous movement of farm families into the city from our less productive farmlands during the past two decades, the steady decrease in the number of farm units, the increase in acres per farm, the rise in the necessary capital investment, and the acreage moving into the hands of foreign and American "tax loss" ownership—then the answer would certainly have to be "no."

This answer, however, does not embrace the entire truth. There are many kinds of soil and crop conditions, many kinds of management skills among farmers, and many objectives for farm life. Drive through almost any farming area of America, read almost any farm journal, talk to any successful farm family—and you will realize that statement is true.

Some family farms remain small and still provide their owners with a tremendously satisfactory way of life. The reason many of these families succeed is no secret. Their owners earn part of their livelihood off the farm. Half of today's working farmers also hold off-the-farm jobs. Often farm families develop management skills until they can compete successfully with the large corporate operations. Still others succeed by becoming specialists who receive unusually large returns from their land.

We read in a farm journal of the experience of two family farmers in widely different parts of the country. One owned a 150-cow dairy operation in Minnesota, the other an irrigated acreage and beef-cattle operation in Colorado. Both farmers had, by management skill and know-how, boosted their alfalfa tonnage from the national average of two tons per acre to six tons or better. Consider that in both cases the alfalfa provided food for cattle, which was the primary source of income, and it is easy to understand why these two family farms were succeeding.

Many years ago we met a family farmer named Roswell Garst from Iowa. He was raising hybrid corn and grass seed, feeding the stalks and hay-straw enriched with urea to his cattle, and making money. Garst was famous as the man who entertained Nikita Khrushchev at his farm, back in 1959. He has since died, but we understand that the Garst family built an agribusiness empire of some eight thousand prime Iowa acres and assets worth an estimated 50 million dollars. This is an example of a family that was not farmed off the land.

The trend in family farming, now that land prices are climbing to astronomical heights, is toward the one-man operation with a maximum of family effort and a minimum of hired help. Sometimes, as in our valley, part of the labor problem is solved by sharing work and equipment with a neighbor, or hiring custom work for certain operations.

On a majority of family-sized farms, specialization of one kind or another is probably the primary solution. Here it may be a dairy or beef herd or a feeder pig or poultry operation or a combination of two or more of these. More and more every day, mechanization makes the one-man farm possible, replacing hired help with labor-saving equipment. More power in the fields, operations handled in tandem or multiple-hitch hook-ups—these make the farm operator an engineer as well as a chemist, agronomist, and livestock expert. The moderately new "no-till" farming method, which actually dates back to E. H.

Faulkner's *Plowman's Folly*, offers many advantages for the one-man farm.

Possibilities in mechanization are growing by leaps and bounds. The chisel plow that helps prepare a seedbed without turning the soil, no-till planting with the elimination of cultivation, new haying methods that mow and condition and windrow the crop in a once-over operation, the new "mini-stack" baler that can drop big fifteen-hundred-pound bales in the field—these are all aids to the one-man operation. The same is true in the dairy barn, feedlot, and poultry house, where machines can be made to take the place of hands.

Many families succeed because husband and wife, often with their youngsters, make an expert management team. This is true, says an Iowa University study, of 46 percent of Iowa family farms, with the husband and wife making joint decisions about such matters as expanding the farming operation. However, with land prices and farm-machinery costs climbing day by day, the best chance for a young farmer getting started is to rent land and buy used equipment and get a part-time job to supplement the family income.

Here in our Ozark country we see land values heading skyward, and much of the demand is from city buyers more interested in the beauty of the countryside than in the price of pigs. However, there is no better grassland anywhere in America when it is well farmed, and the center of most farm operations is livestock, with beef cattle the primary animal unit. While some farms are city owned, the majority are still owned by families, and many of these are young families where both husband and wife have income-producing jobs. Thus one young husband hauls our lime and fertilizer while his wife is the school secretary; another wife is our postmistress while her husband helps in the Ironton post office. Both have active, producing farms with cattle and hogs, and families living the good life. So some family farms are surviving and doing well.

Grass Crop at Possum Trot

Liberty Hyde Bailey, the great botanist and plant explorer, spent his ninetieth birthday on the headwaters of the Amazon, searching for plants to serve mankind. Somewhere in his writings he stated the profound truth that the first man was a farmer and the last man will be a farmer. And as for man's most important crop, we turn to the first chapter of Genesis: ". . . let the earth bring forth grass."

Wise men tell us the most important thing on earth is the green leaf, which through photosynthesis converts sunlight into energy to serve all living things. Without green plants, neither man nor animal could exist—and of all plants, grass is the most universally useful. In his *Fieldbook of Natural History*, Laurence Palmer tells us there are 135,000 kinds of seed-bearing plants, and of these, 500 species are grasses.

On June mornings in our valley, we wake to the sound of tractors warming up for the day's haying. By the time the dew has dried, we hear the clatter of mowing machines and the thump of the balers turning the good grass into winter food for livestock. And we are apt to recall that grasses are still the biggest crop in American agriculture because, after all, they supply 60 percent of animal food and include corn and wheat and other small grains. Moreover, they can return large quantities of organic matter to the soil.

Growing good grass has occupied much of our time at Possum Trot. Yet surprisingly often people say to us: "Grass? Do you mean to tell us that you have to *plant* grass? Doesn't grass just grow?" This makes us wonder how often the average citizen, driving across the great farm- and rangelands of America, can identify even a handful of the plants he sees growing there.

Actually, four divisions of plant life cover the Earth's surface, depending largely on climate. These are forest, grassland, desert, and the Arctic tundra with its mosses and dwarf plants. Grasslands originally covered a fourth of the Earth's vegetated area, but today much of this area is in cultivated crops, some is sacrificed to roads and towns, and too much has been turned into desert through man's misuse.

There are, for man's purposes, two main groups of grasses. First are the eight that, perfected through the ages, today furnish the human race with most of its starchy food: wheat, corn, rice, barley, oats, rye, and the sorghums and millets, in that order. Once perennials, these are now planted as annuals. Another annual grass, sugarcane, is not harvested for seed, but for its juicy stem that produces sugar, man's most efficient energy-producing food.

In America we feed a large share of our annual or grain-grasses to the livestock that produce our poultry, eggs, and dairy products—a highly justifiable use. Perhaps a less justifiable one—and one that causes concern to those who worry about the world's food supply—is the grain used to fatten our meat animals, especially beef. Grain consumption in America approximates two thousand pounds per person, of which only about three hundred pounds are eaten in cereal form. The remaining seventeen hundred pounds go to produce the three hundred pounds of meat in our diet.

The great soil scientist and nutritionist William Albrecht pointed out that man's great migrations through the centuries have been, literally, treks in search of protein. We know, too, that animal protein is a main factor in building the good life. Few areas on the globe are better fitted to producing high-protein grains and meat than America. Yet the perennial grasslands of our plains and prairies originally provided food for uncountable millions of buffalo and other grazing animals.

Certainly one task of our highly developed agriculture today, if we want to do our share in feeding mankind and at the same time maintain a quality diet for our own people, is to rebuild our lands that are best suited to pasture grasses, improve the quality of these grasses, and then produce a far higher tonnage of good meat from these grasslands than we are doing today. We know that this can be done because in our small way we have done it at Possum Trot. On fields built to high fertility and planted to smooth brome and alfalfa, we have turned out steers that went to the packer and produced a better quality beef than some of the fat-larded meat that sells as prime on today's market.

As a great Kansas senator said back in 1872: "Grass feeds the ox; the ox nourishes man; man dies and goes to grass again. And so the tide of life moves onward and upward—and in more senses than one, all flesh is grass."

In America a billion acres are devoted to grass production for hay and pasture. This includes Western rangeland, woodland pasture, cropland used in rotation with grass, and 75 million acres regularly planted to grasses and legumes. Today leafy grasses like smooth brome and orchard grass have replaced timothy, which went out with the horse, while clover and alfalfa feed nitrogen to the soil and add protein to the hay crop.

Through centuries both farmers and writers have sung the praises of grass. Thus we find in Deuteronomy 11:15 the verse, "I will send grass in thy fields for thy cattle, that thou mayest eat and be full." George Washington was a farmer who urged the use of grass in the crop rotation "to restore the land." Horace Greeley, founder of the *New York Tribune* and not primarily a farmer, wrote a book on farming with chapters on haymaking. Author Louis Bromfield called grass "the great healer" and made it the basis of his farming operation. Botanist Agnes Smith said of grass, "it is the meek that inherits the earth."

Like the rest of agriculture, haying has undergone a revolution since we came to Possum Trot, both in the kind of crops and in the technology of the harvest. We well remember our first haying season. The primary grass was timothy, prized as horse feed and introduced from England in 1750 or thereabouts. Small amounts of lespedeza and red clover were present as "volunteers"—but so were weeds such as fleabane, goldenrod, ox-eye daisy (or *Chrysanthemum leucanthemum*), and a dozen others.

Most farmers owned a tractor by the time we settled here, but most also relied on their team of horses for many farm operations. So we mowed with the tractor but used a horse-drawn rake for making the windrows. Hand-wielded pitchforks loaded the wagons for the trip to the barn, where the hay was hoisted up into the haymow with a horse-drawn fork. Then it was dumped and put away with pitchforks.

Now an engine-powered elevator carries the bales into the haymow on an endless chain to where they can easily be stacked away. Many farms, as we do, have the job done by a neighbor whose equipment and haying crew can handle the whole operation in record time. This leaves our days clear for vegetable gardening, fence building, brush clearing, woodcutting, and the countless other chores that manage to pile up on every farm.

Clover. We trudged across one of the meadows recently, making plans for a needed diversion terrace. The grass wasn't quite as high as an elephant's eye, but it was high enough so the pollen dusted off at nose level and started us sneezing. Our dog Maggie ranged far ahead, setting the meadowlarks and blackbirds a-wing. We couldn't help glorying in the fact that we were seeing the month of May in all her beauty.

This was a clover year. Fields that haven't been seeded for a decade are turning out solid carpets of white Dutch (*Trifolium repens*), red (*T. pratense*), white and yellow sweet (*Melilotus albus* and *M. officinalis*), and the little yellow or hop clover (*T. agrarium*). William Albrecht taught us long ago the secret of this sudden appearance of the soil-building legumes.

The seed of the clover has a hard covering and can lie dormant in the soil for many years. As long as the nitrogen supply is high and the grass is lush, the legume seeds find it difficult to get a start because of the competition. But when the nitrogen is low and the grass roots are no longer thrifty, the grass thins out. Then if there is a good supply of moisture, the legume seeds come alive. Millions that are stored in the ground open up, and once again the nitrogen-fixing cycle of the legume family goes into action.

Sometimes the crop is mowed for hay. But since white clover is heaviest in the hardest-grazed fields where grass is short, and since white clover is lighter and less desirable as hay than red clover or alfalfa, it is oftener used for pasture. Then many blossoms mature and drop their seeds. Meanwhile the nitrogen nodules released by the roots have been feeding the nitrogen-starved grass, which starts out the following spring with a burst of energy. This crowds out the tiny clover seedlings, and the seed merely stays dormant, biding its time until another spring when nitrogen is low and grass is no longer dominant. We see that nature rather than man was the originator of crop rotations and that she has long used the process as a soil builder.

Most of us, when we look at a field of fescue or orchard grass, think of the field as growing a single crop. Yet nature's most vital secret is diversity. Thus the great expert on grasses, Dr. John E. Weaver, once made a study of the short-grass prairie that we ordinarily think of as supporting only two or three plant species. Instead, in the small area he surveyed, he listed no less than two hundred plant species—all native to this locality.

Especially interesting to us at this time of year, before the big, hearty flowers start blossoming in the fencerows, are the small beauties hidden away beneath our feet. Among these are the tiny blue-eyed grasses (*Sisyrinchium*), a half-dozen species of six-petaled sky-blue flowerlets that belong to the Iris family; the Deptford pink (*Dianthus armeria*), which is an alien although a true Dianthus with five pink petals spotted with white; and the Venus' looking glass (*Specularia perfoliata*), with small blue star-shaped blossoms cupped within each toothed leaf. This is a relative of the bluebell (*Campanula americana*), although of a different group.

The insistence of plants on growing is doubtless one of the reasons our Earth survives. Yet we found fifty hearty Canada thistles (*Cirsium arvense*) where we cut one head too late last autumn and multiflora roses flourishing where we mowed after the first hard frost.

Multiflora Rose

One of our big jobs at Possum Trot, after we had leased our pastures for three years, was to bring the multiflora rose hedge fences under control, and then to build new fences where the old ones had literally disappeared into the briars. This exotic plant, *Rosa multiflora*, came from the Orient and has been widely used for rooting our hybrid garden-variety roses.

Thirty years ago the idea was conceived of using multiflora rose as a living fence. It would be inexpensive and would restore at least some of the wildlife cover we were losing to close-fence cultivation. All of the agricultural services recommended it. Thus within a few years literally thousands of miles of multiflora had been planted throughout the Midwest, and at least three or four of these miles were at Possum Trot, laboriously set by hand by the owner and his spouse.

The resulting fence generally left the old wire standing inside the hedge, to be overgrown. It was, as promised, inexpensive. It made an attractive cattle-tight fence that some neighbors disliked because they could no longer view our livestock in the fields. As for wildlife, it attracted countless songbirds, as well as cottontails and at least a few bobwhites.

The passage of a quarter-century, however, proved that multiflora rose had drawbacks, as do many other exotic plants and animals. In flat row-crop country like Illinois and Iowa, where fields are plowed each year, the rose replaced the space-consuming Osage orange (*Maclura pomifera*) hedge. Moreover, most plants that might have gotten a start out in the fields were plowed under.

In grass-farming country, however, our "permanent pastures" are, literally, nearly permanent. We seed the fields to a well-fertilized mixture that may contain as many as three or four grasses and an equal number of legumes: orchard grass, smooth brome, fescue, red and alsike clover, lespedeza, and alfalfa.

Our effort is then to graze and mow the pastures conservatively, keeping the fertility level high. Thus the perennial pasture plants persist for many years. But the rose hedges bloom prolifically in late May and then set seed that is eaten by birds during autumn and winter. This seed is scattered across the landscape. Roses spread in the fencerows, show up far out in the fields, and, perhaps worst of all, take root in the woods. Mowing doesn't kill them, and the only answer would be to plow under long-established meadows. In the woods they must be dug or poisoned with 2,4,5-T or other now-illegal herbicides.

Fencerows can be bulldozed, and last summer we successfully tackled a mile of line fence where our neighbor's cattle to the north found our grass so alluring that our neighbor couldn't keep them at home. We took out the entire fence line—roses, brush, and many big wild cherry trees. Then we set six hundred new cedar posts. Woven wire was stretched, with barbed wire atop, and a fence was built that could be approved by every farmer in the valley.

This summer, before the haying started, we tackled a similar fence job along Saline Creek. John Civey came from Caledonia with his small dozer that is especially useful where walnut, cedar, and oak trees must be preserved, while brush, roses, and trash trees are to be dug out and piled for burning next winter. That job is just started, and as soon as the hay is in we'll have John back for more land clearing.

Haying

There is general rejoicing at Possum Trot when our two fields of alfalfa and brome grass are mowed, raked, baled, and stacked safely in the barn without a drop of rain. We usually cut the alfalfa early, in mid-May, in order to beat the deadly alfalfa weevil that strikes this prime legume crop at the time of early bloom. The plan works when there is dry weather, which considerably increases the number of bales of high-quality hay.

Our first hay crop at Possum Trot was harvested in 1946, and the only similarity between then and today is the summer temperature. In that far-off year we had just taken over a farm that, while its production potential was high, had suffered from years of indifferent land use. Thus most of our hayfields were in grass that boasted more "whitetop," or daisy, fleabane (*Erigeron annuus*) than clover.

We did boast some modern equipment: a new Massey Ferguson tractor and mowing machine with a five-foot sickle bar. The rest could only be called primitive. When the hay was properly cured, we raked it into rough windrows with an old-fashioned "dump rake," a tool that today stands rusting in some forgotten corner on many a Midwestern farm. We had two hay wagons, ours pulled by the tractor and Perry McClary's by his faithful team of white horses. We loaded the hay in the field with pitchforks and unloaded it at the barn with a hayfork and rope that ran on a track in the barn roof ridge, then stacked it away with our pitchforks. With each succeeding year the hay crop got better. Orchard and brome grass, clover and alfalfa took the place of weeds. A side-delivery rake did a better job of windrowing. The hay loader came next; a tool that hooked ahead of the wagon and lifted the hay from the windrow to the man who built the load. But soon came the pickup baler that turned the windrow into tight-packed bales bound with wire or strong twine.

Considering today's modern equipment, we are somehow surprised that there is still plenty of hard work involved in haying. One of our neighbors from down the valley has helped us for several years—and if this isn't a fine family enterprise, we've never seen one. Bossman and overseer is Pop Humphrey, the grandfather, although not very old. Son Don mows with the big Massey Ferguson tractor and a mower with a nine-foot cutter bar and conditioner—steel rollers that crush the mown hay so that it cures quickly.

One of Don's youngsters rakes with the John Deere tractor, and a daughter operates the New Holland baler pulled by the big International Harvester. Two wagons are loaded directly from the baler and then pulled by the pickup truck to the barn with their sixty-bale loads. Here everybody pitches in to unload, except for the baler operator and one hand to load the wagons. Day by day the bales mount higher in the barn, expertly stacked under the supervision of Pop Humphrey. And every day, along about noon, Don's wife drives up in the family station wagon with lunch and cold drinks.

We lend a hand, now and then, with unloading. But mostly, Billy Latham and I "open up" the fields by mowing around the outside edge to make sure there are no dead limbs or fallen trees. These we saw up with the chain saw and pile against the fence, to be eventually turned into fireplace wood. And now the harvest is almost over, but plowing and planting lie ahead as the fields are made ready for the coming year.

Cattle

If we are primarily grass farmers at Possum Trot, that effort is to a great extent directed toward feeding cattle. But providing grass, or hay, is hardly the only task involved.

One recent job has been the building of a new pen and loading chute, replacing those we lost to fire several years ago. This was more of a construction job than one might imagine. It started with laying out and digging postholes for two dozen big cedar posts set in concrete; to these we spiked oak timbers. If you've never handled green oak lumber fresh from the mill, you might try it for a new experience. Green oak weighs sixty-five pounds per cubic foot, and the job required twelve hundred board feet, or one hundred cubic feet. Moreover, on the two-inch lumber we started holes for the twenty-penny spikes with the electric drill, because if you miss a single straight "lick" with the hammer, the spike bends and must be cut off with a hacksaw or cold chisel.

If we are primarily grass farmers at Possum Trot, that effort is to a great extent directed toward feeding cattle.

An interesting part of the job was construction of five gates to take care of moving the cattle from one area to the next. These were built with pine lumber from Reed's Mill out at Shirley, while the oak was sawed at Bill Latham's dad's mill close by. Both oak and pine cost today just four times what they did when we came to Possum Trot and had to go only a quarter-mile down the road to the nearest sawmill. Moreover, the five pairs of gate hinges now cost five dollars per pair instead of two. But our gates turned out well and we aren't anxious for visitors to see them, lest they importune us to go permanently into the gate-building business.

As Bill and I worked, we counted up our tool supply: electric Skilsaw, electric Black and Decker drill, Homelite chain saw, level and adjustable square, nail bar, hammers, steel tape, small axes. Then we thought of our pioneer ancestors who not so long ago would have tackled the job with broadax and crosscut saw, square nails, and hand-forged gate fittings—and done a good job of it.

But why all this trouble for just a few cows or steers, asks the visitor. The answer goes like this: Cattle often have to be separated. When the cattle come in to the farm, they must be examined and given shots for blackleg and shipping fever. Calves have to be dehorned and castrated; cows vaccinated for brucellosis. And sometimes on pasture there are problems of pinkeye or foot rot, despite all possible sanitary measures.

*   *   *   *

A cattle farm demands your attention in winter, just as it does in the growing season. And one of the major demands of your livestock is water. Some years as early as November the thermometer has shown close to zero in the morning and gone whole days without ever reaching the thawing mark. Throughout the year, we count on the Big Pond to water our small herd of yearling steers on pasture, and this means ice-chopping, with the ice growing thicker each day.

One thing about raising cattle is that your farm demands your attention in the winter, just as it does during the growing season.

Our partner in this cattle business for a few years was young Bill Latham, who took over the ice-chopping. Since he did this before school, he had to work in the dark, making quite a chore, but that is the mark of a good cattleman. For our part, we have always undertaken the task of gentling the yearlings so they look for us when we drive into the pasture and come when we call. This makes it easy to handle them when they have to be moved or treated for any minor ailment.

Our part of the job is done along in late afternoon, an hour or so before sunset. We take a bucket with a handful or two of high-protein range cubes for each animal and drive down to the pasture on the east side of Saline Creek. On warm days, we can use the tractor, but on cold ones, when we are sure the ground is hard frozen, we take the old truck.

As we turn in at the gate, if the cattle are in sight, we see a white face or two turn our way. In bad weather the cubes are spread in feed bunks, but if the ground is hard frozen or bone dry, we can scatter them on the ground, a handful at a time. We claim to be pretty good cattle callers, and a few calls of "Sook calf, sook calf" start the whole herd our way, even when they are widely scattered across the pasture.

Strangely, while all the cattle come, it takes weeks before all learn to eat. Three or four, in fact, stay fifty yards away, eating grass. Some, on the other hand, become completely gentle, taking food from our hands and nuzzling us for more. But we notice that another steer or two joins the eaters each day—and by the time snow falls, all will be eating. The grass, although dry, is still knee-deep in much of the pasture. Always there is some green growth underneath. And there are swales and wooded areas that provide more feed. Thus, except when snow really covers the ground, there is small need for hay to supplement the ration.

The dogs Maggie and Clyde always make the trip down with us to feed the cattle. Maggie ranges far and wide at field-trial speed and almost always manages to bounce out a covey of quail that take to the woods and deep cover. Generally, too, she finds a few doves still feeding on the aftermath of a milo field on the neighboring farm. As for Clyde, he works the brush piles and soon starts out a cottontail, and Maggie joins in the chase, which soon ends as bunny dives into the next brush pile.

*　　*　　*　　*

At one time, we pastured forty head of Ern Stricklin's cattle down in our big bottom fields. One day in January, we decided we would drive them home on a Saturday and bring in the last of our steers to winter in the barnlot. But Tuesday came with predictions of snow and colder weather, so we had a call from Ern suggesting we get the job done before the weather broke. This was fine with us.

Ern said he and Danny Lashly and Pete would come over on Thursday morning in his pickup, along with Bill McKinney and his dad in theirs. They would pick up Bill Latham and me and we would round up the herd, drive them up the country road to Ern's pasture gate, and from there to his big cutting pen at the barn. There both cows and calves could be looked over, separated, and moved to their final destinations.

I had misgivings about the small calves, some of them no more than a week old, because they have a habit of lying down together in a sheltered spot at a distance from their mammies. But Ern said he didn't think we needed to worry. He had gotten the cattle used to being fed from the truck near the gate, after being called in from every corner of the big pasture. From there, with a little careful urging, we would toll them behind the truck out into the road, across the creek on the snow-covered bridge, and up the hill. There were a few problems: keeping the calves with their mothers, avoiding the open driveways into the Turner farm, getting the herd onto the bridge, and then seeing that they turned south instead of north up the county road.

The success of a job like this depends on having plenty of hands and knowing the need to handle the cattle quietly—but I figured we had three hundred and forty years of cattle-handling experience in our crew. There were enough hands to turn the cattle when they balked at the bridge and scattered into the Turner field—and on the second try a courageous old cow stepped out onto the snow-covered bridge and the rest followed.

On my side it was easy, and with no more trouble the forty head went up the road that ran through the woods. We got them past the Suttons' gate, and across the road Gordon Nickelson's cattle joined us and trotted up their side of the fence. I was a bit worried that they'd scatter out across Ern's big pasture when we turned them in. But again, an old veteran cow headed straight for the barnlot, and soon the job was accomplished.

We had left the task of weighing our two steers until last and now found that each tipped the scales at exactly a thousand and twenty pounds—a good gain for cattle on grass. Our cattle-buying neighbor Charlie Sutton had agreed to take one, and before morning we had made a deal on the other. The McKinneys had a fat heifer ready to go into the locker, so we traded them our last steer to be turned out with their herd, in exchange for the heifer, a trade to our mutual advantage.

This task completed, we headed home up the country road, with our mountain looming dark in the east. The oaks had shed most of their leaves, so the slope was black in the sunset. Our own woodlot close by showed a bit more color, for here the deep alluvial soil provided more moisture than the mountain. Still we knew that the trees were dormant, having finished their year's growth many weeks before, and were waiting for the warmth of spring to set the sap flowing again. There was a remarkable amount of color, nevertheless, in those winter woods—leaf buds on the willows, twigs on the dogwood, a few leaves on the oaks—all these added beauty to the winter day.

Hog Killing

There are, we hear, advantages from living in this technological age; yet we've never known a time when mankind faced more seemingly insoluble problems.

One thing is certain, though; you can't go back to the good old days. We thought of this not long ago when we took our hindquarter of beef to the locker where it would hang in the cooler until we were ready for it to be cut up, packaged, and frozen. The locker plant was working overtime, not only with beef brought in by the farmers but also with hogs that today are dressed and frozen as fresh pork—a sad end for good hams and bacons.

It is also a far cry from our early years at Possum Trot when breakfast on winter mornings was marked by the aroma of sage-seasoned, homemade sausage drifting from the frying pan on the kitchen stove. On a back burner, safe from burning, a skillet of Sayersbrook Jonathan apples sweetened with brown sugar and butter sizzled gently, while Ginnie's biscuits browned in the oven. You don't get that wonderful aroma with supermarket sausage, nor do you get the sugar-cured, hickory-smoked hams and bacons that were our pride and joy at Possum Trot. In those days we maintained a small pigpen at the lower end of the barn lot, and while we never kept sows, it was our custom to buy a pair of shoats—young pigs at a weight of sixty pounds—along in August.

We chose our pigs from a litter that had run with the sow on a good alfalfa pasture, then gotten an early autumn start on acorns, honey-locust pods, and pawpaws—a diet to add flavor to the meat. Once in the pen, they ate yellow corn, ground wheat or barley, and skim milk and were ready for butchering at 180 pounds.

Butchering day was a gala event. We watched for a late November day—crisp but not bitterly cold. Our neighbors came to help, and in return we shared the task at their farm later on. The day before we had rigged the scaffold for hanging the dressed carcasses to chill and had set up the scalding barrel out of the wind, with plenty of wood to keep the fires going. Two big iron kettles heated the scalding water that went into the barrel to just below boiling temperature.

We had also honed our knives and scrapers, set a tub of wood ashes next to the scalding barrel because the lye in the ashes helped clean the carcasses, and pulled in the farm wagon to use as a table for scraping. A small tub or two were set nearby to hold the hearts, livers, and other edible innards—and soon after daylight our neighbor-helpers arrived and the job was under way.

On one record hog-killing day we had a most unusual helper, our friend Chester Davis, president of our Federal Reserve Bank in St. Louis and later director of the Ford Foundation in California. No longer a farmer, he still remembered his boyhood on an Iowa farm. Today his job was keeping the kettles filled from the nearby well and stoking the fires. With all hands hard at work, our two hogs had been scalded, scraped, cleaned, hung, and left to chill by noon.

Possum Trot pork was always sugar-cured in brine; eight pounds salt, three pounds brown sugar, two tablespoons black pepper and one of red, two ounces of saltpeter, and six gallons water for each one hundred pounds of hams, shoulders, and bacon sides. The big stone jars were set on the cool back porch for the required number of days until ready for the hickory smoke. Meanwhile the pork loins and spareribs and sausages were frozen for later use. Today many of our helpers are gone, but we may yet return to the days of curing our own pork.

Gardening

Fairly often folks say to us: "How on earth do you fill your time at Possum Trot—that is, besides going fishing?" The questions come especially from visitors who happen to land here while we're enjoying that twenty-minute nap after luncheon and a hard morning's work, which fires us up for the afternoon's chores.

Among all the other farm chores, there is the half-acre vegetable garden to make ready, plant, cultivate, and harvest. Each season we have great plans for the perfection of that garden, and despite having been at it for a goodly number of years, we still count ourselves in the ranks of the amateur vegetable gardeners. True enough, our garden plot is of considerable size. We feed it plenty of organic matter from manure and compost that is piled throughout the year at the upper end. Little commercial fertilizer is needed, and applications of pesticides are limited to rotenone and pyrethrum.

We have acquired one of the famous Troy-built Rototillers that turn cultivating and working the garden soil from a tough chore into a pleasure. Moreover, after each row of vegetables is well started, we mulch heavily with straw. This has worked especially well in increasing our yield of Irish potatoes, which turn out some four hundred pounds from ten pounds of seed. Aside from this small reliance on modern mechanization, we rely on the high fertility and health of the soil that we have built over the last thirty-odd years.

*   *   *   *

Our Gregorian calendar year may begin January 1, which is

not much of a seasonal beginning. But one compensation January does offer—and in our book there aren't a great many others—is the arrival of the seed catalogs. Handsome books, they are, filled with luscious illustrations of fruits and vegetables that never were, yet are wonderful to look at. Blueberries as big as your thumb. Hybrid tomatoes such as we dream about. Cucumbers guaranteed both tasty and burpless. Chantenay Goldinhart carrots that refuse to do their best in our tough clay soil.

But never mind. If there was ever a year to garden, this is the year. If there was ever a time to try new varieties, this is the time. So we send off our seed order with every vegetable on it that looks like it will grow in the temperate zone. Yet ours could hardly be called a challenging selection. After all our years of gardening in Bellevue Valley, we pretty well know what vegetables give the best return.

Oddly enough, peas do well for us, although many neighbors say they have quit trying to raise them. When we come home from a winter trip in early March, we plant the later varieties and always have a goodly supply for the freezer. Nor is there a better vegetable for the purpose. We let whole rows ripen at one time and then pick and shell them and freeze them in large plastic bags, so that you can pour out any quantity you need and tuck the rest away for the next meal.

One thing we have trouble with is succession plantings, simply because spring is an especially busy time and we just don't get back to planting another dozen feet of Bibb lettuce or row of Bloomsdale Long-Standing spinach.

Meanwhile other vegetables are coming along too fast to keep up with them. Trouble is, you plant a dozen eggplants and a dozen sweet peppers and suddenly have a harvest that is hard to handle, despite the fact that sweet peppers can be hollowed out and frozen for a dozen winter dishes.

We always have a problem with overquantities of squash. Our real favorite is the early white bush called Patty Pan. But hybrid zucchini can be eaten raw, cooked in half a dozen ways, and also frozen. And the little yellow crooknecks have a special flavor that can't quite be equaled. These are all summer varieties, and there are more for fall and winter—acorn and Hubbard, butternut and buttercup, and Turk's Turban. There's no way to keep up with them except to limit the varieties.

Sweet corn has been tough going, the past few years. Just let a groundhog family camp in the multiflora rose hedge—or a family of raccoons wander in from the nearby woods—and your roasting-ear crop disappears like snow in August. Last summer we stretched a miniature electric fence around the corn patch with two wires six inches apart. But we still lost much of our sweet corn.

Some vegetables can be counted on to produce well with minimum effort. Okra is one of these. And ten pounds of seed potatoes divided between Early Ohio and Irish Cobbler will produce enough to keep us going until February. By that time, because we don't have ideal storage facilities, the potatoes sprout and start to wrinkle. But by then, we've eaten most of them. Bush beans are another that do well for us, needing only to be dusted a couple of times against Mexican bean beetles.

Planning the garden is always a pleasant task, especially on winter evenings with seductive, brightly colored seed catalogs laid out beside the living-room fire. Nowadays we seldom try the enticing new varieties but stick to our old reliables. Nor do we ever end up by quite carrying out our plans. We've abandoned some garden enterprises like the strawberry patch and count on neighbor Dick Nickelson for our supply. Yet we can still open the freezer and find, in addition to our beef, a goodly supply of frozen peas, string beans, asparagus, green peppers for stuffing, cherries for an occasional pie, and other dividends of last summer's effort.

February Thaw. There's nothing like a sunny day during the last week of February, with a warm wind blowing straight out of the south, to set a gardener's blood atingling. This morning was such a morning, and after the chores were done we took a turn around the yard to see whether spring is really a month away. We've had no such signs as spring peepers singing in the rain pools or the little Quaker ladies (*Houstonia caerulea*) blooming in the meadows.

Yet we did find that the snowdrops in the wildflower garden had pushed through the deep leaf cover, and now the small flower bells are nodding bravely in the wind. Ours are the small snowdrops with solid flower stalks, *Galanthus nivalis*, which we brought home last spring from the garden of our friends up at

Juniper Hill. An odd fact is that the snowdrops, along with jon-quils and daffodils, belong to the Amaryllis family and are re-lated to the huge sisal hemp or henequen, a giant agave that grows in the mountains of Mexico and Yucatán and is used to make cordage of many kinds, as well as the powerful liquor called pulque.

We found the daffodils up six to eight inches, farther than we like to see them, although they are hardy and will stand a lot of weather. Day lilies are showing and thin leaf shoots of the little *Iris cristata* and old-fashioned sweet william (*Dianthus barbatus*). There are yellow buds on the spice bush (*Lindera benzoin*), and the little dogwood pagodas are starting to swell. Leaf buds are beginning to unfold on the highbush honeysuckle—and as for the pussy willow, the budding twigs are far enough along to bring into the house to mature. Down in the vegetable garden the red rhubarb centers are starting to show, and we'll cover them with straw and rotted manure to prevent them from com-ing along too fast.

There have been years when we managed to disc our garden in autumn; and others when dry days in February let us work the ground into shape. Some years the autumn is wet, making it difficult to take care of this chore. Yet somehow, in the end, the job always gets done—and if planting is late, warmer weather makes for a faster growing season.

March—Bee Keeping. It is little wonder that many ancient cul-tures—the Greeks and Egyptians, for example—began their year in March. Our own American Indians also had a good idea for their calendar in which March was the "Moon of Planting," as other seasons were "Moon of the Hunt" and "Moon of Rains."

March is indeed the time of awakening when no countryman can afford to be long absent from his fields and wood and ponds. Thus it was that one year we abandoned a long-planned journey into Mexico that would not have brought us home until mid-April and substituted a shorter trip to Arizona. On the last day of February when we came home to Possum Trot, we stood on the terrace overlooking our valley and heard the evening note of the mourning dove and the thousand small silver bells of *Hyla crucifer*, the little spring peeper, singing in the rain pools.

In March the days and weeks are filled with a hundred tasks. Each morning at breakfast we add to the list of chores that loom ahead. But no matter how many of them we manage to complete during the day, tomorrow morning's additions will leave us with a list longer than yesterday's.

Moreover, unexpected tasks are always turning up. On one warm morning when we went to remove the protective straw bales from our beehive, we could hear no reassuring hum from inside. We had known, when we put the beehive to bed for the winter, that the colony was weak, but we then forgot that it might not survive until spring. This is exactly what happened, and now we must order a new queen and worker bees in order to start another hive. At the same time we make an inventory of our bee equipment, so that we can also order what is needed to start the new colony.

The two winters of 1977 and 1978, with their long spells of near-zero and even subzero weather, wiped out thousands of honeybee colonies across the Midwest. This has created serious problems for orchardists who depend on the bees to pollinate the blossoming trees and thus guarantee a bountiful fruit crop. During these years not only the orchardist but also the beekeeper with only one or two hives has been faced with the problem of making a new start.

This is generally not too difficult for the small-scale beekeeper. He makes certain that his hives are clean and that the frames inside are filled with clean honeycomb. Then off goes his order to one of the big commercial apiaries where thousands of mated queens are produced, along with a goodly supply of worker bees. The difficulty is that, in such seasons as this, the apiaries are flooded with more orders than they can handle, so packages are apt to arrive too late for the early harvest of pollen and nectar.

This happened to us last year with the new bees arriving in June. Then followed a dry summer so that, even though our colony built up fairly well, the bees were never able to store enough honey to take them through the winter. Somehow, it is sad to open a hive in spring and find the small colony still in its winter cluster but lifeless.

Once a new colony of bees is installed in its hive at Possum Trot, we begin feeding them sugar syrup.

This year we were able to get our order off a bit earlier, and the package of bees with its queen arrived in mid-May. Even then the spring honey flow was nearly over. Still we got the bees properly installed in their hive and are still feeding them sugar syrup. Meanwhile the sweet and white clover and alfalfa are blooming and will soon furnish an ample food supply.

Getting the new colony settled is a comparatively easy task. The bees arrive in a small wooden cage with sides of screen wire. The package contains from six to eight thousand worker bees and the mated queen in a small separate cage. First step is to paint the sides of the cage with sugar syrup so the bees can feed until they are full and contented.

The beehive is in sections; a body approximately twenty by sixteen inches by ten inches deep, with supers the same size except six inches deep. Body and supers are equipped with ten frames that hold the sheets of beeswax that the workers draw into cells. In the hive body the eggs are laid, while the honey is stored in the supers.

The colony consists of the queen and eventually upwards of thirty thousand workers and a smaller number of drones whose only purpose is to fertilize the queen. When this is accomplished during her nuptial flight, drones are destroyed by the worker bees as useless baggage for the hive. We start our operation with only the hive body, set on a firm floor board and with a double cover ready. The cage containing the worker bees is now opened and the bees are firmly shaken down into the hive body. Meanwhile the small container with the queen, which is sealed with a small block of sugar candy, is fastened between two frames at the top of the hive body. Immediately the workers start eating through the candy block to release her.

As soon as these operations have taken place, generally without arousing any anger from the worker bees, the hive is closed and the queen goes to work. She is unbelievably prolific, laying up to six times her weight in eggs every twenty-four hours—or four to six eggs per minute. Thus if there is sufficient food, building the colony to its thirty-thousand size is an easy possibility. Our new Midnight strain of bees is remarkably gentle. We use our veil and gloves when going into the hive, but small matters such as feeding can be done without this armor and with little danger of being stung.

Germination. There is a law of nature that we call "the will to life." One response to this law has recently astonished us. As do most vegetable gardeners, we always end the season with a few seeds left over. Generally, these are thrown into the pot and planted the following spring, but we have never checked to see what success was achieved with the old seed. This year, following a suggestion in *Down-to-Earth Vegetable Gardening Know How* from Garden Way Publishing in Charlotte, Vermont, we decided on a germination test.

The method we followed, with a few minor variations, is simple. First, we took six varieties of leftover seeds: bush beans, cucumbers, okra, and three varieties of sweet corn. Ten seeds of each variety were then laid on dampened paper towels, on which we had identified the seeds while the towels were still dry. Then another damp paper towel was laid over the seeds and the towels were rolled up. Next the rolled towels were placed on a dampened bath towel, which was itself rolled and placed in a plastic sack.

Our amateur laboratory was then placed in a warm spot in the kitchen for a week and finally taken out for examination. To our amazement, practically 100 percent of the seeds had sprouted. Moreover, these sprouts had not only penetrated the paper towels but in many instances were also pushing their way through the bath towel, plainly determined to reach the life-giving sunlight.

Next my gardening spouse, who is nothing if not an experimenter, chose several husky-looking sprouts with their seeds still attached and transferred them into small pots filled with rich garden soil.

Although we again felt that this was asking too much of the seedlings and would probably be the end, we were once more surprised. The infant plants took off in fine shape as though determined to survive and thrive.

Thus once more we are convinced that "the will to life" is an immutable law governing the plants and animals that inhabit our globe.

Spring Planting. Ozark summers, when they get under way, are apt to be hot and dry, and this makes succession plantings a gamble. Thus the hardy frost-resistant varieties go in first; lettuce, radishes, spinach, onions, and four rows of peas, which are our favorite for freezing but seldom succeed if planted too late.

Our 150-by-150-foot garden plot is really oversize for a family of two and, moreover, the doyenne of Possum Trot's kitchen has laid down the law. She is no longer interested in finding our freezer half-full of last summer's vegetables while her horticultural hired hand is busy planting the new season's provender.

We've taken care of this by retiring a third of the garden to a green manure crop that will be plowed under in the autumn. Meanwhile our first spring fruit or vegetable is ripening. This is rhubarb, a hardy perennial that hasn't failed us for a quarter-century. Our four plants are kept well composted, and this autumn we must divide the roots for replanting.

St. Patrick's is the time-honored day for planting potatoes, and we try to get them in by the end of March. Yet in 1976 the tops froze to the ground twice and we were sure the crop was lost. But each time the potatoes put forth new growth and by mid-May we mulched our three rows with the usual eight inches of straw and raised a bumper crop.

Other vegetables follow in succession: beets, bush beans and limas, okra, cucumbers, and squash—with sweet corn when all frost danger is over. Last of all come the plants: tomatoes, sweet peppers, eggplants. We long ago abandoned some members of the genus *Brassica*—cabbage and cauliflower—but still raise broccoli and Brussels sprouts. The others ripen all at one time, and what do you do with twenty-four cauliflowers or fifty heads of cabbage? Moreover, they need heavy dusting or spraying, and both are readily available in the winter market at reasonable prices.

For the second year we have "planted" the praying mantis in the garden, with egg cases that come from the seed house but were built by the females last autumn. These are the big Chinese mantids that have been naturalized in America with females that grow to five inches. They are entirely predaceous, feeding on larger and larger insects as they grow to maturity and often on their husbands after mating.

In mid-April our faithful asparagus bed sends up its succulent spears, and now for five weeks there is a daily harvest. We should add that now we keep a sharp eye out for our first wild harvest, pokeweed, or *Phytolacca americana*. This perennial is odd in that its roots, berries, and even the mature plant are poisonous, while the shoots, harvested at four to six inches, cooked in two waters, and served like asparagus, are delicious.

We remember to follow a few rules from year to year. One is to properly balance the varieties of each vegetable. Thus we know that the thin-skinned potatoes like Early Ohio are delicious for early eating but do not keep well. Varieties like Irish cobblers are best for baking and for winter storage and thus make up three-fourths of what we plant.

When it comes to garden pests, our problems are the usual ones. Aphids like eggplant, chinch bugs like cucumbers, box tortoises like tomatoes—and so do the big green hornworms that eventually turn into sphinx moths. Corn earworms and raccoons vie for the sweet corn, and Mexican bean beetles can clean up a crop of bush beans, while cutworms are enemies of the cabbage. Rotenone, pyrethrum, and 5 percent Sevin are the safest insecticides—but we believe a big population of English sparrows, purple martins, house wrens, and other songbirds is a help.

Many garden vegetables produce big crops, and a top producer is the zucchini squash. Our squashes are planted in hills that measure six by six feet. Three hills of zucchinis should fill the needs of the average family, especially when you plant one or two other squash varieties.

Summer and Harvest. Few things in nature are handsomer than a well-tilled vegetable garden on a June morning—with its orderly rows of sun-drenched peas, spinach, lettuce, and string beans sparkling in the morning sunshine. One forgets the hours of labor, the aphids on the eggplants, the failure of the giant sunflower seeds to sprout.

But, after all, each year there comes a season, close to midsummer, when the distaff side of our household looks up with foreboding whenever she sees the lord and master approaching from the east. For in this direction lies Possum Trot's vegetable garden. If we may credit what the distaff side says, the lord and master expects all the produce of his fertile half-acre to be picked, dug, cut, washed, cleaned, peeled, cooked, and eaten for every meal of the week—including breakfast.

Sometimes we believe she would prefer to go back to the ancient world of the hunter—when man spent his days pursuing the mammoth, mastodon, and musk-ox, while only woman knew the secrets of the digging stick and the fruits, roots, and seed plants that could be eaten.

The biggest successes of our summer's gardening were the four or five Big Girl tomatoes that Ginnie planted by her kitchen terrace. Both the size of the crop and the size of the individual fruits were amazing; fruits weighing two to the pound and often with single branches bearing four or five tomatoes. We let these go as long as we dared, picking the ripe ones each day. Finally on the day before the first hard frost, we stripped the vines. We know from experience that many of the green tomatoes, wrapped in newspapers, will ripen perfectly, furnishing us with fruit until long past Thanksgiving.

The sweet green peppers produced an early crop, and we froze many of these for winter use in salads and for stuffing with meat or rice. There's a limit to the pickles and relish a family of two can use, but the peppers can be stored in a part of the cellar that is not too dry and will keep almost until Christmas. Eggplants are always a gamble, extremely sensitive to cold but liking both heat and moisture. Aphids are a problem for eggplants during their first month, and they may stop producing in dry weather. But the fall rains often start them up again and supply a dozen or more for freezing.

Weeds. Working in the garden made us think about plants that grow there in addition to our vegetables. "Weeds" we call them—and a nuisance because they interfere with plants we are harvesting. Yet if we trace those weeds back to their origins, we find that many were used as human foods long before the vegetables we plant today.

First we might list lamb's quarters, or *Chenopodium album*, from South America, which makes excellent early spring greens but eventually grows into a deep-rooted, five-foot giant. Sour dock, or *Rumex crispus*, might come next; an immigrant from Europe that is also cooked for greens in spring.

Purslane of the Portulaca family is another European invader that is often cooked as a vegetable or eaten as salad or pickled.

Green amaranth, *Amaranthus hybridus*, often called careless weed or pigweed, probably originated in South America but is naturalized everywhere. In spring it can be cooked like spinach for greens. We are fortunate to have the amaranth study made by the great botanist Jonathan Sauer and thus know the plant is still highly edible. Its leaves stay tender all season, while the seeds can be ground into meal to make good bread and pastries. Until five hundred years ago it was a staple in the Aztec diet in Mexico because it contains an excellent protein balance and a concentration of lysine, a valuable amino acid lacking in most vegetables.

The Amaranth story is strange. Aztec priests toasted the seeds and from these fashioned statues of their gods of fire and war that were molded together with the blood of victims of sacrifice. This pagan rite was too much for the Spanish conquistadores, who banned amaranth and the Aztec religion. Thus an important Central American food crop was lost, along with the quarter-billion bushels of seed paid in taxes each year to Montezuma.

As every Midwestern vegetable gardener knows, amaranth can be a weed to contend with. It is vigorous, needs no cultivation, and gets along with minimal moisture. If its nutritional qualities and flavor could be developed, it could be a lifesaver in the underdeveloped countries where fertilizer, water, and good soil are lacking. Four hundred varieties of amaranth have been identified, while research on yields, plant density, leaf quality, and volume of seed production is being carried out. Research groups today are working in Mexico, Puerto Rico, the Netherlands, Nigeria, and in nine American educational institutions. It is hoped that this ancient plant of high nutritional value may find its way back into cultivation and to a place on the supermarket shelves.

Final Harvest. Anyone knocking at the door of the kitchen porch at Possum Trot during the fall is apt to be greeted by baskets of big green tomatoes, rows of tomatoes turning red in the sun, trays of tomatoes wrapped in newspaper to ripen in days ahead, buckets of green sweet peppers, a dozen small eggplants,

Anyone knocking at the door of the kitchen porch of Possum Trot during the fall is apt to be greeted by the bountiful fruits of the garden harvest.

and a supply of okra. Thus we manage to outwit the first killing frost and salvage some produce before putting the garden to bed for the winter.

Rains in late September gave a new lease on life to all the vegetable plants that were still producing. Moreover, seeds of unharvested cucumbers, lima beans, and tomatoes were all sprouting young plants, although we well knew none of these could mature a crop before cold weather. Four vegetables did remain to furnish a daily harvest—tomatoes, eggplants, sweet peppers, and okra. All are highly susceptible to frost, and we

Ginnie and the giant sunflower heads.

knew the harvest would end on the first clear night when the thermometer dropped into the twenties.

Not everyone develops a taste for okra because of its slightly mucilaginous character. Yet it has many uses and is widely grown, especially in the South where it is called gumbo. Actually, okra is a tropical annual hibiscus of the Mallow family, with large yellow blossoms attractive enough that it is sometimes planted as an ornamental. We pick the green pods no longer than two inches when they can be cooked as a vegetable alone or with tomatoes, rolled in cornmeal and fried, or added to soups and pot roasts. Okra can also be dried, and we remember from years ago the long strings drying in the summer kitchen for winter use.

*   *   *   *

In late October, Possum Trot puts its vegetable garden to bed for the year, leaving only the strip of soybeans, milo, and millet along the edge, which is already furnishing a harvest for bobwhites and songbirds returning from the north. First step is to chop up all vegetable matter with the bush hog. Then we disk this in and follow with a subsoiler to stir the ground to a good depth.

With most of the garden plowed, we'll wait for it to dry out enough so we can work it into shape with our Rototiller. We've hulled out the sunflower seed, sharing some of it with the chipmunks as the heads were drying out in the tool shed, but we managed to fill a couple of five-gallon cans that will help with the winter's bird-feeding program.

It won't be long before it is again time to peruse the seed catalogs in search of next year's fare.

3

Animal Companions

Our domestic animals—dogs, horses, cats—are so much a part of life at Possum Trot that we forget to report on them. There is one sad circumstance. The life cycles of these devoted friends are shorter than ours, so we are recurrently faced with the loss of one or another of them. Despite this, it has been our good fortune through the years to know the companionship of a succession of great hunting dogs, no less than a half-dozen horses, and countless cats.

Dogs

Many pleasant years shared with a succession of fine dogs often set us thinking about man's relationship with this most faithful of animals, which stretches back to the beginning of recorded history and far beyond. Eskimos and American Indians trained their dogs to carry packs and pull the sled and travois. Doubtless other primitive peoples did the same. But long before, when man was a food gatherer and hunter, the dog was his companion in the pursuit of game.

A collection of specimens studied by Darwin shows two wild dogs, although he decided it would be impossible to date the origins of the domesticated dog. Excavations of primitive villages in Iran dating to 7000 B.C. show the goat and dog as the two domestic animals, and some anthropologists set the beginning of domestication at twenty thousand years ago. Mutual fondness between man and his hunting partner is clearly shown in a photograph we have of an Australian aborigine sitting with his yellow dingo dog.

The dog's history is one of usefulness, companionship, and devotion to his human masters, in addition to hunting. He guides the blind, protects the weak against theft and injury, makes the lonely feel needed, satisfies our yearning to relate to other life forms, even teaches us patience and kindliness.

All our dogs have been partners in the field, until we finally racked up our guns in favor of binoculars and the camera. The succession began with a young Llewellin setter from Illinois who lived fourteen years to become "Old Mac." A better bird dog and a finer companion never quartered an autumn field. Next was Mike, an Irishman from Oregon whose age and background we never knew. But he was perfectly trained, and we roamed the fields together for ten years before he was called to the Happy Hunting Ground that is the reward of all great dogs.

Next came Tiger Kilkelly of Windy Hill, named for a Dublin swordsman of the 1700s. Leo Odom of Arkansas trained him, and he was our third great hunting companion. During his

Tiger Kilkelly of Windy Hill was our Irish setter named for a Dublin swordsman of the 1700s.

reign at Possum Trot he was joined by our only hound, half beagle and half bluetick, whose name was Sassafras. She was too fast for cottontails, but we've never hunted cottontails so speed made little difference. Finally came Shannon, who flew in from California at the age of six weeks. He was the biggest of our Irishmen and, like all other setters, loved nothing so much as riding the Current River in our canoe and camping with us on the gravel bars.

We've never known a dog with so many friends, for they included everyone who came to or lived near Possum Trot. The neighborhood youngsters had long ago named him Big Red and reached through the car windows to pet him, for he loved to ride with us. Shannon and I didn't hunt much as his life progressed, at least not with a shotgun. But he knew every covey on the farm and pointed every bird faithfully. He was a great companion and a great gentleman and we hope nothing disturbs his rest.

Shannon was killed by a car out on the highway, one of those useless and cruel accidents that nevertheless seem always to be happening.

There was a fire in our fireplace that evening, and after supper, when the room grew warm, the big setter asked to go out. Perhaps an hour later, just as I stepped outdoors to see why Shannon hadn't returned, a car turned into the drive and a young fellow came to the door. We will long remember his kindness and that of his wife. They asked if we knew who owned a big Irish setter and said they had seen one struck down on the highway, a quarter-mile south of our road.

They had stopped, determined that the dog was dead, and moved it onto the grass where it couldn't be struck again, then headed for the nearest house lights. We told them it could only be our Shannon, and they went back with us and the friends who'd had supper with us. We brought Shannon home and next morning buried the old fellow where he can look out through the woods and down to the creek and across the valley where he loved to run.

Shannon's death on the highway was a real tragedy. But before we'd chosen a successor there came in off the road a waif, perhaps six months old. Like a million others in an America that claims to love animals, she had been thrown from a car by her owner and abandoned. She won our hearts and has paid her way in returned affection. She is white with faint brown ticking, and a tail that sometimes curls over her back.

Maggie is a born hunter, willing to tackle anything from a mouse to a moose, and the fastest thing on four feet. She catches bullfrogs and butterflies on the fly and tackles the biggest groundhogs deep in their dens. Robins, wild hen turkeys, and bobwhites are all the same to her, and when we picnic on the creek in evening, she spends the entire time in the water stalking bluegills.

A good many dogs have wandered in to Possum Trot throughout the years; dogs turned out onto the highways to starve by a type of American who deserves this same kind of treatment. We've cleaned them up and assuaged their hunger and found homes for some, with the help of our old friend Jay

Maggie (*left*), fishing with her friend Molly, is a born hunter, willing to tackle anything from a mouse to a moose, and the fastest thing on four feet.

McColl. Others were taken to the Humane Society of Missouri or the Animal Protective Association, who in their turn found new owners for practically all of them.

We recall one trip into St. Louis just before Christmas some years ago, accompanied by a husky and fairly attractive mutt of obviously rich and varied ancestry. We had put on him an old brass-studded collar, and our friends at the Humane Society desk said, "If you can just leave that collar on, you'll be surprised how it will help us find him a home." Sure enough, only a few minutes later, as we were getting into our car to leave, here came a family proudly leading our stray with his handsome collar.

As for Maggie, she grew and filled out, although it was obvious she'd never be a big dog. Once we'd won her confidence, it was plain she considered herself the mistress of Possum Trot. We had her vaccinated and spayed, not wanting to increase the canine population. But it was clear from the beginning that Maggie was a country dog. Her speed was equal to that of any field trial champion we've seen, so she is often called "The Streaker." She is obedient up to a point, answering the whistle until we reach home, but then sometimes deciding she needs another round.

Maggie knows every groundhog hole on the farm. She swims like a trout and for hours at a time. She needs deticking twice a day in summer but has a wonderful knack, when she comes in covered with mud, of cleaning herself like a cat. She even likes her dog pen, going voluntarily to sit atop her house in the sun when we are busy at the typewriter or in the garden or must be away for a few hours.

Our Maggie is not elegant, as bird dogs go. She must be about 98 percent English setter, small for the breed and with a dark patch over one eye and white eyelashes on the other that give her a quizzical look.

It was more than two years after she took up residence that we found out, quite by accident, that Maggie didn't like guns. In fact, gun-shyness may have been the reason that she was abandoned. But while our guns are kept oiled and perhaps loaded, we long ago racked them away beside the fireplace as decorative furniture. Thus Maggie's gun-shyness bothers us not at all.

As with most dogs, Maggie is devoted to her master and mistress. Her whole life revolves around this association. Thus she will wait patiently all day, hoping the time will arrive for a round of the fields and woods, yet not holding it against us if we cannot go.

Ever since she came to live with us, she has been one of the easiest animals to manage in all our experience. When we are out hiking, she covers endless miles, circling back every quarter-hour to make sure we're with her. She knows every bobwhite, bullfrog, squirrel, and groundhog on the farm and comes in ready to sleep.

Incidentally, Maggie sleeps on a small rug in the kitchen after spending her evening with us in front of the living-room fire. Only on the few occasions when she has been awakened by coyotes running close to the house has she ever barked at night. But the good times seemed to have ended when she began her affair with Clyde. It was a platonic affair, since she has been spayed. As for Clyde, he was a friendly mutt who lived across the road at Dick Nickelson's farm. He is big, brown, short-haired, nondescript, and useless, and he fell for Maggie.

Starting one December, every morning for more than a month, well before daylight Clyde would arrive at our house. Actually, he hid out around the horse barn, feed room, or machine shed where we wouldn't see him when we let Maggie out for her before-breakfast run. Then for a half-hour or until I would call her, they played like pups in the yard. But my call must have been a signal, for they would hear it, and off they'd go, heading for the woods or the creek.

Mornings weren't so bad, for Maggie would get hungry, bite Clyde hard enough to send him home, and come in to eat. But afternoons were something else.

If Maggie got out, the two dogs would head happily for the bottom fields. There they would dig for groundhogs or muskrats, chase rabbits, or do whatever occurs to a pair of young dogs with hunting instincts. They would have so much fun that we hated to break it up. But on several occasions when Maggie wasn't along, we had spotted Clyde out on the highway. And that could end in only one way.

The alternative to breaking up the affair was a tough one. It meant that the moment I got to the kitchen, an hour before daylight, I would pull on boots and coat, hook up the leash, and head with Maggie for her morning walk. There were compensations when the sky was clear, because never are the stars so bright as on a February morning. A planet climbs the eastern horizon that is so brilliant it shines long after all the stars have gone to bed. Planets always confuse us, but this must be Venus, becoming the morning star.

As for poor Maggie, she spent much of the day in her pen. Then on fine afternoons after our work was caught up, or at least well along, we took her on leash for a long hike through the woods and fields. It wasn't much fun for either of us. She pulled like a steam engine, covering little of the territory she normally would. She continually tangled both of us in thornbushes. Our only hope was that Clyde would find another girl friend so we could give Maggie her freedom again.

By October Clyde had decided that the daily trip to see Maggie was a nuisance and had moved in on us.

For a while we refused to feed Clyde. We didn't need another dog and we heartily hoped he'd go home. Moreover, Dick still put out food for Clyde along with that for a couple of others that had taken up residence with the Nickelsons. But finally Clyde stopped going home and started to grow thin. Our resistance broke at last and he became a permanent resident at Possum Trot. He was, in fact, an entirely amiable country dog except that we didn't need him. Moreover, we still worried that one day he might lure Maggie onto the highway.

The association between these animals was unusual, and we would have liked for our friend Michael Fox, who is the authority on dog behavior, to observe it. Maggie would tolerate no other dog than Clyde and barked ferociously at every dog she saw, even when she was riding in the car. She was very plainly dominant in this "two-dog pack."

Maggie came indoors for meals during this time, as she always does. Clyde ate in the garage. Maggie slept in the house on an enclosed porch that Clyde never attempted to enter. Although Clyde was slow, when following Maggie through woods and fields he managed to keep up, after a fashion.

There is no doubt that Maggie got bored with Clyde at times and preferred our company to his. Yet they communicated in ways beyond our understanding. One evening we drove down to cook supper beside the Big Pond, from which we have a magnificent view of the surrounding woods and fields, with the brilliantly colored mountain in the distance. We drove down, in fact, by a devious route so we could take Maggie in the car and leave Clyde at home.

Once we'd set up the charcoal hibachi under the cypress trees, Maggie took off for a round of the fields at her usual lightning speed. She flushed a dozen meadowlarks, then came in for a swim, disturbing a beautiful great blue heron, a bird that has become quite rare with us.

Then, while Ginnie put her skillet over the charcoal and I mixed the toddy, Maggie settled down to frogging along the pond's edge. This is quite a sight, and we once saw her catch a leopard frog in midair. But she soon tired of this and came in to have her ears scratched while we watched a half-dozen big turtles lazily surface on the pond and then disappear from sight.

After a few moments an interesting thing happened. From the house, a full mile away by the route we had taken, came the faintest bark. Maggie's ears went up as she listened intently. Then she left, circled the pond dam, which brought her a bit closer to the house, and barked sharply for a moment or two before heading out for another round of the field. Supper was ready by this time, and we went to work on broiled mushrooms and a tomato and zucchini casserole. Twenty minutes passed and I looked up to see Clyde trotting across the field toward us. Soon Maggie came in and the two dogs went happily out to hunt for a groundhog den. Their long-distance communication had worked.

The Maggie-Clyde affair ended happily. The youngsters of his rightful owners had originally been too small for a pet of Clyde's robust size. But they grew apace and, when a year was out, wanted him back again. The affection they showered on him soon won his allegiance. As for Maggie, she had never been dependent on Clyde and seemed glad enough to transfer her loyalty back to us, where it remains.

Cats

Farm cats come and go. Some live out their nine lives, while others suffer the same vicissitudes as humans. Farm cats also arrive in devious ways. A full-grown tom appears one day to take up residence under the granary; wild as a March hare but welcome as a potential mouser. For days we leave his food where he doesn't have to come into the open to eat. Then one morning we find a present of a furry-tailed pack rat on the back stoop and know that tom has adopted Possum Trot.

Some cats arrive in a different fashion. On a cold, rainy night in autumn we hear a kitten crying and go out to pick up a starved, bedraggled waif at the kitchen door. Such orphans of the storm are gifts tossed by kindly folk from cars on the high-ways. As Herbert Spencer pointed out long ago, man's treat-ment of animals is an accurate guide to his treatment of his fel-lowmen and, we would add, to his sense of humanity.

Another way of acquiring a cat is to glimpse a lean and hun-gry tabby at the edge of the woods or up at the barn where the mousing is good. Shortly thereafter she takes over at the granary and in due course a couple of kittens appear. Two of our most satisfactory cats arrived in this way. When mother had weaned the youngsters, she disappeared again into the woods that were her natural habitat. The progeny were handsome young toms, soon christened Sugar and Spice. Cat food plus mice got them off to a running start. Then they developed a taste for the high-protein range cubes fed to our beef cattle and grew to tremendous size. Spice finally expired from overeating; but Sugar survived to become boss of the valley. Then he took to patrolling the highway south of the farm, which proved his undoing.

Between the cats that happen to chance our way, we are con-tent to go catless, especially during the spring bird-nesting sea-son. Cats catch mice, but most are also inveterate hunters, and we have watched a tabby spend hours stalking a sparrow. The best technique is to keep a hunting cat overfed, but even then it will capture an occasional bird or lizard. When a farm is catless, however, mice multiply and move indoors. Thus we were re-lieved when our last cat appeared out of the woods, a big fellow of bright gold color. He gradually grew tame and finally slept on the back porch. But he was a fierce fighter and frequently came in with tattered ears and other scars; a highway encounter finally brought him home with a broken leg and other injuries we couldn't cure.

A longtime resident cat at Possum Trot started out as Buttercup, but the name gradually changed to Butternut because the last syllable fitted her personality. She is, like most cats, a remarkable personality. We'd gone to the nearby airport to bid farewell to our flying niece and her husband. From somewhere close at hand we heard a kitten crying and finally located it, up in a tree. It was bedraggled, full of burrs, and starved; when I rescued it, niece Priscilla sacrificed a sandwich from the luncheon Ginnie had packed for their trip. Soon the plane took off, and we headed home with the squalling kitten under the car seat. Yet within hours after reaching Possum Trot it had made itself at home, filled itself with warm milk and cat food, cleaned itself from head to toe, had been vigorously defleaed, and generally had become part of the household. It spit at Shannon, climbed a tree, came down, and five days later rubbed noses with the setter.

There was no handsomer cat in the valley; pure white with a thick Persian tail and heavy fur that ended below her knees like boots. The fact that she was well fed didn't blunt her hunting instinct. Her diet included young rabbits in season, plus moles, shrews, and a fair quota of birds, mostly English sparrows. She kept the horse barn free of mice and loved to walk with us in

Butternut found us when she was a starved, bedraggled kitten.

the woods. She always turned up on our hikes, now and then getting ahead to hide behind a bush and spring out as we passed.

Butternut maintained a peaceable if armed truce with Maggie, as she did with Clyde. Since Maggie, when she isn't covered with mud from a groundhog hole, spends her evenings by the living-room fire, the two were forced to coexist. When the cat came in to take her place at the end of the sofa, she carefully approached the sleeping Maggie to rub noses, and Maggie froze until the ceremony was over.

While Butternut was a resident for several years, there have been other cats, if less reliable. Some time ago, in the fall, we had traveled to Newport, Rhode Island, to talk at the Audubon convention. On our return, after picking up our car at the St. Louis airport, we headed south through the familiar foothills of the Ozarks. To our delight and surprise, autumn had stolen into Missouri during our five-day absence. Seldom have we seen such color. In the fencerows, sumac was brilliant red and dark purple, with bunches of fruit starting to turn brown. We returned to an Ozarks with trees of colors that could only be painted on an artist's palette—tints and hues, from palest yellow through gold and orange and crimson, to deepest magenta.

Once home at Possum Trot, we made our usual round. Shannon had been, we knew, perfectly content with our friends who were holding the fort during our absence, yet he greeted us as though we'd been gone a year. Butternut admitted only her allegiance to the farm, its fields and woods for mouse hunting and its kitchen for food when she wanted it. Yet even she rolled on her back in the barnyard dust and made us welcome.

Along toward dusk, Ginnie went out to say "hello" to Penny and Ha'Penny, our horses, and suddenly called me to come in a hurry. But this story must go back for about two weeks. A small stray cat, starved nearly to death, had taken up residence in the horse barn—and as usual, we'd been feeding it back to health and prosperity.

We didn't need the new cat, however, so when friends a few miles away said they had run short of barn cats and would welcome an addition, we loaded puss into our travel crate and delivered it. An old mother cat in the barn made it welcome, our friends fed it warm cow's milk, and we came home delighted.

On our return from the East, when Ginnie walked down to pet the mares, she heard a meow from the hayloft. And down climbed the little cat, once more almost as thin as when it had first arrived. It rubbed delightedly against her legs, came up to the back stoop, and got under my feet as I took milk and cat food down to its regular quarters in the safety of the hay bales. Butternut paid it only scornful attention. Shannon saw that it didn't come into the porch through the "cat and dog" door. It put up its back fur and hissed at the big setter for a day, then settled into its old routine.

This was our second "cat that came back" from a distance of several miles during our years at Possum Trot, and we had the same experience with an English setter that was stolen and turned up nearly three weeks later with a ragged piece of rope around its neck that had plainly been chewed in half. Is it possible that these animals, like migratory birds and homing pigeons, have a mysterious sense of direction that brings them home again?

Penny and Ha'Penny

The residents at Possum Trot are hardly horse-mad, yet horses shared the farm with us for years. For a while the equine tribe consisted of Penny, a huge and fairly elderly strawberry roan matriarch with blaze face and white stockings. In the pasture she looked like the matron she was, but under the saddle she was a wonderful traveler and ready to give you a real ride from the moment your foot touched the stirrup.

In due course we mated Penny to a chestnut Tennessee walker, and she produced a strawberry roan filly whom we named Ha'Penny. Full grown, she was as big as her mother but handsomer, a beautiful creature who much preferred the company of humans to that of horses. She needed little training to make a satisfactory saddle animal for our leisurely kind of riding. "She's lazy," I told our old horseshoer and trainer, Frank Crocker, one day. "Just keep her that way," said Frank, "and she'll make you a good saddler as long as you're able to ride."

When Ha'Penny was two, we bred Penny again; this time to another strawberry roan Tennessee walker, but smaller than the first, in hope of getting a smaller foal. Eleven months went by

The equine tribe of Possum Trot, Penny and Ha'Penny.

from the time of mating, and one June afternoon Ginnie and I came home from the village to see a white dot at the far end of the pasture. We decided it was a new calf or perhaps a white English setter. But soon Penny went over and nuzzled it and we hiked out to find a pure-white colt with long, spidery legs. We lent a hand as he struggled to his feet, and soon he was at work on his first meal.

We searched for some red or chestnut hairs in the white coat, for we've heard of strawberry roans being born white. But not a colored hair was to be found. Old Penny was a bountiful mother, nursing her progeny for twelve months if we let her. So Tuppence grew like a weed and, like his half-sister, developed a strong preference for people. As we rode about the farm that autumn, he followed along on legs that were wobbly at first but gained strength by leaps and bounds.

Tuppence proved as easy to train as the filly and soon made a mount for Ginnie, seeming to prefer feminine companionship. But by spring we decided that three horses were a horse too many, and Ginnie made up her mind she couldn't part with old Penny. Thus the problem was to find a home for Tuppence, and at that moment, as it now and then does, good fortune came our way. Our old friends Dave and Pearl Bruhn from up near Pevely dropped by for a visit. They're folks who love the country and horses, and, a week later, they came back with Dixie and Rusty Hill and their dad.

Dixie is a fine young horsewoman, and we sensed that with her and Tuppence it was love at first sight. That was on Sunday, and on Tuesday they were back with Dave Bruhn's horse trailer to take the colt to his new home. Although he had ridden in both horse trailers and pickup trucks, Tuppence decided he would have none of this. We coaxed and cajoled, brought a bucket of oats, and finally put the bridle on old Penny and led her into the opposite side of the trailer, but to no avail.

It was during this process that we really knew Tuppence had found a happy home. The one way to load a horse is with patience. In our day, we have seen it a hundred times. When an animal is shy of the truck or trailer, let him take his time. Push, tempt with oats, lead him around the lot, try again. Get his front feet in and let him stand. Keep some pressure on the rear end, but not too much. Don't hammer the horse or apply a nose twist. Talk him in. Finally, in he goes and the chore is done. One interesting thing happened, entirely aside from the fact that Tuppence backed up and came within an inch of sitting down in my lap (it's a husky lap but not up to a thousand pounds of horse flesh). By the time he was in and his halter tied, the colt's name had been changed to include one or more signs of the Zodiac, maybe including Aquarius. One of these days we'll expect to see Dixie and Aquarius (or whatever his name becomes) proudly carrying the flag at the head of a black-horse show parade.

*   *   *   *

Unlike the British gentry or western cowboy, riding appeals to us a bit less as the years roll by. Western saddles grow heavier, and the distance up to the stirrup grows higher. Yet we've ridden many an hour in rounding up our cattle, moving them from pasture to pasture, and searching for newborn calves. Finally, Virginia let another horseman have her Ha'Penny for a brood mare, and we had only Penny for the morning bait of oats.

It wasn't long until the old girl would lie down to roll and be unable to get up. We'd raise her head, wedge a bale of hay under her forequarters, and get her to her feet. But the tumbles grew more frequent, and we weren't always there to help. We called our friend and veterinarian Wayne Sheets and asked him to come put Penny to sleep. He promised to come and didn't, and we suspected the reason. Wayne had cared for all our animals, including Penny, for twenty-five years. Next time we called, he asked if we'd mind getting our animal doctor over from Potosi so he wouldn't have to end the career of an old friend. Since that day Possum Trot has gone without equine companions—although Virginia is tempted to ride again.

4

Flowering Fancies and Forest Feasts

That our blossoming trees and wildflowers do not choose their dwelling places at will is a fact we do not deny. Yet from the moment the primordial seas began to cool and primitive life appeared in the water, plants started to move. First they were carried by ocean currents, then they moved into estuaries and rivers, and finally out across the land until all the earth was covered with the green mantle so movingly described by our astronauts from the moon's surface.

Eons would pass before the flowering, seed-bearing plants evolved to make possible our modern flora—and still more eons would go by before the first ancestors of man appeared. But those long-ago ancestors were tree-dwellers, and thus man's association with the forest began. If we were to use a time-clock of twelve months to represent the 3.5 billion years since life appeared on our planet, biologists calculate that late on December 29 the first tree-dwelling ancestors of man appeared.

As for modern man, his arrival must have been less than a half-hour before midnight on New Year's Eve. Anthropologist Loren Eiseley described these primitive forebears of ours as strange, old-fashioned animals, hesitating on the edge of the forest. Their bodies were the bodies of tree-dwellers—yet they had prehensile hands and a passion for lifting themselves up to see about them. These anthropoids became men because, in the inscrutable wisdom of Nature, plants began to produce flowers that produced fruits and seeds in such tremendous quantities that a new and totally different store of food energy became available to the animal world.

Wildflowers

There are some who say that the sound of bird song or the sight of wildflowers is enough to make one appreciate their beauty. Yet our enjoyment of nature grows in direct proportion to our knowledge of the things we see and hear. Nor need we carry this quite as far as did Emerson when he wrote of those scholars who love not the flower they pluck, and know it not—for they know only the Latin names.

Perhaps the greatest delight of country living is the opportunity it gives for close association with Nature throughout the seasons. The paths we follow through woodland and field grow daily more familiar. We come to know where and when to look for certain wildflowers and nesting birds and to note where the white-tailed buck has polished his antlers on a cedar tree or the beaver has cut willows for his food supply.

Wildflower Names. Wildflower names are a cause of endless discussion and some controversy. The amateur flower lover who goes wildflowering is satisfied with a "common name" and leaves the finer points of name definition to the more serious botanist. Yet this causes problems, since many plants have a half-dozen common names and many have the same name. Thus we find Julian Steyermark, the author of *Flora of Missouri* and our ultimate authority, listing twelve plants of one kind or another called snakeroot. Eldon Newcomb lists eleven, while Asa Gray's *Manual of Botany* has eight. Finally, Edgar T. Wherry and Roger T. Peterson each come up with a modest five snakeroots. From this it can be seen that common names can be an unsatisfactory way of identifying wildflowers.

It it weren't for an old fellow named Linnaeus who lived in Sweden from 1707 to 1778, we'd find it impossible to identify and give knowledgeable names to many of the wildflowers we bring in from our walks through the woods. Linnaeus's father, as was the Swedish custom, took a Latin surname—adapting it from the linden tree, which in Swedish was called *Linne*.

The labors of Linnaeus as scientist were phenomenal. He perfected the binomial system that is used today throughout the world for naming not only the plants, but also the animals and minerals. A great field naturalist, he also found time to write some hundred and eighty books and to teach at the University of Upsala. Most important of his books were *Genera of Plants* and *Species of Plants*.

While it is not easy for the amateur to describe the terms *gen-*

era and *species* simply, it seems essential to understanding. Thus *genera* or *genus* relates to a group of structurally related *species*, which in turn is a group having common characteristics. Each genus is a member of a *family*, while below the species are the *varieties*, with differentiating characteristics too trivial to be classed as separate species. Add to this the Linnaean system of plant sexuality, based on number of stamens and other factors, and we have the method of plant identification in general use today.

One example may illustrate the way in which the method works. In the Rose family (Rosaceae) we find the genus *Pyrus* (the fleshy fruits) and thereafter the species *Malus* (meaning apple). Following this might come any number of varieties, as *paradisiaca*, or paradise apple. Every plant and every member of the animal kingdom including the insects may be charted in this manner.

Although serious students soon learn the botanical nomenclature, common names have a certain charm. The great Pennsylvania botanist Edgar T. Wherry, who was still alive at ninety-four and interested in his science, had a faculty for inventing or discovering happy names for wildflowers. Thus he called the beautiful member of the Buttercup family named *Cimicifuga racemosa* "fairy candles"—a pleasant description of this plant when in bloom. And here are a few others worth remembering: *Monarda fistulosa* is "bee-balm," while "angel-wings" describes *Houstonia pusilla*. "Wet dog" and "toad" describe two trilliums. Certainly "enchanter's nightshade" is more poetic than *Circaea quadrisulcata*—and "snow-on-the-mountain" has a pleasanter sound than *Euphorbia marginata*. Thus we'll agree that common names for wildflowers have much to recommend them.

Examining Wildflowers with a Hand Lens. Few implements used in the outdoors provide us with as much pleasure as our binoculars and small hand lens. With the binoculars we identify the birds, bring wild animals up to within speaking distance, and examine the distant landscape. With the hand lens we open up a whole new field of the beauty of our wildflowers, mosses, lichens, and ferns.

The hand lens is actually no more than a small magnifying glass, often with fixed focus and varying magnifying power. It enables us to examine and study not only the smallest wildflowers but also the smallest flower parts. Our own hand lens is a simple one that can be acquired at almost any scientific or optical supply house. It is often called a thread counter because it was long used in the fabric industry to count the number of threads per one-eighth inch in the warp, which runs lengthwise, and in the woof, which runs crosswise, in the material.

Soon after we started examining blossoms under our hand lens, we began learning more about them and about flowers in general. There is, after all, some similarity in the parts of all flowers. Rather naturally we find ourselves concentrating on small single blossoms like those of the bluet (*Houstonia*), Deptford pink (*Dianthus armeria*), or small agrimony (*Agrimonia*)—and next on members of such families as the Composite, which includes the goldenrods and dandelions, or as the Parsley, which includes such cluster flowers as the Queen Anne's lace, or *Daucus carota*.

Bluets are one of the earliest and smallest flowers of spring, often showing up in March. If we examine a half-dozen blossoms picked from different patches of bluets, we are surprised to find two quite different kinds of flowers. Seen under our hand lens, both flowers are funnel-shaped with four petal-like lobes. But when we open the corolla tube, one blossom has its stigma at the very top while the four anthers are halfway down the tube. The second blossom, to all appearances like the first, has its anthers at the top of the corolla tube, while the stigma is halfway down inside.

The reason for this, of course, is to insure cross-pollination of the bluet flowers. The small pollinating insect visiting Flower A gets its tongue dusted with pollen from the anthers at the middle of the tube, and this is dusted off by the stigma of Flower B. Conversely, the insect visiting Flower B gets its tongue dusted with pollen that is removed by the protruding stigma of Flower A. Yet only under examination with the hand lens is this process easily detected.

One of the most conspicuous autumn flowers in Missouri is the goldenrod of the Composite family. The name *Composite* means, as might be guessed, many-flowered, and here in Missouri the goldenrod family has twenty-five members. If we detach a single flowering stem from the cluster and examine it

The goldenrod, of the Composite family, is one of the most conspicuous autumn flowers in Missouri.

with the hand lens, we find a row of tiny gobletlike blossoms, each a complete flower in itself.

Queen Anne's lace or wild carrot is a conspicuous flower of midsummer with large, flat-topped flower clusters often six inches across. Even looked at casually the flower cluster is interesting, but under the lens it becomes a thing of real beauty, containing many flowers, all of varying sizes and yet each with five tiny petals, five stamens, and two styles. Most interesting is the floret at the very center of the cluster with delicate wine-colored petals. It is set separately from the white flowers on its own isolated stalk. Nowhere in our flower books can we find any explanation for this floret.

We have introduced many flower-loving friends to the hand lens, and all of them agree that it is a unique way of getting

Bloodroot, *Sanguinaria canadensis*, is one of spring's earliest blossoms, with eight to ten white petals and "orange juice" in the stem.

more pleasure from their adventures with wildflowers. The amateur entomologist will find it equally rewarding, as will any naturalist interested in going for a walk in the country.

March Flowers. Now we come to the time of year when any day lost without a hike through the woods is a day that may never be recovered or duplicated. First warning that the season is at hand may come at the end of February when only the yellow buds of the spice bush have begun to show. You hike the woodland path, kicking aside the deep cover of oak leaves to see what secrets may be hidden beneath. Suddenly, if your eye is sharp, you note a tiny cluster of white and purplish black blossoms that seem to hug the moist earth.

This is *Erigenia bulbosa*, often called pepper and salt, from its appearance, but more aptly named harbinger of spring. No other herbaceous native plant blooms earlier in Missouri, although one introduced plant, the little snowdrop of the Amaryllis family, has small white bells that often vie in beauty with the late snows. Yet harbinger of spring is a warning, for now within a few days we're sure to find a half-dozen others. All too often if we're away for a week, we may miss the entire blossoming season of some of our favorites.

Perhaps the next we see is a single creamy white, many-petaled bloodroot, *Sanguinaria canadensis*, looking lonely as it pushes above its still-curled leaf. Then we find one *Anemonella thalictroides*, or rue anemone, touched with pale lavender, and then a clump of Dutchman's breeches (*Dicentra cucullaria*) hidden among the gnarled roots of an old chestnut oak. This is the time of year for flooding down along Saline Creek, which leaves a jumble of fallen trees and drifts that make hiking difficult. Yet the soil is deep and alluvial, fed by eroding limestone from the base of the high bluff. It is a great place for wildflowers, and on the first warm and sunny day we go down to explore.

Everywhere are signs of advancing spring—bluebells (*Mertensia virginica*) pushing up, a carpet of violet leaves, new columbine (or *Aquilegia canadensis*) plants, yellow spice bush in flower. Then under a giant sycamore we discover a shower of bloodroot blossoms that cover a quarter-acre. Here also, where some huge stones had tumbled from the cliff, is a favorite habitat of the hepaticas and now their odd liver-colored leaves from last year still dominate, while the furry mouse ears of new leaves and the beautiful blossoms are unfolding.

Hepatica nobilis, also called liverleaf, is a lovely wildflower that appeared in our woodland only after we had protected it for a dozen years against the grazing that had wiped out many native plants. Now we find hundreds of hepaticas that bloom in the full color range of white, rose pink, lavender, and the vivid blue that is our favorite.

April. Along toward April's end, we begin to notice a change in our woodland. Now the paths that had been open since last summer begin to close in. Plants have sprung up in the path, while our way is blocked by new twigs on shrubs and on young trees. The sun, moreover, no longer shines brightly through the bare branches overhead to provide light for the early wildflowers.

As we look upward, we realize that new leaves on most of the softwood trees are already large enough to cast their shadows, even though the oaks and walnuts are still almost bare. Meanwhile, underfoot we see the foliage of those early blossoms turning brown or even disappearing. There are a few like hepatica on which this season's leaves unfold after the flowers are finished. But others like Dutchman's breeches, false rue anemone (*Isopyrum bitenatum*), and bloodroot literally "fold their tents like the Arabs and silently steal away."

Since we try to walk our woodland paths for at least a half-hour each day, we realize that the early wildflowers reach their peak in number and color before the tree leaves block out the sunlight. Then for a week or more there is a pause in the blossoming, after which a new group of shade-tolerant plants puts in its appearance. Since these include some of our most unusual and beautiful flowers, we look forward to them with special interest. One that blooms freely along the path edges, especially where moisture seeps down from above, is the swamp or marsh buttercup, *Ranunculus septentrionalis*, with its deeply indented leaves and shiny butter-yellow five-petaled flowers.

Two modest wildflowers blooming in great masses are sweet cicely (*Osmorhiza claytoni*), and the closely related anise root (*Osmorhiza longistylis*), both growing erect with small white flowers and the second, especially, with a strong and pleasant aroma. Another that completely blankets large areas of rich, moist land along stream banks is *Phacelia purshii*, or Miami mist. Its small fringed flowers grow in terminal clusters of as many as twenty blossoms and are a pale blue verging on white.

Three oddly colored but unrelated flowers that seem not to mind the deep shade are wild ginger, purple trillium, and pawpaw. The ginger, *Asarum canadense*, whose root has been used as a ginger substitute, hugs the ground with two big heart-shaped leaves, between which hides its small, deep brownish red, cuplike blossom. *Trillium sessile*, or wake robin, stands erect to twelve inches, with three whorled leaves from the center of which rises the three-petaled blossom. It, like the ginger, is a rich brownish red or purple. The third member of the unrelated triumvirate is the pawpaw, *Asimina triloba*, of the tropical custard apple family. It flowers before the leaves unfold, and its six-

Trillium, or wake robin, seems to grow well even in the deep shade.

petaled blossoms are deep purple brown, which closely matches the others we have described.

Late April is also time for the jack-in-the-pulpit, or Indian turnip (*Arisaema atrorubens*). It, too, likes rich ground of the deep woods or stream banks, and its brilliant red seed head in autumn, if bitten, will burn in your mouth for hours. Closely related is the green dragon (*Arisaema dracontium*), which grows to two feet or more and has a fan of five to fifteen leaves from which rises the long-tailed spadix. The root, or corm, of the green dragon—and that of the jack-in-the-pulpit—was dried by the Indians and grated into flour.

An equal pleasure is the search that starts each spring for new flowering plants—especially for rare and endangered species. It is true that as our list grows we make fewer new discoveries. Yet rare plants have an odd habit of appearing suddenly in some favored habitat, staying for a season or two, and then disappearing. Sometimes they seem gone for good, and then a year rolls around when we discover them again.

Two such plants have appeared and been identified during our years at Possum Trot. Both happen to be vines. The first is the climbing milkweed, *Matelea decipiens*, which is different from all other milkweeds. Often called angle-pod, it has an odd deep brown, ragged blossom. The vine grew quite prolifically in our woods for several years, then disappeared. But we are hopeful of finding it again. The other vine was the *Clematis viorna*, called leather flower. It has a bell-like reddish brown blossom and is listed among Missouri's rare and endangered species. We have found it in our woods only once.

There are other, more common, wildflowers to add to the list: fire pink (*Silene virginica*), golden ragwort (*Senecio aureus*), Jacob's ladder (*Polemonium reptans*), shooting star (*Dodecatheon meadia*), blue phlox (*Phlox divaricata*), and true and false Solomon's seal (*Polygonatum commutatum* and *Smilacina racemosa*)—until we reach the summer solstice and the festival of color moves out into the meadows and fields for the greatest display of the wildflower year.

May–June. No season is more fascinating than spring—nor any month more beautiful than May. True enough, most of the early wildflowers must feel the sun's warmth reaching down through the bare tree limbs to the woodland floor in order to put forth their blossoms. Reaching a crescendo in mid-May, they bloom in endless succession. Then when the trees come into full leaf and the forest floor lies in deep shade, one by one the early spring flowers disappear. First the blossoms go and then even the foliage.

Our woodland by early May is a jungle of new growth that the sun hardly penetrates. Some flowers, however, persist; Solomon's seal, fire pink, phacelia or Miami mist, May apple (*Podophyllum pelatum*), thimbleweed (*Anemone virginiana*), Indian paint brush (*Castilleja coecenea*), shooting star, marsh buttercup, and a few more.

The deep shade in the woodland by no means marks the end of the flowering season, for now the blossoms move out to the fencerows and meadows. For many years it was believed that wildflowers merely blossomed when they got good and ready. Now botanists have discovered that the governing factor is day length. Soil, moisture, and temperature bring the plant to maturity, but minutes and hours of daylight determine when the flowers will open. So spring flowers might be called "short-day plants" and summer flowers "long-day plants."

Our area has two peak flowering periods—the first toward the end of April and the second toward the end of June. Records show sixty or more species in blossom on the longest day of summer, although some may be holdovers from spring.

On our last hike out along the bluff we found our buttercups at the height of bloom, their five yellow petals as shiny as though freshly waxed. Buttercups are hardly spectacular, but they have a legitimate claim to fame. They give their name to the oldest wildflower family (with the alternate common name crowfoot) with the scientific name Ranunculaceae, which translates from the Latin as "little frog." The Roman botanist Pliny discovered the plant in marshy areas where frogs abounded and so named it.

The Buttercup family is a basic flowering family, and Gray's *Botany* lists some thirty species as family members, including some of our most beautiful and familiar wildflowers. Among those recorded at Possum Trot are hepatica, larkspur, columbine, clematis, meadow rue, anemone, marsh marigold, isopyrum, and black cohosh. Clear sign of the antiquity of the family is that all their flower parts are separate—with five petals, five sepals, and numerous stamens and pistils attached in a spiral arrangement in the center of the flower.

All these arrangements may change as evolution advances, with composites at the apex of plants having two seed leaves and orchids at the peak of those with one seed leaf.

Wildflower Garden. Years ago we started a small wildflower garden just inside the front fence at Possum Trot. It is an area perhaps ten feet by a hundred, bordered by five ancient sugar maples and sloping gently toward the road. Spring beauties, or *Claytonia virginica*, and violets grow here naturally—and gradually each spring, without definite planning, we have brought in other flowers from our own woodland.

Since this is no more than digging a bluebell or two from a bed of many thousands—or a trillium or trout lily (*Erythronium albidum*) where hundreds grow each year—we have no twinges of conscience at this small disturbance of nature. Since the plants have been brought in as they bloom in the wild, we have gradually acquired a succession of blossoms as they are found in the woods and in field borders.

Plainly some species like the bluebells, or *Mertensia virginica*, try their best to crowd out the others by scattering a big seed crop across the whole garden each season. Meanwhile the spring beauty has moved out into the lawn, while trillium and wild ginger establish compact beds. No fewer than fifty species of spring wildflowers have found a home in our small bit of wild land under the sugar maples. This is a bare handful compared with the total number that bloom in our woods, but there the space is a thousand times as large. It is also interesting that most of the plants are natives, despite the huge number that have moved in from Europe and the Orient during the years.

On walks through our woods, we have brought in specimens of two unusual plants that have blossomed profusely. Both plants are excellent examples of the reasons for learning the correct names of our wildflowers.

The first plant belongs to the buttercup family but looks nothing like a buttercup. Above a cluster of large notched leaves it sends up a four-foot flower stalk topped by long, narrow, cylindrical sprays of white blossoms. Often these sprays form a three-pronged candelabrum, and this may well have inspired Wherry to name the plant "fairy candles."

Other names are less aesthetically pleasing: black cohosh, black snakeroot, and bugbane. We find plants by the name snakeroot in the legumes and the parsley, composite, milkweed, and birthwort families. Thus, to identify our fairy candles accurately we must trace it down to its scientific name, which is *Cimicifuga racemosa*. The first word means, literally, "to drive bugs away," while *racemosa* describes the long flower sprays.

Our other plant has few names, but the true one is just as hard to trace down. This is the false hellebore or Indian poke of

Although a member of the buttercup family, black snakeroot looks nothing like a buttercup.

the Lily family, which sends forth its cluster of large, heavily ribbed leaves in early spring. Sometimes these disappear without ever putting up a flower stalk, as Steyermark has stated. In other years, however, many plants have sent up five-foot flower stalks bearing hundreds of small six-perianthed blossoms. Our Missouri species of false hellebore has the scientific name *Veratrum woodii*, and the blossoms are dark maroon—well worth examining under the magnifying glass.

Summer Flowers. In nature all things have their seasons. Thus the wildflowers of spring are promises—promises of showers and warm weather. Blossoms of late summer and autumn, on the other hand, are fulfillment, urged along by bright sunshine and rain. Spring flowers as a rule are woodland flowers, delicate in color and often fragile and with foliage that disappears soon after the blossoms fall. Summer and autumn flowers, on the other hand, love open fields and fencerows. Most grow on husky plants, and their colors are apt to be definite and bright.

One of the pleasant things about these later wildflowers is that they are generally large and highly visible, so you see them in profusion when you drive the country roads. Moreover, they are apt to belong to big plant families. Thus if you are abroad in our Ozarks from July through August, you can identify no fewer than a dozen goldenrods of the great family Compositae, although you may need a good field guide. All are bright yellow and all will be attracting their odd firefly-like pollinating insects.

Also blooming along country roads at this season will be even more members of the Labiatae, or Mint, family—again, these may require a field guide for identification. Here are the *Monardas*; tall, sturdy plants with lavender to purple blossoms piled up the stem in pagoda fashion. Then come the *Blephilias*, or mountain mints, also with blossoms piled pagodalike. And if you picnic on an Ozark creek, you will find the *Pycnantheums*, also called mountain mints but with sharply fragrant leaves and blossoms verging on white.

Still another member of the mint family that blooms in late summer is the beautiful *Physostegia* that loves the shaded gravel bars along the creeks. It has two common names—false dragonhead and obedient plant, this latter because when the flowers on their stem are moved, they remain in the new position.

Physostegia has the square stem of all mints and is a delicate shade between pink and violet. It is one of our wildflowers that has been domesticated.

Along the wooded borders of our pastures, the tall bellflower, or *Campanula americana*, grows in four-foot spikes with a succession of five-lobed flowers that open down the stem. It belongs to the Campanulaceae or bluebell family, along with the lobelias, and is a clear, deep blue that makes it one of the handsomest flowers of late summer. The related blue lobelia (*L. siphilitica*) is darker and blooms about a month later. It likes any moist place in the meadows and along the creek banks.

A half-dozen yellow sunflowers start blooming in late summer—all grouped under the species name *Helianthus*. There is Jerusalem artichoke (*H. tuberosus*), ashy sunflower (*H. mollis*), and sawtooth sunflower (*H. grosseserratus*). All help brighten the country roadsides where they like to bloom. And there are three more yellow flowers of the *Gerardia* group—all called, for some reason that escapes us, false foxgloves.

Gerardia like the dry woodland, but the other plants prefer the stream sides or similar low, moist locations; the brilliant cardinal lobelia (*L. cardinalis*) and the purple fringeless orchid (*Habenaria peramoena*) are two of our favorites.

Sabatia angularis is the scientific name of the rose gentian, a beautiful plant that is scattered irregularly throughout southern, east-central, and northeastern Missouri and is most common in the Ozark counties. This is one of our most spectacular wildflowers, growing up to three feet tall with a sturdy, square, broad-leaved lower stem. The many flowering branches are paired and are topped by large five-petaled blossoms that are delicate rose pink in color. Although the plant is a biennial, rose gentian is hard to maintain in the wildflower garden and generally requires resowing each autumn.

The purple fringeless orchid, which is on Missouri's "rare and endangered" species list, has been found growing in three locations at Possum Trot. We have recently been informed that its name has been changed, but we'll stick to the old name, *Habenaria peramoena*, until further evidence of the change arrives.

No name change can disturb the beauty of this rare plant, a tall many-flowered stem of lovely rose pink blossoms. It grows and blooms in damp soil in low-lying woodlands and meadows.

The purple fringeless orchid, although rare, had been found at three locations at Possum Trot.

We found the orchid in time to photograph it for our *Ozark Wildflowers* and to let a dozen flower-loving friends bring their cameras. The locations were quite far apart—two in the woods and one at the edge of our pasture pond.

The orchid in all locations had competition from blackberry briars and marsh grasses so that its numbers diminished and one year we failed to find it. But the next year toward the end of July we made a careful search with our helper Jeff Latham, who has an eagle eye for birds' nests, all sorts of wildlife, and flowering plants. To our delight we found the orchid in two of its old locations and are still searching for the third.

Plants with blossoms so small they often escape notice are of special interest to us. Often on our morning woodland walks we collect them and are reminded of an elderly friend with whom we have walked the beaches of Florida's Captiva Island. We saw her first with her small collecting pail, bending down to retrieve marine objects too small for us to identify. Curiosity got the better of us, and we introduced ourselves and asked the objective of her search.

"I collect littlies," she said, and showed us her morning's haul of tiny shells, none much more than a quarter-inch in diameter. So we've come to call our tiny wildflowers "littlies" and carry a magnifying glass to examine their perfection and beauty.

Autumn. Early September brings a subtle change in our Ozark valley. At first daylight a heavy mist hides the mountains and shrouds the creeks and may not burn away until an hour after sunrise. On the sunniest afternoons there is a suspicion of haze in the air—a promise of Indian summer to come.

Autumn brings a multitude of wildflowers, some of them among the handsomest of the year. One year Bill Latham and I built fences in the bottom fields, driving down with the tractor each day, and we found the road down the hill and across the creek a regular botanical garden. Most of the flowers were familiar, and we counted no less than fifty species in bloom. Some of these, however, lack common names, while the scientific names are easily forgotten from year to year. Or as my good wife puts it, "I can forget those names from bush to bush."

As for color, yellow certainly dominates the autumn scene, although the whole color spectrum is touched upon. Thus there are whites, pinks, reds, and blues, with a few even verging on browns and greens. Among the yellows are the sunflowers, sneezeweeds, silphiums, goldenrods, rudbeckias, St. John's-worts, tickseeds, and the primroses. Reds are scarcer, although we'd include trumpet vine, cardinal lobelia, butterfly-weed, or *Asclepias tuberosa*, and off-reds like false dragonhead, or *Physostegia virginiana*, and swamp milkweed, or *Asclepias incarnata*. As for blues, there are the tall bellflower, blue lobelia, aster, dayflower, chicory, and at least one vervain.

Perhaps the greatest triumph of the Ozark autumn is the magnificent cardinal lobelia. It has a tall stem down which the intensely red blossoms open in succession. When a hundred or more cardinal lobelias open in unison, they make a brave sight equaled by few other Missouri wildflowers.

Two *Verbesinas*, whose common names, if they have any, are not well known, grow to be seven feet tall and are among the autumn wildflowers. Both are sometimes called frostweed because of the beautiful ice curls or frost flowers that form from liquid rorced through the cracks above the root system. Another name is crown-beard, for what reason we do not know. One *Verbesina* has a cluster of small white flowers atop its stem, while the other has a multiple sunflowerlike yellow head, almost completely lacking in the rays we generally refer to as petals.

Another interesting group is the *Silphiums*, with three members along our woodland borders. Most spectacular is the eight-footer with square stem, yellow flowers, and hugh leaves clasping the stem to form a cup; hence the names carpenter's square and Indian cup. Next is the seven-foot rosin-weed with paired leaves and yellow flowers—and finally the prairie dock with two-foot basal leaves and a tall stem that, like the others, bears yellow sunflowerlike blossoms. We've even learned to pronounce its tongue-twisting name, *Silphium terebinthinaceum*. One of these nights a killing frost will bring the flowering season to an end; meanwhile we enjoy it and make the most of every September day.

Out in front of the old house at Possum Trot, which faces south, is a pokeweed of noble proportions. This is, to use its scientific name, *Phytolacca americana*—a perennial herb that comes up each season from a taproot big as a man's leg. The first shoots in spring are excellent eating, much like asparagus, when cut at six inches and boiled in two waters. Stems not cut will grow into husky reddish branches two inches in diameter that bear big bunches of dark purple berries with scarlet juice. The whole plant, except for those early shoots, is poisonous, although the berries were once used as a primitive dye.

Pokeweed is truly a weed, seldom favored by landscape gardeners. Yet ours has held its place between the dogwood and black haw for many years, and thereby hangs a tale. Back in the early days of the soil conservation movement in the late 1940s, we drove east in early autumn for the National Audubon con-

Prairie dock, one of the silphiums, brightens our autumn, lasting until the first killing frost of winter.

Although the berries of the pokeweed are poisonous, the first shoots in spring are excellent eating.

vention in New York. On the way we stopped for a long-promised overnight visit with friend Louis Bromfield at his Malabar Farm near Mansfield, Ohio.

Louis was a national leader in the conservation movement, a successful novelist turned successful farmer. He had built a handsome home on a rise of ground above his pond with the dairy barn nearby. It was late afternoon and the herd was being milked, although Louis had not yet come in from the fields. While waiting his arrival, we surveyed the home-ground plantings and were surprised to find a hugh pokeweed by the front porch, loaded with ripe berries.

We had a pleasant visit, staying long enough next morning to ride across the farm with Louis in his Jeep, accompanied by three hugh boxers. It was, sadly, our last visit with this talented and energetic man. But when we came home to Possum Trot and found that a young pokeweed had found a place near our front door, we decided that if weeds were good enough for Bromfield, this one was good enough for us—and it has been here ever since.

One morning as we were deciding whether it was time to cut down this year's pokeweed in favor of more conventional shrubbery, an interesting thought struck me. Our landscaping is ragged at best, and we knew there were many more weeds making themselves at home in our flower beds and shrubbery. So I got a notebook and pencil to list them.

First, beside the front stoop, on one side we found an ancient *Desmodium*, a legume with pink, pealike blossoms that turn at last into beggar's lice to stick to our clothing. On the other side was another prolific perennial, the *Polygonum virginianum*, or knotweed, with its long sprays of tiny flowers and the intriguing common name dooryard weed.

From there things got out of hand. One of our favorites is the little sky blue, three-petaled *Commelina*, or Virginia day-flower, of the Spiderwort family. It can take over a flowerbed and will bloom all summer long. Next are the wild four-o'clocks, or *Mirabilis nyctaginea*, big hardy plants with woody stems and countless tiny blossoms that actually do open at four o'clock. Still another that likes to take over the flower beds is the little yellow *Oxalis* or wood sorrel with small pickle-shaped seed pods that give the plant the nickname sour grapes.

No doubt a good flower gardener would do away with the beggar-ticks, Spanish needles, smartweeds, crotons, elephantopus, mints, frostweeds, and even poison ivy that creep into the flower beds and lawn. If we took care of those, even discounting those with attractive flowers, there'd never be time to cultivate the garden or pick Ginnie's Better Girl tomatoes that run two to the pound; not to mention the eggplants, sweet peppers, okra, broccoli, and Patty Pan squashes that ripen each day.

* * * *

One of our great woodland pleasures is the discovery of a new wildflower—and this happened not long ago when we picnicked with friends who have a forest hideaway on the headwaters of a small stream that ripples down over limestone ledges; a wonderful habitat for wildflowers and with a flora amazingly different from ours, a dozen miles away.

As we hiked up their creek, I commented on the profusion of autumn blooms; cardinal and blue lobelias, bouncing bet (*Saponaria officialis*), blue mist-flower (*Eupatorium coelestinum*), the magenta-colored false dragonhead (*Physostegia virginiana*), and many more. Then we noted a new flower scattered in pockets of moist soil. It stood fifteen inches high with a rosette of long-stemmed round leaves at the base and a single leaf clasping the flower stem. The flower itself was five petaled and white, lined with green veins.

The plant was a stranger, but it didn't take long to identify and we soon had it nailed down as grass-of-Parnassus, or *Parnassia grandifolia*, of the Saxifrage family. It is quite rare, found in five Ozark counties, but several other species are scattered across eastern America from Newfoundland south and west. As for the name grass-of-Parnassus, for an entirely ungrasslike plant, this one does thrust its flower head up above the grassy meadows and likes the higher elevations, which might account for Parnassus. At any rate, we brought a specimen home, planted it in a moist crevice beside the creek, and hope it will adapt there to give us a new and interesting wildflower.

*   *   *   *

Early on a Sunday morning in November, before the sun had topped our mountain, we looked out toward the west. Nearby the valley was still shrouded in shadow, but the higher hills with Logan Mountain in the distance were a blaze of golden light such as we have seldom witnessed. On the previous Saturday night, a real cold snap had dropped our thermometer to twenty-five degrees, putting ice on the water buckets and a heavy coating of white frost across the meadows.

After breakfast we hiked out with Maggie and found the first ice curls around the six-foot stems of the *Verbesina virginica*.

The sun was well up when we realized there was a constant rustling murmur throughout the woodland. Soon we realized it was made by leaves falling from the trees in a steady rain, so that before we came back to the house, the woodland paths were already ankle-deep in the bright foliage. We realized, too, that the frost had brought an end to all blooming wildflowers except the smallest white and pale blue asters. Gone now are the other late bloomers; the wild blue ageratum, or mist flower, the white snakeroot also called ageratum, and the dittany, or *Cunila origanoides*, which is one of the smallest mints, with tiny lavender flowers.

Some plants put out new leaves in autumn, and among these we found the heart-shaped foliage of wild ginger, the three-lobed leaves of hepatica, and the leaves of Virginia waterleaf, or *Hydrophyllum virginianum*, splashed with gray dots in autumn and making a thick mat on the floor of the woodland.

Ferns also remain green, at least through autumn. In a dozen colonies out along the bluff and in the deep woods, we find the Christmas fern, *Polystichum acrostichoides*; *Woodsia*; the grape fern, *Botrychium dissectum*; several spleenworts, or *Asplenium*; and, most interesting, the walking fern, of the genus *Camptosorus*. Walking ferns are fairly rare and quite small in size. Their long, narrow leaves shaped like a spear point are armed with thin, threadlike tips that radiate out from the parent plant. When the tips touch a crevice with a bit of organic matter, they take root. Thus you often find the parent plant surrounded by a colony of small plantlets.

But the sun has climbed high, and we recall that the martin houses must come down and be made ready for winter, the woodboxes must be filled, and a dozen other tasks are waiting, so we whistle for Maggie, who is barking at an imaginary squirrel in a tall oak tree, and head for home.

Wild Harvest

Our Ozark wild harvest extends over eight months of the year, and its fruits can be enjoyed for a full twelve. It begins with the early spring greens, a few of which we gather each year. These include the shoots of the pokeweed (*Phytolacca americana*), a real native; lamb's quarters (*Chenopodium album*), which came from Europe with the first settlers; and sour dock (*Rumex crispus*), another foreigner. Countless others can be eaten as salad or cooked like spinach; they are so numerous it would take all of two people's time just to hunt, harvest, and cook them.

Today huckleberries are rare, and so are youngsters who'll trek to the piny woods to pick them. Wild blackberries are dependable, and dewberries are even more delicious in wet years.

We pick what we can eat of both, with a few quarts frozen and a few more boiled down for juice that makes delicious pancake syrup or can be turned into jelly when the summer rush is over.

The 1975 season bore a tremendous crop of wild elderberries, and we decided for the first time in years to make jelly. Euell Gibbons, who wrote *Stalking the Wild Asparagus*, recommends the Sure-Jel recipe, and we figured we couldn't go wrong on that one. So we picked nearly a bushel of ripe berries, merely clipping the coarser stems from the dark purple fruit. This fruit went into a big kettle, was crushed to start the juice flowing, then set to simmer over a low fire. Next step was to put the "mash" into a cotton bag to drip into a crock, a process that must be guarded against fruit flies.

When the juice was well drained, it was mixed with an equal amount of blackberry juice along with the juice of two lemons. Sugar was added, along with Sure-Jel, and the whole was boiled until it "spun a thread" when dripped from the spoon. Lemon and blackberry gave the rather bland elderberry the necessary "zing," and, when finished, the mixture was poured into jars, sealed, and set to cool. The result is beautiful in color and delicious to taste.

Persimmons come next and offer many possibilities. One is persimmon chiffon pie made in a graham-cracker crust. Prepare the persimmon pulp by working the fruit through a colander. Then in a saucepan combine one envelope unflavored gelatin, 1/2 cup brown sugar, 1/2 teaspoon salt. Beat three egg yolks with 2/3 cup milk, stir into the brown-sugar mixture. Bring to a boil, remove from heat, stir in one cup strained persimmon pulp, and chill until it thickens. Beat the three egg whites stiff, add 1/4 cup granulated sugar, and fold in the persimmon mixture with 1/4 cup chopped nuts. Turn this into the crust, chill, and wish you'd made two pies.

The Ozarks boast three varieties of *Vaccinium* with a dozen species and subspecies. All answer to the name *huckleberry*, although they are also called deerberry, southern gooseberry, squawberry, and lowbush huckleberry. Sadly, the wild cranberry (*Vaccinium macrocarpon*) is missing. This is the species that Euell Gibbons recommends we take home to spread on cold cereals, and that he describes as tasting like wild hickory nuts. We do, however, boast nine species of hickory nut; all except the pecan, which has been widely domesticated. Of true hickory nuts, shellbark and shagbark have the most delicious fruits, and in early days both were tapped for sap to make syrup and sugar.

Recently our friends Lester and Maria Mondale came up on a rainy day for early dinner. Since we couldn't walk the woods, we showed them the wildflower garden where at least half of the forty-odd plants are edible or were used medicinally by our forefathers. Still, it takes a lot of spring beauty bulbs, which Euell calls fairy spuds, to make a mess. He claims that in a half-hour he could dig all the tubers that two people could eat. The effort expended must be carefully considered as we realize that even when the spuds in our vegetable garden are what my great-aunt Lucy called "small potatoes and few to the hill," one push of the spading fork will turn up enough for supper for four.

But we shouldn't downgrade the late Euell Gibbons, who has introduced many to our wild fruits and vegetables. These add variety to our viands, although we feel some require a tremendous amount of searching, gathering, and cooking time with

The bulbs of the spring beauty, or fairy spuds, are one of the true feasts of the forest.

results that are hardly Lucullan. A few, however, are worth trying.

There's one more bit of wild harvest worthy of mention. Back under the limestone bluff beside the creek is a small wet-weather spring, and here we found water cress growing. It was short-stemmed because the water is shallow, but we brought home enough for two or three delicious salads. Then we had the happy thought of taking the roots back to the spring again, and in a few days they were putting forth new leaves. Whether or not they thrive depends on summer rains to keep the spring flowing. Meanwhile we'll enjoy our wild harvest.

Mushrooms. As we've said before, wildflowers bloom in endless succession. The hundreds of trout lilies disappear to be followed by bluebells. Rue anemone clings to every rock crevice. Bloodroot and hepatica are followed by purple trillium, merrybells (also known as bellwort, *Uvularia grandiflora*), and blue phlox. Soon it will be May apples and jack-in-the-pulpit. In April mushrooms show up, and Dick Nickelson came by on Saturday to share a gallon of morels he had gathered. Next day in an opening among the white oaks on the bluff, Ginnie and I discovered a new species of sponge mushroom we couldn't identify.

There must have been thirty or more of these, many as large as a grapefruit. The color of the deeply pitted head was a dark mahogany brown; the stem, almost invisible in the deep leaves, was a thick pure white. We were sure it belonged in the morel family but called our friend Lester Mondale who is something of a mushroom expert. That afternoon he drove up with Maria, his wife, and armed with four field guides to mushrooms, two in color.

A half-dozen species resembled our mushroom in one way or another: *Verpa bohemica*, which our authority Alexander Smith urges be eaten with caution; four Morchellas, of which *M. esculanta* is the true morel and the most delicious; and *M. crassipes*, which we're convinced is our mushroom—but not quite convinced enough to eat it. Trouble is, the next family of the Helvellas is rather chancy and in several species quite poisonous. Want to try *Morchella crassipes*?

In the yard is a big old sugar maple stump that is perfect

In wet seasons, mushrooms will form a fairy ring in the fields.

mushroom habitat. Growing at its base was a clump of fungi that Mondale greeted with enthusiasm. "Pleurotus ostreatus— oyster mushroom," he said, and proceeded to kneel on the wet ground to gather a double handful. "Not the best but worth trying." So they went into the refrigerator.

Next evening we carefully trimmed away the edges, cut the remainder into small pieces, and set them aside. Then into the skillet went a small onion sliced thin and plenty of butter with salt and pepper. When they had browned, we added the mushrooms along with a sprinkle of basil, chives, and parsley. The results turned our humble hamburgers into a feast.

Rainy weather in mid-June is seldom welcomed by the grassland farmer who may be caught with fresh-cut hay on the ground. Then, unless the sun shines, a whole cutting may be lost. Only consolation is that during seasons of good moisture the grasses and legumes keep growing. This generally insures a second cutting.

The Ozark mushroom hunter, on the other hand, welcomes

such weather. It is now that the woodland mushrooms appear, many growing only at this season. Mushroom hunters, moreover, are an odd clan who delight in trying specimens listed in the field guides as "questionable" or "inedible for many people."

As for us, we let the other fellow do the mushroom experimenting and stick to such old reliables as morels in spring, inkcaps in early summer, giant puffballs as summer wears on, and meadow mushrooms as autumn approaches. Yet even here it is well to study each species thoroughly. The morel or Morchella has a similar looking family in the Melvellas that are inedible or even poisonous. Deadly Amanita (*A. phalloides*), known as the destroying angel, may grow in fields with the meadow mushrooms, and even the Lactarius with the deceptive name "delicious milky cap" (*L. deliciosus*) is poisonous for many.

Few outdoor folk call themselves real experts in the identification of "safe" mushrooms, for the simple reason that individuals differ widely in their tolerance of the subtle substances found in the seventy thousand fungi that scientists have described. Edible species belong chiefly to two classes—Acconycetes and Basidiomycetes. All fungi lack the chlorophyll that enables plants to manufacture food with the help of sunlight. Thus they secure nourishment from other sources. Among edible species this occurs in three ways. Some are parasitic and depend on living hosts; some are saprophytic and live on dead organisms; and some are symbiotic and both give and take from their associated organisms.

Last week we had opportunity to try (with reasonable safety) some of the gourmet species prized by the collectors. Our nephew, Peter Schramm, drove down for a visit. Pete is a zoologist who also teaches biology and ecology and is an expert on prairie flora. Thus a primary objective of this visit was to join me in botanizing one of the limestone glades common to the Ozarks.

Pete arrived in his camping Volkswagen bus with Cholla, the big black retriever, and an elderly nondescript dog named Old, for the simple but logical reason that he is old. We got in our day of botanizing. But then the rains came; a mushroom opportunity too good to miss. After a thorough spraying with Ticks-off against the chiggers and our special breed of Ozark "throwing ticks," we were off to the woods.

On the first day, mushrooms weren't too plentiful, though we knew there would be more next morning. We did gather the delicious *Cantharellus*—orange-yellow and a favorite in many countries of the world. Others we found were a *Russula*, some of the bitter *Boletus*, and two or three other species. Which went into the mushroom bag and which were discarded, we won't specify here, but our hunt provided the accompaniment for two delicious dinners.

During the dry weather before the rains of late August, almost the only fungi to be found in the woodland were the "shelf mushrooms" on the tree trunks. Then the rains came and suddenly mushrooms appeared in countless sizes, shapes, and colors including red and green. The fact that few of these are poisonous does us little good unless we belong to that breed of mushroom hunters who have learned to know those that are not only edible but, because of size, fleshiness, and flavor, are worth searching for and collecting.

All mushrooms are, of course, fungi. They belong to an order at least as old as the green plants and are older than most animal species. They perform a service without which few, if any, life forms, could survive; they carry out decomposition. Without this service, green plants would soon tie up all the atmospheric carbon that makes their lives possible and so would die of starvation.

Green plants through chlorophyll have the ability to build carbohydrates from water, carbon dioxide, and light, and thus to form living matter. Mushrooms, without chlorophyll, cannot build organic from inorganic matter. They thus depend, through the process of decomposition, on using organics already manufactured by green plants and animals. This process of decomposition carried on by mushrooms also prevents overpopulation of many plant species, for example by shortening the life of old trees through an attack on their wooden skeletons.

The history of mushrooms as food goes far back into antiquity. Thus there has never been and will never be complete agreement among mushroom hunters as to which species are the best for eating, or even as to which are edible and which are not. Much depends on taste and on custom, except for a few well-known deadly species.

Europeans have eaten mushrooms for much longer than we have, although the American Indians and natives of Central and South America have long been familiar with many hallucinatory mushrooms used in their religious rituals. Many species, both edible and poisonous, grow throughout the world, and in 1937 the Czech Food Codex published a list of fifty-eight mushroom species not only edible but safe to put on the market. In this list only the *Russulae*, generally edible, were omitted because they are too easily confused with some poisonous species.

Our own mushroom hunting is too limited to take chances, and this makes our woodland hikes somewhat disappointing. Possibly because we no longer have grazing cattle to enrich the pastures, we seldom find the delicious meadow or common field mushroom that we gathered in quantity for many years. These are much like the variety purchased in the market and raised commercially. At least three other members of the *Agaricus* group are safe and good eating.

Another late summer favorite is the puffball *Calvatia gigantea*, which can be gathered and used as long as it is white clear through when sliced for frying. Some other members of this group are good, although too small to be worth gathering, but some like the stinkhorns cannot be recommended, even though not violently poisonous.

In spring we hunt the delicious morels, which seem to have an association with dying elm trees in our woods. In late autumn at least one of the coral mushrooms, *Clavaria botrytes*, is excellent, though it has some poisonous relatives. Another large group worth learning are *Boletus*, members of which are found from spring until autumn. Alexander Smith, the American mycologist, lists fourteen good *Boletus* and only one that is poisonous. As for us, we'll hope to learn more of the ones listed "edible and choice" to add to our list of gourmet recipes.

Pawpaws. The pawpaws are ripe in fall, a season enjoyed by many forms of wildlife and by the few humans lucky enough to be able to gather the fruits at the moment of ripening. Although pawpaws are found in small-town fruit stands in the South, they turn soft and black so swiftly that they can hardly be classed as marketable. This is a pity, since they are delicious when you can gather them fresh every day or two.

Asimina triloba, the pawpaw tree, is the only northern member of the Custard Apple family, which has many tropical relatives. It grows in low bottomlands along the streams and in moist, shady ravines. Thickets are formed by suckers sent up from the roots of established trees, so the old saying about "the possum in the pawpaw patch" is quite accurate.

The trees are small, seldom reaching thirty feet and with soft, brittle wood. The odd purple blossoms open in spring ahead of the leaves; when the leaves do appear, they grow to twelve inches in length and are a clear dark green. In early autumn they turn bright yellow, thus with the spring flowers, summer foliage, autumn color, and curious fruits, the pawpaw makes an attractive ornamental.

Pawpaw fruits somewhat resemble short, fat bananas and are generally borne in clusters of three or four. Being heavy, they break their twigs and fall to the ground as they start to ripen. The skin, which is pale green, then turns to yellow and soon thereafter becomes black. The best time to gather them is when the fruits are barely soft to the touch. But you must be "Johnny-on-the-spot" because the competition from every form of wildlife is keen.

Since the skins often break when the fruit falls to the ground, insects are first to arrive at the banquet. Often we'll find two species dining busily, along with sweat bees, yellow jackets, and wasps. The fruits seldom last long on the ground, since they are enjoyed by possums, raccoons, squirrels, groundhogs, foxes, coyotes, and even deer and cattle.

Pawpaws have a heavy, sweet aroma that can fill a kitchen in minutes and, while not unpleasant, can become cloying. We like ours best raw, peeled and sliced from the big seeds to place atop cold cereal, or eaten with cream and sugar, or sliced with sugar and a bit of lemon juice. They can, however, be made into pie fillings or, combined with sugar, beaten egg, and milk, be eaten as a pudding.

We also like to harvest enough to make pawpaw jam, a delicious concoction that originally came from an Illinois reader in jars but whose secret he finally released to us. The pawpaws are peeled and worked through a colander to remove the big seeds. The pulp can then either be stored in the freezer until wanted or made up into jam at once. Add 1/2 cup water to 3 1/2 cups pulp and the juice of one lemon. Add a box of Sure-Jel and bring to a boil, then add 5 1/2 cups sugar and bring to a roiling boil for three minutes. Remove, pour into sterilized jars, cover with paraffin, and cool.

The insects, birds, wild and tame animals, and humans that feed on the pawpaw are a good illustration of the intricacy of the food chains that make all life possible. The fruit has absorbed energy from sunlight, nutrients and water from the soil, and carbon dioxide from the air. It is part of the underlying plant layer in the great pyramid of life; one of the uncountable plants that capture sunlight and start the marvelous upward energy circuit that we call the biota.

Thus we see that the meadow and stream surrounding our pawpaw patch contain countless plants of many kinds, millions of insects, thousands of birds and rodents that depend mainly on insects for food, hundreds of herbivores like the deer and cattle, dozens of omnivores such as the raccoon and man—and perhaps at the top of the pyramid one pair of Cooper's hawks that are the true carnivores. The lines of food interdependency between all these life forms, which we call "food chains," are complicated and diverse beyond description.

Maple Sap. There are books on our shelves that explain how autumn colors the foliage, although not all accounts agree completely. We can understand how, as the cells at the base of the leaf stem harden in autumn, the flow of fresh sap to the leaf is gradually shut off. This in turn stops the manufacture of green chlorophyll that, trapped in the leaf, is now destroyed by sunlight so that other chemicals take over. Among these is carotin, which, in the sugar maple, is rich in yellow and orange and chrome. Yet we still do not understand why the date of coloring in our dozen sugar maples varies—or why there is a wide variation of coloring in the individual trees from year to year.

When we first came to Possum Trot we heard that maple sugar was the main money crop of this farm during Civil War days. We have no way of knowing about this, but we can still find the ragged remains of a few ancient monarchs that could have been producing a century ago. The present trees in our yard date to 1900; most of the others scattered through our woodland are a bit younger. Sometimes in spring we've been tempted to tap our trees, but adding one more chore to our spring enterprises would undoubtedly break the camel's back. More than this, sugarmaking requires a lot of time and equipment for a period of two or three weeks, and we're sure considerable experience is needed to tap the trees, insert the spiles, gather the sap, and boil it down. Romeyn Hough, who wrote the *Handbook of Trees of Northern States and Canada*, says three to four pounds of sugar per tree is average but that he once made twenty-three pounds from a big sugar maple in a single season. He also gives twelve to fourteen quarts of sap as the amount needed for a pound of sugar. There are still a few producing sugar groves here in the Ozarks, however, and in most seasons we manage to acquire a quart or two of good syrup.

The last days of October are the days of clouds and mist that grow heavier as daylight strengthens. Those sugar maples look like pure gold as we step into the yard before breakfast. Mist closes the view in every direction, but the air is filled with birdsong. A flight of grackles passes overhead with a silken rustle. Dozens of robins move from tree to tree with a cheerful chatter. A towhee calls from the woods, and the mockingbird in the dogwood reviews softly all the new melodies he has learned during the summer. All the time the yellow leaves come drifting silently down like gentle rain.

5

Little Creatures Everywhere

Nature has a way of providing something new each day. If one is willing to take the time to look, some of the most interesting phenomena in nature occur among the small creatures that exist there. Certainly everything in nature has its purpose, a fact that must be true of the smaller creatures, and of some of the less physically attractive to man. Thus the handsome migratory monarch butterfly pushes north in spring, laying its eggs on the leaves of the butterfly-weed that later serves as food for the caterpillars. Likewise, the bumblebee has an attachment for the hollyhock and even more for the red clover field that it seems especially designed to pollinate. This same thing is true of the honeybee that, although it feeds on many blossoms, is a valuable ally of the orchardist and alfalfa grower. There's no doubt that nature has a place and task for all her creatures.

Toads

One June morning a flash of blue out in the yard caught our eye. Looking more closely, we saw a blue jay on the ground under the big sugar maple, pecking at some fairly large object that moved a few inches at each peck.

We count the blue jay as a predator, even though colorful, and we were afraid this fellow might be harassing a young bird that had fallen from a martin house, or even a newborn cottontail. So I hurried out to the rescue. The jay took off, and after a bit of searching I found the object of his attack. It turned out to be a small garden toad, too big for the jay to carry away and not badly injured but plainly dazed by the treatment it had received.

The toad is among our most valuable creatures in the flower and vegetable gardens, capturing countless harmful insects with the lightninglike thrust of its long tongue. Often in spring we've wondered how the infant toads, no more than a half-inch in length, manage to survive. Yet obviously they do. And during the mating season the adult males at the shallow breeding ponds have a prolonged trilling song that naturalists have called one of the sweetest sounds in nature.

Toads aren't handsome. Yet in addition to their usefulness and the beauty of their mating song, they have been celebrated in literature by no less a poet than Will Shakespeare. The toad's eye is large and black, surrounded with a broad gold border and in ancient times was considered a talisman to ward off evil. Said the great bard, who was certainly something of a naturalist: "Sweet are the uses of adversity, which, like the toad, ugly and venomous, wears yet a precious jewel in his head."

Bumblebees

"Busy as a bee" is a good, homely country expression. Nobody is busier than a bee at her appointed task of gathering pollen to feed the young in the hive and to store as nectar for the winter. The task goes swiftly, and when bumblebees are hard at work, they pay little attention to any hulking human figure watching them. This led to a favorite summer sport when we were youngsters.

Every farmstead in those days had hollyhocks growing in the fence corners. This plant with the scientific name *Althaea rosea* arrived from overseas with the early settlers and became naturalized. It belongs to the Mallow family and is a perennial. Because of this, plus the fact that hollyhocks are brightly colored, it was a favorite of the busy farmwife.

The big open blossoms were visited by bumblebees; while they were busy at their pollen gathering, we could cautiously grasp the big petals, fold them in, and thus become the proud if temporary owners of the bumblebee. It was only much later that we learned the name did not mean a bee that "bumbles" clumsily, as certainly seems the case, but that *bumblebee* derives from the early English word *bumblen*, meaning to hum.

Some disease has attacked the hollyhock of late, so the root seldom survives the winter. But bumblebees are still with us. On a recent morning when our wisteria was bursting with hundreds of blooms in late spring, the air was heavy with the humming of bumblebees. Wisteria is a legume and each blossom in the flower cluster resembles a sweet pea with three flower parts called the keel, wing, and standard. The latter is like a lid that closes tightly to protect the interior of the flower. As I watched, a bumblebee lit on a blossom and literally forced the standard to open. Then it reached down with its long "tongue," or proboscis, to sip the nectar and meanwhile gathered a few pollen grains on its legs and back.

The bumblebee has need of this long, tubelike proboscis to reach the nectar tubes of other flowers, such as lobelia, wild columbine, or *Aquilegia canadensis*, and larkspur. Red clover with its tight head made up of many small tubular florets can only be pollinated by the bumblebee. But these bees are by nature a bit lazy, so the honeybee is a harder worker and covers a much larger territory in searching for pollen and nectar.

Bumblebees and honeybees, however, are not the only pollinating insects. In this division of life forms, the Arthropoda, science has described 670,000 kinds of insects since the day of Linnaeus. Yet new ones are constantly being discovered, and the total will probably run eventually to 2 million. Some forms, like the cockroach, are extremely old and have changed little during the past 200 million years. Many species are discovered in fossil form, and some have been beautifully preserved through the centuries in amber.

One morning we carried out a bit of totally unscientific research in this relationship between blossom and insect. Within a dozen feet of our back door we gathered blossoms of five wild plants. Two were yellow and three were white, and none of them was more than a quarter-inch in size. They included yellow agrimony, yellow wood sorrel, white avens, white Virginia knotweed, and white euonymus patens. We watched in the garden for a time and soon found that the euonymus attracted two or three species of large flies, although none that bother either humans or livestock. All the others seemed to attract small insects of the type we farmers call sweat bees.

Nature's Singers

It is all too easy for city dwellers to neglect the after-dark hours outdoors that we spend enjoying the night music of the countryside. It is, of course, impossible for anyone who lives out of hearing of the city and its traffic and who is interested in nature not to be conscious of the insistent rhythm of insect sound that fills the air after dark from early summer until autumn. Yet we become so used to it that we seldom try to separate the symphonic score into individual voices, or, to be more accurate, into individual instruments.

Enjoyment of these sounds of nature is one of the pleasures of country living. Who opens the spring chorus, for example? Is it the spring peeper, or an early cricket, or our first bluebird? Is there really an accurate sequence of dates on which we hear *Hyla crucifer*, the peeper; or *Hyla versicolor*, the tree frog; or *Bufo americana*, the sweet-voiced garden toad? Among insects the entomologist knows he will probably hear, first of all, the chirp of the little black cricket, *Gryllus assimilis*; nor will he mistake this for the very similar song of *Acris gryllus*, the tiny cricket frog.

The singing of the tree frog, *Hyla versicolor*, is one of the sure signs of spring.

Just as there are spring sounds for which we listen—the first whip-poor-will or mourning dove—so other sounds identify the start of summer. The phoebe calls as she feeds her youngsters over the back door, and the chickadee and house wren are vocal as they fuss at their enemies and the world in general.

Crickets. Probably the most constant insect sounds in early summer are those of the crickets, although in due course these will be followed by the katydids and later by the cicadas that are daytime singers. All the crickets belong to the large order of Orthoptera that also includes mantids, roaches, grasshoppers, and walkingsticks. The cicadas, which we often but incorrectly call locusts, are great singers but belong to a different order, the Homoptera.

Most of the insect choristers make their music by stridulation, which merely means that they rub one part of the body against another. In the case of crickets there is a sort of file on the right-hand wing and a scraper on the left-hand wing, thus there are what we call right-handed and left-handed singers among the musical insects.

We have two principal singing crickets, but several varieties of each. There is the common cricket with a relative that gets into the house where it sings loudly. The snowy tree cricket, *Oecanthus fultoni*, is slender, pale green, and quite another sort of creature. Its chirping is a complicated yet decidedly melodic performance, when we can separate it from other night sounds. Rachel Carson makes poetry out of the snowy tree cricket, calling it the "fairy bellringer" that makes a whispered chiming; a silvery bell held in the hand of the tiniest elf—ghostly and faint, yet clear.

The mechanics of the singing of crickets is less romantic yet equally interesting. The male snowy tree cricket, barely a half-inch long, raises its narrow wings perpendicular to the body when singing. This exposes a gland that emits a liquid with an odor attractive to the female. She climbs onto the back of the male to imbibe this liquid and mating takes place. Since the female has no hearing organs with which to hear the musical chirping of the male, mating clearly depends on some chemotropic response.

Another interesting thing about this night music is that the chirping depends upon temperature. On hot nights the song is rapid and high-pitched; on cool nights it is slower until it becomes a mere rattle. One entomologist has actually worked out a formula for determining the temperature by the number of cricket or katydid chirps per minute. Thus the formula for the snowy tree cricket can be written as follows: temperature Fahrenheit equals 50 plus (number of chirps per minute minus 92), divided by 4.7. For the mathematically minded naturalist, this should certainly provide a summer evening's entertainment.

Frog Chorus. We are greatly entertained at this time of year by the frogs that are attracted to the small pond only a few yards west of the yard, while even the horse trough behind the house may eventually turn up with countless small tadpoles of *Hyla versicolor*, the tree frog. Later in the summer we'll find these small frogs high in the trees, but at this season they repair to quiet, shallow ponds to sing and mate and lay their eggs.

Katydids. Along in mid-July comes an evening when we are suddenly conscious of a new sound. We may not stop at once to identify it, but we realize gradually that we are hearing the first katydid of summer. Unlike the cicada, whose sad summer whirring is produced by a sort of drum inside its body, the katydid belongs to a large family of singing insects that produce music by fiddling; that is, by rubbing one part of the body against another.

Our bush katydid, *Scudderia furcata*, is actually a long-horned grasshopper, a pale green creature about two inches in length with rather broad wings. At the base of one wing cover is a large vein with a rough, filelike edge. On the other wing a thickened area serves as a scraper. Thus the "katy did, katy didn't" song is produced by rubbing the scraper against the file. More remarkably, the file develops only on the left wing and the scraper on the right wing, so our katydid is a left-handed fiddler.

The katydid's music, if we may so characterize it, makes us realize how many and wonderful are the sounds produced in nature; and how fortunate we are that we have ears to hear them. The cycle of seasons can be gauged by these sounds if we are methodical enough to record them on our calendar. In the insect world alone, it could be a lifetime hobby to identify and record the sounds and then classify them as to purpose. One sound might be to frighten away enemies; another to call the social insects together to protect the hive; still another to charm a member of the opposite sex.

Cicadas. August is the month of dog days. It is also the peak season of singing insects; we generally become conscious of a few cicadas in midafternoon on hot, windless days. Although singing in unison is probably accidental, it is still a fact, and the chorus rises to a crescendo as dusk approaches and often continues far into the night.

Most of the singing, incidentally, is done by the male insects. This fact was noted in 500 B.C. by Xenarchus, who wrote this comforting bit of verse: "Happy the male cicadas' lives—for they have voiceless wives."

Moths and Butterflies

Moths and butterflies of the order Lepidoptera are the most beautiful insects and, from the standpoint of plant pollination, extremely valuable. Collecting butterflies is a hobby almost as old as man, and there are legends of a Persian king who trained sparrows and starlings to act as falcons to hunt butterflies and bring them back unharmed. Many of the insects in the larval stage are destructive of plant life valued by man. At the same time, some are useful as scavengers or as eaters of parasites on other insects. When the moth or butterfly reaches adulthood, however, it becomes a valuable pollinator. Anyone who has watched the great hawk moths of the family Sphingidae, as large as hummingbirds, visiting the deep, trumpet-shaped flowers of the jimson weed (*Datura stramonium*) at dusk, has seen one of nature's countless wonders.

August is the month of butterflies and shooting stars. During the long dry spell before the rains start, nights are crystal clear and our eastern sky at four in the morning can be a thing of incredible beauty. Venus is at her brightest, shining like a blazing lantern, with Jupiter almost as spectacular. Also in the east, although not as bright as the others, we can see Mars.

The butterflies are as tantalizing as the stars. Now we drive through the fields where ironweed (*Vernonia*), blue vervain (*Verbena hastata*), chicory (*Cichorium intybus*), tall bellflower (*Campanula americana*), and swamp milkweed (*Asclepias incarnata*) vie with the yellows of goldenrods, sunflowers, silphiums, and hawkweed (*Hieracium gronovii*). Everywhere we look are butterflies of many sizes and colors. Some drift in pairs, while others move lazily from blossom to blossom. We note one here and there with wings broken at the tips and know its season is ending.

Swallowtails, Fritillaries, and others. The butterflies in August seem to like best the black-eyed Susans (*Rudbeckia hirta*), sunflowers, and ironweeds. Even an amateur can identify the most numerous, and among our favorites are the swallowtails of the family Papilionidae. The beautiful tiger swallowtails, *Pipilio*

Swallowtails are among the most numerous butterflies of late summer.

glaucus, are spectacular, but we have also identified the black (*P. polyxenes asterius*), with yellow wing spots and bands of metallic blue in the lower wing; the spicebush (*P. troilus*); and the zebra (*Graphium marcellus*).

The skippers, or Hesperioidea, are the first in the order of butterfly families, and most of them are harmless. Yet this cannot be said for the Pieridae, which include the cabbageworm (*Pieris rapae*), alfalfa butterfly, and some others. Lycaenidae include the small coppers, blues, and hairstreaks; many quite beautiful and even beneficial because they feed on aphids and scale insects.

Of other families, there are monarchs, viceroys, and other Nymphalidae, which are numerically the largest butterfly family. They include the regal fritillary, which loves the thistles, and the mourningcloak (*Nymphalis antiopa*), red admiral (*Vanessa atalanta*), and question mark (*Polygonia interrogationis*).

Our most common fritillary is the spangled or silverspot. Some years ago we had a hedge of flowering privet, removed when it grew too large. When it bloomed, the silverspots came in hundreds, and now that the hedge is gone, we have lost most of them. But there are a dozen or more species that remain. Along with the moths and dragon and damsel flies, all add interest as well as problems to the summer scene.

Monarchs. During our warm spring days of April and May, we see large numbers of moths and butterflies, most of which live out their entire life cycles in the area where they are hatched. One that especially attracts our interest, however, is the monarch, or milkweed butterfly. This is a true migrant; a handsome brown creature with four-inch wingspread that lays its eggs on the leaves of the milkweed, *Asclepias tuberosa,* commonly called butterfly-weed because of its association with the monarch butterfly.

Probably no other butterfly is better known, because of its wide distribution, its interesting migratory habit, and its connection with the bright orange butterfly weed. It is found all across America and from Mexico far up into Canada and is the only member of the family Danaidae that is found here in the Midwest. Feeding on the milky, poisonous juices of the night-

The monarch, or milkweed butterfly, is perhaps the best known of all the butterflies.

shade and the milkweed, the monarch is distasteful to birds and is avoided by other predators.

An interesting side note is that the viceroy butterfly resembles the monarch so closely that it is thought to be an evolutionary mimic. The monarch is notably distasteful to most birds and so is safe from predation. The viceroy, on the other hand, is a tasty morsel but may be safe because of its appearance.

Anyone who has ever captured and fed the monarch caterpillar in a mason jar will remember its tremendous appetite for milkweed leaves as it makes ready for its metamorphosis from larva to pupa to butterfly again; a process that requires three weeks. The pupa is bright green and is fastened securely to a support, and if we watch closely as the days go by, we can see the process of change, even to the development of the spots on the wings.

Few butterflies are more interesting to watch as the summer progresses, although we also have some other favorites. The

Asclepias tuberosa is commonly called butterfly-weed because it is a favorite habitat for the monarch butterfly.

monarchs are strong, rather deliberate flyers with powerful wings, as they must be to accomplish their remarkable migratory journey. Along in September, we see them gathering in numbers, and on windless days the air is literally filled with the brown beauties, all trending southward.

It has long been known that Pacific Coast monarchs winter in certain areas on the Monterey Peninsula. But the myriad hatched in the Midwest were a mystery, although it was plain that many crossed the border into Mexico. The mystery was finally solved by a professor at the University of Toronto, aided by a young naturalist named Kenneth Bruggers who lived in Mexico City. These two, searching in the Sierra Madre, finally came upon the resting place of the monarchs. In an evergreen forest up at about nine thousand feet, they found trees literally blanketed by countless butterflies. Here the monarchs live out the winter in a fairly dormant state and start the long journey northward in early spring. Along the way, the females start laying eggs on the milkweed plants, and many of those that hatch will mate and produce more butterflies before summer ends. Those that make the journey, however, will not live out the new season.

Sphinx Moths. There are more moth families than butterfly families, but most of these are night flyers and few are seen on our afternoon walks. An exception is the sphinx moth of the family Sphingidae that produces the tomato hornworm and feeds by daylight. It flies with incredibly fast wing-beat.

One day in August our good neighbor Audrey McClary, whose farm is up toward the foot of the mountain, stopped to show us a pair of strange-looking creatures she had dug up in their potato patch. These were dark brown, cylindrical, nearly three inches long, and with an odd stemlike appendage curling out from one end. She knew they must be "creatures" because they moved.

Although we hadn't seen one of these oddities for a long time, they somehow reminded us of the chrysalides of smaller moths and butterflies that we find at this time of year. So we got out Ralph Swain's *Insect Guide* with its beautiful color illustrations, dug through to the illustrations of large moths, and the problem was solved. There was the sphinx moth, largest of the hawk moths, along with its chrysalis, or pupa, and its caterpillar, the big green and highly destructive tomato worm with the fierce-looking but harmless horn at its rear end.

Following the sphinx in the illustrations came the beautiful Saturniidae, the pale green Luna (*Actias luna*) called queen of the night, as well as Io (*Automeris io*), Promethea (*Callosamia promethea*), Cecropia (*Hyalophora cecropia*), and Polyphemus (*Antheraea polyphemus*). These are our largest moths with six-inch wingspreads and are mostly night flyers. The adult moths seldom if ever feed. Their caterpillars feed mostly on tree leaves but are seldom numerous enough to cause serious problems.

As for the sphinx, it is a strong flyer with five-inch wingspread and is active mostly at dusk or later. It has a long proboscis, or feeding tube, so that it can pollinate deep-belled blossoms. We see the sphinx in evening in the barnyard, where it may be mistaken for the hummingbird because its wings can be heard. Often it is feeding on the pale lavender, deep-tubed flowers of the jimson weed that blooms at dusk. The sphinx is one of the few insects that can pollinate such deep-belled blossoms.

When the sphinx caterpillar, the tomato worm, is ready to pupate, it burrows into the ground and here the chrysalis is formed. This was the creature found in Audrey's potato patch, and we put the pair into a carton with six inches of soil, in hope they would hatch. It has always seemed to us that this business of raising moths and butterflies is better carried out by youngsters than adults, yet in due course our sphinx moths hatched.

Dragonflies and Damselflies. Often on September afternoons, when the chores are done, Ginnie packs her basket and we drive down to eat supper beside our favorite picnic spot. Saline Creek runs northward beneath a limestone bluff that is heavily timbered along its crest, so we have shade there on the hottest afternoon. Eastward is another strip of woodland, beyond which stretches a broad meadow with cattle grazing, and beyond this, perhaps a mile away, the mountain raises its forested crest.

The edge of the creek is a narrow bit of beach, just wide enough for building a small Indian fire and setting our chairs and an old bench to serve as a table. If the day is hot, we may take a dip, for the stream is spring-fed and cold. But whether we swim or not, we pour the small evening libation and Ginnie crumbles a piece of stale bread to feed her pet bluegills that seem always to be waiting.

The fringe of weed growth along the water's edge is a favorite resting place of damselflies, those delicately contructed insects that along with the dragonflies make up the order Odonata. Damselflies hold their four wings erect above the body when at rest, while the dragonflies come to rest with the wings extended horizontally to each side.

Both damselflies and dragonflies, we have observed, travel a regular beat, coming back to rest on the same twig or plant time after time. Our common damselfly, *Calopteryx maculata*, has black wings, although those of the female are tipped with white dots that may trigger the male mating impulse. The males have brilliant green bodies while the females are more dull. Eggs are deposited in the shallow water of a quiet pool and hatch into long-bodied nymphs that go through many molts before reaching adulthood. They are highly predaceous, feeding on tadpoles and small fishes.

As ·for dragonflies, they spend much time hunting farther from water and have accumulated such wonderful names as darning needle, snake doctor, and mosquito hawk. The family has more than five thousand members, and a fossil form has been found with a two-foot wingspread. Dragonfly nymphs swim by jet compulsion and may spend years as water creatures. The final change from water-dwelling swimmer to air-breathing flier is one of nature's miracles. The adults are not harmful and destroy millions of insects as they hunt. On one or two occasions we have watched them playing their part in a fascinating pageant of nature.

This pageant has for its setting an unusually large hatch of some small flying insect. Thus on an August evening, we found hundreds of dragonflies hunting in the air above our meadow. They are, incidentally, master flyers, with multilensed eyes and a head that moves in every direction. As we watched, we became aware of a flight of chimney swifts, hunting at a slightly higher altitude above the dragonflies. They too are remarkable fliers, with extremely long wings and big mouths to capture prey.

Whether the swifts were trying to capture dragonflies, we could not determine, although it seems likely they were both feeding on the smaller insects. But then this picture became complete when, high above the swifts, came a flight of nighthawks hunting the upper sky in their erratic flight.

Spiders

September is the season for spiders. Misty mornings find dew-jeweled webs of gossamer silk swung like miniature fishnets where the orb weavers have been at work. All across the meadows, half-hidden in the grass, are webs of the trap-door spiders and others that live at ground level. If we wander through the woodland, we must constantly brush from our

On misty mornings we find dew-jeweled webs of gossamer silk
swung like miniature fishnets.

faces the tough strands woven by the silk spiders that seem to
float suspended from the trees.

Spiders are not, in general, popular. Yet they are tremendously interesting and here in America, with the exception of
three species, are quite harmless. The bad ones are the black
widow, brown recluse, and less dangerous tarantula. Fortunately, these are fairly rare, while all the spiders are valuable
destroyers of harmful insects.

We often think of the spiders as insects, although they belong
to a class of their own: the Arachnids. These differ from insects
in having only two body sections and four pairs of legs instead
of three. They vary in size from the big tarantula and trap-door
to the tiny triangle spider whose male is only one-twelfth inch
long. Laurence Palmer states that there are thirty-six thousand
species in eleven orders.

Web spinning or building is probably the best-known activity of spiders, although the "hunting" spiders catch their prey without trapping it. Most spiders, however, secrete the web-spinning fluid in their abdomens whence it is shot through many jets onto the spinnerets. Here on contact with air it hardens into silk. Entomologists list four primary cobwebs or spider webs, and seven common groups of spiders: tarantulas and trap-door spiders, funnel-web weavers, comb-footed weavers, orb weavers, crab spiders, wolf spiders, and jumping spiders. For us, few sights in nature are as fascinating as watching the big black and yellow garden spider spinning her geometrically perfect orb web that may be six feet across and is strong enough to hold a katydid, grasshopper, or praying mantis.

French naturalist Henri Fabre writes at length of this spider, but we shall quote more briefly from our favorite naturalist, our biologist brother Thomas Hall, on the construction of the garden spider's web: "The female fixes her line to one spot, then walks or swings to another spot, playing out line and drawing it tight as she lands. Having built several such bridges, she then lays down the spokes in the same way. Next step is to form a strengthening mesh near the center of the web and finally to lay down the continuous spiral. This, unfortunately for intruders, is covered with a sticky glue. After this she sits at the hub of the web, awaiting an incautious insect."

The word *gossamer* is quite accurately used in describing the spider's web. It derives from a medieval English word meaning "goose summer," or Indian summer when the geese are fat and ready for roasting. At this time, just before the first frost, you may have experienced warm days when the sunny autumn air seemed filled with floating gossamer threads. These come about in quite a remarkable way, and if your eyes are sharp, you will see that many of the floating threads carry a small, and probably young, spider.

These threads are of the spider's own construction, produced in this manner: the tiny spider, having climbed to the top of a grass stalk or other elevated spot, attaches itself securely by several threads. Then it spins another strand that it allows to blow freely in the wind. The strand grows longer and longer, crisscrossing until a tiny raft is formed. Finally, the wind lifts both raft and spinner into the air for a journey that may last for a half-dozen yards or for miles. Perhaps, as one naturalist has put it, the little ship lands in some spot where the spider can spend the winter in security. The ballistics of this flight, says Henri Fabre, may not be in accordance with current teaching, but instead suits the plan of the Universal Planner whose compass measures all things.

6

The Contemplative Art

We have a theory we've never quite been able to carry out. This is that any sensible person should spend a third of his life camping in the back country. There are reasons: to keep close to nature and to observe her wonders; to learn the value of solitude; to put the complexities of civilization into perspective by learning how easy it is to live without them. Our back country may be as distant as the Yukon or as close as the nearest state park, provided the latter does not force the tent-peg-to-tent-peg camping so common today in America. Under primitive conditions there is the opportunity to learn about nature, to get beyond hearing of this horn-honking culture, to shed artificial camp gadgets, and to practice the ancient techniques of woodcraft.

Something of this feeling came to us in a letter from a friend who agrees with our basic philosophy, describing one of those rare moments that reward folk who love the outdoors. "Yesterday," he writes, "I saw what I believe must have been the prenuptial flight of a pair of broad-winged hawks, with one repeatedly diving to the ground, then soaring in a beautiful arc to sweep by his mate—the whole time twittering. They were smaller than our red-tailed but definitely bigger than the sparrow hawks. They passed over our lake, then slowly drifted down toward your pasture and pond. It was a truly inspiring sight—the freedom of their flight, a ballet of the skies."

One sight like that can make an outdoor weekend, but how much better to increase the number of outdoor opportunities. All of our camping through the years has been under canvas, and we do not envy those who have traded the tent for the van, trailer, or cab-over camper. For us, one of the essentials of successful camping is a measure of solitude, a thing hardly possible in a campground filled with a hundred motorized vehicles, no matter how many conveniences it offers.

Two things are essential to successful camping, equipment and planning. Taking that second essential first, we want to plan where we are going, by what route, and how long it will take to get there. Here such things as national park, Forest Service, state recreational, and road maps are all helpful. There are also excellent materials available such as Rand McNally's *Campground and Trailer Park Guide* and the camping and tour guides of the auto clubs of America.

Equipment can be listed under five headings: shelter, bedding, cooking gear, food, and emergency kit. Unless we are backpacking, in which event every ounce counts, we like a tent of ample size to hold our bedrolls and all other gear in case of stormy weather. Ours is a 9'6" × 9'6" umbrella-type tent of flame-retardant material with outside aluminum poles, screened windows, insect-proof ground cloth, dining shelter, and pegs. Also included in this category are such items as a shovel for trenching when necessary and a small ax.

Comfortable sleeping is essential, and we have long used light, three-pound polyester-filled sleeping bags and three-quarter-length air mattresses. We prefer these to the foam-rubber pads often used today. Fewer and fewer campgrounds have wood supplies, although some state and Forest Service campgrounds do. However, we have long depended on our two-burner Coleman stove, even if we have a campfire. Late models burn propane instead of white gasoline, but this cannot be purchased everywhere. Our cooking equipment came from L. L. Bean more than a quarter-century ago and still does the job.

Other important items include an ice chest, a two-gallon water jug, a butane or propane latern, a good flashlight, and lightweight camp chairs if space and weight permit. Add paper towels and toilet tissue.

We have long planned the food department on a menu basis—so many breakfasts, luncheons, and suppers for so many people, plus a standing list of such basics as salt, sugar, soap, washing powder, pot cleaners, and an extra ten-quart bucket. Finally we include bird and wildflower guides, cameras and film, binoculars, and a good first-aid kit, and we are ready to go. But remember, finally, that your objectives are fun and comfort, not a competition with Mother Nature, and have a good time.

*　　*　　*　　*

Aldo Leopold had ideas about time spent in the outdoors. "Advertisements on rock and rill," he said, "confide to all and sundry the whereabouts of new retreats, landscapes, hunting-grounds, and fishing lakes just beyond those recently overrun. . . . To him who seeks in the woods and mountains only those things obtainable from travel or golf, the present situation is tolerable. But to him who seeks something more, recreation has become a self-destructive process of seeking but never quite finding."

This describes in a nutshell the charm, to us, of floating the Ozark rivers in canoe or johnboat; especially the smaller streams and at seasons of minimum traffic. Thirty miles of downriver paddling give you more solitude to observe nature than three thousand miles of roaring around an artificial lake, deaf from your own 75-horsepower motor. Drift in your canoe around any bend and you are alone with your companion. Pitch camp on any clean, windswept gravel bar, and when the fire burns low and the stars wink into being you could be in un-touched wilderness. Only the music of hounds running or the thunderlike rumble of a far-off jet tells you there are other mor-tals on your planet. Soon only the singing river and call of whip-poor-will break the night silence.

Study a topographic map of the Current River country in the Missouri Ozarks and you can understand why this stream, more than many others, maintains much of its wild and un-spoiled character. The Current runs through an ancient land, the riverbed itself cutting down through a channel of dolomite limestones, with now and then an outcropping of rhyolite por-phyry. Geologists give names and dates to those formations. The limestones are chiefly those called the Eminence or older Bonne Terre, laid down during a succession of ocean inunda-tions that covered the Ozark highland during a period of many millenia, perhaps a half-billion years ago. Fossil life in these limestones is primitive but includes many marine forms. This period is known as the Upper Cambrian. As for the porphyry, it is rock fired by the internal heat of the earth and contains no

Thirty miles of downstream paddling give you more solitude to observe nature than 3,600 miles of roaring around on an artificial lake.

fossils, having been pushed up a billion or more years ago in Precambrian time.

Lands surrounding the river, including the beds of the creeks that feed it, are somewhat younger. Here we find residual cherts, sandstones, and limestones of the Gasconade and Roubidoux formations, dating from the Ordovician period, 450 million years ago. These explain the gravel that washes down the little valleys in quantities that sometimes choke the parent stream. This geological background tends to produce a rugged terrain, where cultivation is only possible in small areas of alluvial soil in the river and creek bottoms. Chief natural resource has always been the forest that covers 85 percent of the watershed.

We started floating and camping on the Current River more

than forty years ago, and in digging back through our files, we found this description of an expedition of the early 1930s:

> We camped on a high gravel-bar opposite a beautiful bluff hole and slept under the stars, for the night was clear. One joy of this Ozark stream is its almost complete freedom from mosquitoes in summer, provided the swift-moving water keeps the air stirring. Early next morning I rolled out of my blanket and slipped away down river with the fly rod. Dawn painted the eastern sky and mist rolled up in long streamers from the valley. The whip-poor-will still called and a wood thrush sang in the deep woods across the river. As I reached the bank, a band of teal beat the water to foam as they took off downstream. High on the bluff a hickory nut dropped and a fox squirrel barked, and over at the head of the bluff hole a big bass rose to an insect on the water. A wonderful time of day to be up and about.

Johnboat

The craft we took on our first float trip was quite unlike the thousands of canoes that crowd today's waterways on weekends. Midwestern canoeing was still considered an adventurous sport and was confined mostly to near-city streams like Missouri's Meramec and Big rivers

More distant waters—Piney, Gasconade, Niangua, and Osage on the north Ozark escarpment and Current, St. Francis, Eleven Point, James, North Fork, and White rivers to the south—had long since developed their own special craft. This was the johnboat, designed and modified through the years and ideally suited to the swift and often rock-strewn waters.

We've never determined just where the name *johnboat* originated, but every farmer in the river valleys owned one, and most were built from "patterns" carefully preserved from one generation to the next. The boats are flat-bottomed and canted slightly upward at bow and stern. Sides slant outward and are generally made of a single board. Johnboats are of slight draft, but deeper on the lower rivers where they are powered by outboard motors. Upstream they are paddled or poled from the stern. It is possible to sink them, but normally they do not tip as easily as a canoe.

We built a small johnboat in our backyard—a clumsy affair, I must confess—and trucked it to Cedargrove on the Current.

The Current River.

During that first season we ran it by easy stages clear down to Van Buren, some 120 miles. We didn't haul it back and forth but tied up wherever our weekend float ended. Here we would arrange for our car to pick us up, and such was our faith in the honesty of the river folk that we were certain our craft would be waiting exactly where we'd left it when we came the following weekend to run the next stretch of river.

That boat dumped us more than once, not being perfectly designed. But on the last weekend of summer a fourteen-foot rise came down the Current, tore our small craft loose from her moorings, and carried her downstream to Arkansas or perhaps even to New Orleans. We never saw her again, but we learned considerable about river running from her, and our next craft was a canvas canoe. When we hauled it to the river the following spring, atop our car, our friends along the valley looked at it askance and allowed we'd never make it through the first riffle. But it surprised them.

Floating

Floats were almost always of more than one day, so we gradually developed the camp gear that suited us best and would make a reasonable cargo. A light floor rack of our own construction kept the load dry and served as a table in camp. One tent followed another until the day of the lightweight "umbrella" over an aluminum frame. A waterproof canvas duffle bag carried extra clothing, a light aluminum icebox kept perishables. One thing that hasn't changed is a pair of two-compartment wooden orange crates fitted with rope handles in which we carry the grub and cook kit.

We floated in those early days for love of the unspoiled wilderness, and to fly-fish for bass that still abounded in the Ozark rivers. Often a whole day passed without seeing another boat or more than a bank fisherman or two. The bow man fished, and the stern paddler handled navigation, although at noon and in evening we'd fish with live bait for jack salmon, as the walleyed pike is called in the Ozarks.

When wildlife moviemaking became part of our expeditions, we traded the old canvas canoe for a square-sterned aluminum Grumman with a three-and-a-half-horsepower motor so we could get back upstream when we needed a second sequence of a worthwhile scene. All this came to mind the other day as we put a fresh coat of green on the canoe and set up the tent to make sure it was still waterproof. Nowadays, if one wishes to duplicate the opportunity for solitude that we found back then, it is best to float the river during midweek.

Camping gear at Possum Trot is always close at hand, though in some years it might be August before we can get to our first Current River float of the year. We found ourselves in this position ten years ago and decided it was time to get to the river. It was a lazy man's trip with outfitter Willie Parks of Van Buren running his big commissary boat and two fishing boats with guides Roy Reed and young Jeff McSpadden. We have been floating with Willie since he was sixteen. Our companions were two friends of long-standing—Ed Cherbonnier and Lew Stuart, both veterans of a hundred Ozark floats.

Only member of the Possum Trot family who didn't go was Shannon, the Irish setter. He stayed home as companion for another friend of equally long-standing, Lexie Hill, who was holding down the fort during our absence. She and Shannon had been good companions since he was a pup, and while he likes float trips, we didn't explain to him exactly where we were going. Thus once we'd taken off, we knew he wouldn't be disappointed.

It takes most of the morning to assemble our gear, but by the time Ed and Lew arrived, I had tent, duffle bags, baskets of fresh vegetables, and fishing tackle assembled in the yard for easy loading. Then after an early lunch we were off for our meeting place, south to Ellington, west across Highway 106 past Powder Mill Ferry, and onto county road V, which runs to the junction of Jacks Fork and the Current.

We'd made arrangements for Will and our boats to arrive there in time to float downstream and set up camp on the Gauge Hole Gravel Bar, named for the gauging station maintained here for many years by the Geological Survey. Meeting time was four o'clock, and we arrived on the minute. Willie had already left to set up camp, and we soon had our luggage transferred to the fishing boats. Willie's wife and our car driver headed home for Van Buren, and we stepped aboard, glad to be afloat after a year's absence.

You couldn't have found a more beautiful Missouri afternoon. The river was clear and dropping slowly. Along the banks, wildflowers of many species were in bloom. Green herons took off ahead of us, kingfishers rattled, and pileated woodpeckers came winging across the valley with their wild calls. We rounded a bend, saw the smoke from Willie's cooking fire, and pulled into the gravel bar where our tents were pitched, ready for occupancy. The supper menu was settled upon—fried chicken, garden vegetables from Possom Trot, peaches and cookies, good boiled coffee. But there was still time for a long, cooling swim and toddy before the cook called, "Come and get it."

Leonard and Ginnie Hall at Powder Mill Ferry.

At supper I retold an incident that had taken place on this gravel bar on a summer evening forty years before. We were floating the river with only a precious pint of medicinal grog to use in case of snakebite. As we beached our johnboats, I asked my guide, a great riverman and coon hunter now gone to his reward, if he might find us a small jug of mountain dew. He allowed he might, went off up the hollow, and finally came back with an ancient mountaineer whose long beard waved in the breeze and who carried a large kerosene can painted red. I was introduced, and the following conversation ensued:

"Be you the feller wants the whiskey?"
My answer was, "Yes."
"Well, how much will you want?"
"Depends on the price."
"Would six bits a quart be all right?"

There is nothing to compare with the quiet of a night spent on a gravel bar with close friends.

And I said, "Sure, if it's old enough."
"Well, by crickety, it ought to be. I made it Tuesday."

At this point the sale was consummated by pouring the mountain dew from the kerosene can into a couple of quart mason jars, and the old man retreated into the woods.

*   *   *   *

One sure way for an outdoorsman to know that youth is on the wing and midddle age is at his doorstep is when the drumbeat of raindrops on taut canvas at night ceases to sound like a Schubert symphony and takes on a sinister note. If this analysis is correct, on one night in September about ten years ago, we heard the approaching footsteps of Father Time.

We had planned a trip to the Current with Ed Cherbonnier and Sarita Van Vleck of Captiva Island, whose book *Growing Wings* is a delightful account of the annual cycle of bird life. Ginnie and I had made arrangements for the trip with Willie Parks and had asked for Roy and Bennie Reed to run the fishing boats while Will handled the commissary. We had also planned the grub list to provide gourmet eating. This was our first float of the season, so assembling camp gear, checking tent and fishing tackle, and making sure air mattresses didn't leak and that mice hadn't nested in the bedrolls all took time.

It rained three inches the night before we left, a real "trash raiser" that sent the creeks out of their banks. But an early call to Willie brought word that they'd had no rain and the Current was running clear. We loaded our gear, saving room for Shannon in the backseat. At ten-thirty we rendezvoused with our companions in Ellington and a half-hour later were at Powder Mill Ferry where guides and boats waited.

Another half-hour saw the commissary boat loaded and headed downstream with its outboard purring. We rigged spinning, casting, and fly rods, got our personal gear aboard, whistled Shannon in from the shallows where he was fishing, and were off.

Current River was running a foot above normal and decidedly dingy; a poor condition for any lure except live minnows. There was an overcast and an occasional touch of mist in the air. We pulled in below Blue Spring for hot coffee and a bite of lunch and found the gravel bar clean of any trash. This was true on the entire trip, which speaks well for the Ozark National Scenic Riverways staff, considering the heavy summer traffic.

We tried many lures with little success. Yet despite poor fishing, there were always things of interest along the way. Swift rapids alternated with deep pools running silently beneath towering bluffs where wildflowers and gnarled old cedars flourished. Small bands of teal, wood ducks, and shovelers rose ahead of us or came whistling overhead. Pileated woodpeckers were almost constantly in sight or hearing. Turkey vultures rode the updrafts.

At four o'clock, with the sun still high, we found Will and his commissary boat already camped at the last fairly high gravel bar for a good many miles; in such uncertain weather only the novice camps at water level. But it was hot enough for a swim before toddy time, and soon we sat down to a delicious dinner of smallmouth bass, cooked perfectly in Willie's big black skillet.

After supper we made camp snug, got the bedrolls ready, and soon turned in. Within an hour, lightning was playing across the entire sky and the wind was rising. Then came the drumbeat of·rain in recurring squalls, just hard enough to bring us awake each time it started. When I looked out at midnight, stars showed and the waning moon was bright.

By midnight it had cleared and four barred owls started serenading, up and down the river. One finally came too close and set Shannon barking in his dry shelter under the cook tent. At dawn, we wakened to cool air and a heavy mist that we knew would burn away with sunrise. The promise was for a good day, for the river was clear and dropping.

Breakfast was a modest affair of fruit juice, coffee, bacon and eggs, cold fried chicken, and stacks of hotcakes. Thus it was after nine when we pushed the johnboats into the stream and headed downriver. There was time, on this float, to loaf a bit and enjoy the scenery, bird life, and wildflowers. The spectacular cardinal lobelia (*L. cardinalis*) had been hard hit by recurring floods, yet we glimpsed its rich vermilion color on gravel bars and along the bluffs. Blue lobelia (*L. siphilitica*) was plentiful, along with asters and the wild ageratum or blue mist flower (*Eupatorium coelestinum*). There were also the lavender obedient plant (*Physostegia virginiana*) and clumps of swamp sneezeweed (*Helenium*), coreopsis, Spanish needles (*Bidens bipinnata*), and rudbeckia.

We lunched on a gravel bar that, like the others, was free of litter. Here we noticed an interesting thing, that these arid-seeming areas develop their own flora, including some strange plants along with miniature specimens of many common species. Among these were day-flower (*Commelina communis*), spiderwort (*Tradescantia*), blue morning glory (*Ipomoea hederacea*), and a dozen others. As always on our trips, we came up with new plant specimens. One species that we finally keyed out, *Erechtites hieracifolia*, was a homely flower with the homely name of pilewort. It is also called fireweed, although no relative of the beautiful fireweed of the evening primrose family that we've found in the Yukon and the high country of the Sierras and North Cascades. Pilewort is a tall plant with greenish-white flowers, resembling and related to the Indian plantain, or *Cacalia*.

A second new plant was a fruiting vine with grapelike leaves that grows in the river bottom. This we finally had to take home to run down in the big Steyermark *Flora of Missouri*. After some puzzling, we identified it as *Passiflora lutea*, or passionflower, quite common to our Ozarks. It has an inconspicuous green white blossom and grapelike fruits called "May-pops" (with one seed), which are edible although sour.

Our most interesting wildlife were the beavers. We saw them first in a small bay as we ate lunch, and they soon took off upriver. These are bank beavers that build in small backwaters and cutoffs that they often dam up. Most farmers dislike them, saying they destroy good timber along the riverbanks and sometimes flood the low-lying fields. Yet their favorite foods are small cottonwoods and willows that have little value as timber.

On this morning Ed Cherbonnier's guide decided, after every sort of lure had failed, to resort to plastic worms. These are about six inches long in red, brown, or black and have a small lead head to give them casting weight. Fished without a spinner, they are allowed to sink and then retrieved with a slight jerking motion. The choice proved a winner, and in the space of two hours, Ed took the best string of smallmouth we've seen on the Current in many a moon. Then the action stopped, and Ginnie and I hardly managed a strike all day.

Now that Labor Day was past and school had started, the river was deserted; in fact, we saw not a single boat nor even a bank fisherman for our entire trip. Our commissary boat pushed on downriver to set up camp, and we loafed.

At three-thirty as we came down past Paint Rock, we saw a pickup truck parked by the mouth of the creek. The driver said he was waiting to haul some canoeists and their gear back to their starting point at Akers, forty miles upstream. More than this, he told us that Akers had gotten a five-foot rise from the big rain. This was worrisome news and we pushed downstream, hoping to find camp set on a high gravel bar above possible floodwaters. This was where our adventures really started.

We filled our water jugs at Gravel Spring and pushed on to find where Willie, with the commissary boat, had decided to camp. Guides Roy and Bennie weren't happy with the news, nor did I relish the idea of a flood rolling downriver. The guides knew what we didn't remember—that Paint Rock was the last high campground for miles. Sure enough, four miles downstream we found the commissary boat pulled up on a low bar. The tents were pitched, the cooking fire going, and Willie had even cut driftwood logs for a "sit around" fire.

Smallmouth bass make a good catch along the Current River.

When the commissary boat had passed Paint Rock, our high-water informant hadn't yet arrived there, so Will knew nothing of the flood and had elected to chance camping on this fine, open bar, even though it was only eighteen inches above river level. We held a war council, delaying the toddy while we made our decision. Upstream was Paint Rock, four miles of swift water above us. The next high bar downstream was a long hour away, and striking the tents, packing, motoring down, and pitching camp again would have put us well into dark.

In the end we took the optimist's view. With luck the promised high water might not reach us until morning. So we made
camp snug, laid out the bedrolls, quaffed our toddies, ate our
steaks and fresh garden vegetables, watched the stars come out,
and turned in. The boys promised to rouse us in case of a rise,
and we discussed a safe spot in case of emergency. They agreed
on an old deer hunter's cabin a mile downstream and high on a
bluff. It was a cabin they'd built, years ago, and now unoccu-
pied from one deer season to the next.

Ginnie and I had hardly turned in before we were sound
asleep. Moments later, it seemed to us, a shout awakened us.
The river was rising—so fast you could see it creeping up the
bank. All hands turned out, and with campfire light and the
Coleman lantern, we rolled our gear, crammed it into the duffle
bags, struck the tents, collected the fishing tackle, and loaded
the boats at lightning speed.

During all this, Shannon remained calm; confident that with
his folks close at hand all would be well. Soon we shoved off
into the pitch dark, for starlight has little candlepower. To guide

Even with a flood threatening, there was still time to enjoy fresh-
cooked steaks and watch the stars come out.

us, I held aloft the one lantern, which lacked its glass mantle and flared in the wind like a giant torch. We strung out, Will in the lead, our boat second with the light, Ed and Sarita behind us. We hit the current with motors almost idling and finally swung in alongside the bluff where the cabin was located. But our troubles weren't over. The river was swift and a giant oak had fallen to smash the wooden stairs that climbed the perpendicular bank.

Thanking our stars for the three expert rivermen who handled the boats, we somehow made fast. Soon we had scaled the cliff, found the cabin locked, forced an entrance. Inside were two old beds with mouse-riddled mattresses—and half a hundred wasps' nests that occupied our first attention. Somehow the boys made another trip down the bluff, located our sleeping bags, and were back. Then they moved the two fishing boats to a safe mooring across river and tied the commissary securely, high alongside our bluff, allowing for a further rise.

Sleeping arrangements for seven in the sixteen-by-sixteen-foot cabin were too complicated to detail here, and Shannon got the best night's rest. Once I woke to see stars shining and hear the roar of the river, and at dawn the yellow flood stretched into the woods on the far shore. We packed our gear, made the descent to the water's edge, boarded our craft, and were off on the crest of the rise. Later we found a bar high enough to cook breakfast. Rain threatened, and we decided the better part of valor was to wind up the outboards and head for Van Buren. We were there before noon and had soon packed the cars, bid good-bye to our good companions of the river, and were on our way home to Possum Trot. Here's to better luck, next time we float the Current.

Angling

There comes a day each year, along toward the end of May, when we suddenly realize it's time to go fishing. This is quite different from long-ago years when we used to take off in early March for the Current River down below Welch Cave Spring to fish after dark for the giant rainbow trout that inhabit those swift, chill waters. The road in to the river was an adventure in itself, but somehow we'd make it.

These cannibal trout fed mostly after dark on big dead minnows, and it wasn't unusual for ice to form on the fly line as you stood hip-deep in the rushing torrent and floated your lure down against the rocky bluff where the big trout hid. The record of my years there was a monster that tipped the scales at seven pounds eleven ounces; a real "bragging fish." We'd camp close to the river, build up a big fire against the night chill, and wake at dawn with heavy frost on the bedrolls. First one awake would chunk up the fire and put on the big coffeepot.

There's one tale we've told about the Welch Cave trout for so many years that I can no longer vouch for its veracity. We had hiked up the Welch Cave Spring branch one morning and climbed to a shelf on the bluff where we could peer down into the crystal water. Suddenly below us—can this have been only a dream—we saw a rainbow trout that seemed nearly a yard long pursuing a full-grown muskrat with the obvious intention of eating him. But the muskrat reached a sunken drift and disappeared into safety.

Well, that was long ago and we no longer go "frostbite fishing." We have somehow never gotten used to the excellent elbow-to-elbow trouting furnished today by our fish and game managers. We know it is good sport, but angling has always meant for us wildness and solitude, or at least only the company of a good companion or two. There is, moreover, something special about a "native" quarry—even a small "born wild" pan-sized fish. And there is art in luring him into striking an artificial fly or bug or minnow as it drifts past his hiding place.

*　　*　　*　　*

It is a sorry summer when you get too busy to go fishing, but it happens. We generally make out in such seasons by occasional evenings along our creek with the fly rod or by casting to the fish rising at sunset on the Big Pond. But some summers drought drops the level of the Saline until the pools are low and the riffles barely run. Moreover, in those summers we water cattle at the pond, so fly rod and spinning rod stand neglected in the corner.

If anyone suggested to us that a summer month could go by without our wetting a fly line in some Ozark stream, we would have simply said that they were off their rocker. Yet such are the vicissitudes of life in our times that the pumpkinseeds, goggle-eye, and smallmouth bass in Saline Creek have swum unmolested by us for many a day. But a Saturday evening will finally arrive when we find time to rig the fly rod, tie on a small spinner and bucktail with a bit of pork rind, and head down the hill to wade our half-mile of water.

There are many years full of contrasts for small Ozark streams. Heavy spring rains may cause flooding that brings down fallen timber and, sad to say, litter dumped into the headwaters by the village of Belleview some miles to the south. There is no doubt that the higher nitrogen runoff from fertilizer has caused a growth of algae that covers the gravel with a slick coat of organic matter and clouds the pristine clarity of the spring-fed water.

These are things we want to examine firsthand, and how better than to spend a few hours up to one's waist in one's own stream. Nor does our concern as to water quality lessen our enjoyment of the summer afternoon. For one thing, pursuit of the "big" fish has always seemed to us to belittle angling, both as a pastime and as an art, just as the pursuit of "record" heads does the sport of hunting. Yet this is a matter of controversy on which we cannot hope to find agreement.

There's no doubt, however, that the charm of wading a small Ozark stream does not come from capturing giant fish. It is, rather, an occupation for the naturalist. The banks of Saline as it flows through Possum Trot are heavily timbered, often flanked on the western border by the limestone bluff. The heavy vegetation here helps prevent erosion, just as it increases the food supply for the whole life complex from water-striders and dragonflies through minnows and panfish to the occasional bass at the top of the pyramid.

The green growth would interest any botanist, for it includes all the wildflowers that like shade and moist earth, shrubs of many kinds, and the rich assortment of trees that our Ozarks boasts. We note the big walnut crop and, to our delight, clusters of pawpaws that are still green. Among wildflowers, the vivid blue of tall bellflower contrasts with the pink of the obedient plant, or *Physostegia*, and the violet blue of the monkey flower, or *Mimulus*. Yellow is also a dominant color with St. Johnswort, sneezeweed, tickseed sunflower, and a variety of coneflowers.

Birdlife here is richer than anywhere on the farm. Phoebes carry food to nests hidden in the bluff. The big pileated that nests in a dead sycamore comes winging above, giving its wild call.

The afternoon is hot, and so it is not unpleasant when, now and then, we wade into a pool that hits above the waistline. This is "wet-wading" with heavy-soled canvas shoes that L. L. Bean calls their Maine Hiking Shoe. The rocks seem slicker than in earlier seasons, but bank cover is so heavy we stick to the stream channel. The creek is low—a succession of pools and small rapids that barely run. Thus a single rise in each pool is the best one can expect, since the fuss kicked up by the smallest sunfish when hooked sends larger quarry scurrying for deep cover. Small panfish keep us busy releasing and returning them to the water, and we put two or three small bass back to grow for another day. So the creel is still light when we climb the bluff and head for home, but at least we've made a start on the new season.

*   *   *   *

Late August often brings new life to summer fishing in our creek. One particular year, the August rains, which break the droughts and bring temporary floods, had subsided. Streams were running faster, higher, and cleaner than at any time that year. Little wonder, then, that an afternoon arrived when I could no longer think of any excuse not to go fishing.

This was enough to bring the old willow creel down from its place on the deer antlers. I checked the supplies: fish knife, plastic boxes of flies and popping bugs, spinners, fresh leader material, a bottle of new pork rinds. Out came the fly rod, and I reeled off a bit of line to make sure it had not gone brittle, then tied on six feet of two-pound-test nylon.

Shannon watched these proceedings with perfect under-standing, and Ginnie said she would take her reading and drive me to the creek if I'd gather wood and build a bit of a fire against the unlikely mosquito. We parked at the edge of the woods along the creek, under a pawpaw tree where big green fruits were showing. The fire was soon made, and I waded off down-stream after admonishing Shannon to do his fishing several yards behind me. Since he seems not to mind never catching a fish, he offered no objection.

As I took off, a kingfisher rattled up the long pool under the limestone bluff that still drips moisture from the rain. From their nesting area downstream came the fussing of a young pileated woodpecker. Blue jays crossed overhead, carrying acorns to be hidden in knotholes. The yellow-billed cuckoo gave his throaty "ka, ka, ka, ka, kow, kow, kow, koup, koup," which all country boys know means rain.

Flowers now blooming along the stream are mostly composites: verbesina, goldenrod, Spanish needles, swamp sneezeweed. But on wet banks are masses of jewelweed, or *Impatiens capensis*, where hummingbirds feed, and on gravel bars we find blue lobelia, star bellflower, and the delicate lavender pink obedient plant.

In years when we have time to wander the creek banks, we locate hiding places of smallmouth bass. Yet these are so wary that taking them on any lure except a live minnow is a rare accomplishment. In deeper pools are schools of white suckers that seldom take a bait in midsummer. But when snared or gigged in season, deeply scored down the sides to cut the small bones, and dropped into bubbling-hot fat, they make a meal to be enjoyed.

Our quarry this afternoon, however, was more modest. Bright orange sunfish that we call pumpkinseeds seldom grow bigger than six inches, but they charge out to do battle with the gameness of fish several times their size. Equally game, and an even better panfish because larger and fatter, is the green or black perch, also a sunfish. Occasionally we pick up a rock bass or goggle-eye, another battler but rare in our creek.

Each of these small adversaries requires a certain amount of skill, a matter of knowing where they live, of placing the lure in just the right place, and of retrieving it at just the right speed and depth. These are matters that cannot be learned except by wading the streams throughout the years. Suffice it to say that as the sun slanted its long afternoon rays down through the trees, I found the creel heavy enough to guarantee a good dinner. Back at the fire I found Shannon frog hunting in the woods and Ginny ready with the evening toddy. Something told me it wouldn't be so long before I went fishing again.

* * * *

Every angler has his pet theories as to why fish strike and when and where. Some depend on solunar tables, some on the moon stages, some on thermometers to check the water at various depths, some on electronic fish finders, some on magic fish oil. Come to think of it, we aren't any different from the rest, although we incline to go along with the country boy who spits on his worm before consigning it to the stream. Yet we know that theories, scientific or not, furnish a handy excuse when we come home with an empty creel.

The truth of the matter is that, like many another angler, we go fishing wherever and whenever the opportunity arises. Certainly this was the case when we enjoyed one perfect Current River float trip that didn't yield enough bass, goggle-eye, sunfish, or suckers to fill the skillet for a single meal. We have our theories as to why this happened, and certainly it wasn't for lack of angling skill or effort, with spinning, casting, and fly rod lures going steadily for the better part of two days.

Ginnie is the hardest working fly fisherman we know, dropping her lure into every swirl and pocket of the stream and fishing steadily even through the hottest hours of the summer day. Of our companions, Ed had fished many waters and been high rod on more than one Ozark float. Bill had taken every species of giant deep-sea and game fresh-water fish from northern Canada to Mexico and the tip of South America, with New Zealand and other "angler's heavens" thrown in. My own fishing career started sixty years ago on the creeks of Washington County. When we added up the angling years of this quartet and found that it came to a total of 225, we'll admit that it was a bit of a shock.

A Gentle Appreciation. There are some occupations and occasions within daily reach of the countryman whose flavor is seldom enjoyed by the city dweller. One of these is the opportunity to slip off occasionally for a late-afternoon hour to some nearby creek where the fish may be only pan-sized but were planted by God rather than by the fish-hatchery truck. The angler's equipment for such an expedition may be a cane pole and can of worms, or a four-ounce fly rod and the finest lures of the fly tier's art. The aim of such an hour, however, is not a trophy fish, a fact that has been recognized by anglers for centuries.

Another "sport" we have enjoyed for many years is collecting books about fishing, generally called angling. The word goes back to the Greek *ankos* meaning barbed hook, rather than to angleworm. A great thing about fishing is that it has produced delightful literature, which can be said about few other sports and least of all about hunting. Moreover, we agree with one fly fisherman who said that "master angler" is meaningless because a degree of mastery could only come down to pounds of fish caught, an ideal uncherished by any true fisherman.

So our shelves devoted to the gentle art contain fifty volumes or maybe more. They range from an ancient and treasured volume of Izaak Walton's *The Compleat Angler or the Contemplative Man's Recreation* to a modest little work by Herbert Hoover. Izaak Walton's classic was published in 1653 when he was already sixty years old, and no fisherman should be allowed to publish before that mature age. As for Izaak, he lived to enjoy his sport to the fine old age of ninety-three.

Some of our pleasantest and most rewarding angling hours have been spent exploring the dusty shelves of old bookstores. Here our trophies have been volumes by fishermen of an earlier day.

Many a pleasant hour we spent in those collecting days, browsing through the dusty shelves, and many a small treasure we discovered. There is, for example, a thin volume by Bliss Perry entitled *Fishing with a Worm* and published in 1918 by Houghton Mifflin, although it had run in *The Atlantic* in 1904. He starts, as do many works by fishermen, with a quotation from Walton, "The last fish I caught was with a worm." The Rev. Henry Van Dyke has furnished us no less than three volumes on angling, while Washington Irving said that there is certainly something in this gentle art to produce a pure serenity of mind.

Angling literature is a treasure trove of good writing. This cannot be said of hunting literature, which necessarily deals with the destruction of creatures we have no real reason for killing. We once read an account from our Conservation Department, detailing the exploits of a Missouri marksman who had killed four hundred squirrels during the 1972 hunting season. We wondered as we read how such an unpleasant exploit might be incorporated into an account of "sporting" literature.

Many things about modern-day recreation disturb us, and one is the highly commercialized "fishing tournaments" promoted on both big artificial reservoirs and natural waters across America. These tournaments are specifically aimed at the limited supplies of predator game fish such as our largemouth bass, which play a natural role in controlling the excessive·production of bluegills and other panfish.

First of all, we question the quality of such "sport." Moreover there is increasing evidence that we can kill out the game fish in even the largest reservoir with this kind of fishing. In addition, the explosion of panfish populations under such conditions results in severe stunting of those species that provide the vast majority of recreational angling.

Have we forgotten that for many centuries angling has been the "gentle art," serving usefully as our foremost form of contemplative recreation? Is angling to be limited to a small group of "big-fish killers" while the interests of the millions who fish for pure recreation are forgotten?

As we peruse the volumes that make up our growing library about angling, we note there is nothing on our shelves about the competitive fisherman, for angling is truly the contemplative pastime. Let us hope that bass boats and tournaments will never destroy the charm of fishing.

Another Approach to Angling. Every autumn, in about September, the noon mail brings us a mouth-watering Christmas catalog from Orvis, one of America's great producers of sportsmen's gear. This lets us know there are still bamboo fly rods that list for a mere three hundred fifty bucks with an extra tip thrown in for another two fifty. Things of marvelous beauty these rods are, but if we go in for featherweight tackle, we'll turn to the new Orvis graphite rods, many of which weigh under two ounces.

Outdoor magazines offer all manner of expensive gadgets, and now we may open to a color advertisement for something called a "bassboat." We had always thought a bass boat could be any craft without holes in its bottom that would hold a fisherman, his tackle box, and a paddle. But apparently "it ain't that way" any more. Today's "bassboat" is an elegant affair with a price tag of $3,995.00, and what's more, it needs a new 175-horsepower Mercury or 200-horsepower Johnson outboard to push it along at a reasonable fifty miles per hour.

Digging deeper into the magazine, we learn that one of these fancy bassboats is indeed essential to catching big bass, although we had always believed that anything bigger than a 15-horsepower outboard would scare every bass in a fair-sized lake. Neither had we realized there are professional bass fishermen who earn a fair living winning fishing tournaments plus doing a bit of guiding.

Once we did have a guide who was a ring-tailed whiz at catching big bass. Trouble was, he knew every fish in the river, and while we were facing downstream in the fore part of the boat plying our fly rods, this fellow would slip a plug over into one of his hot spots where an old grandpa bass hung out. On one occasion he had caught two smallmouth scaling seven and a half pounds before we told him to put his rod under the seat and lean on the paddle unless he wanted to swim back to our starting point.

Somehow this contest fishing bothers us. We've been anglers for well over a half-century and rate the quality of bass fishing something like this: First a back-country creek to wade in mid-summer in jeans and Bean's Maine Hiking Shoes. Next to the small creek but close to it comes a bigger stream with plenty of fast water and a canoe loaded with camp gear. Third is an Ozark johnboat and a good Ozark guide with a long paddle to jab into the river bottom so we can get in another cast. Prime tackle is the fly rod, although bait casting and spinning tackle will do in a pinch.

We will long remember our first sight of a fly rod and, for that matter, of a fly fisherman. Four of us youngsters were camped in 1914 in a spring branch hollow under Sugar Loaf Mountain on Mineral Fork in the Ozarks, a dozen miles west of Potosi. There were brother Ralph and his friend Goddard, both sixteen, brother Arthur, who was eleven, and myself in between. Our old tent turned water fairly well and was bedded down with two feet of straw and a full quota of patchwork quilts.

Mineral Fork in that day was one of the finest smallmouth bass creeks in the Ozarks, fed by a dozen spring branches and ending up in Big River, which was noted in that day for its lunker bass. Our fishing tackle was primitive, although nobody could have convinced us of that fact.

Our rods were twelve-foot bamboo poles supplied by Boyer's Hardware Store in Potosi. To these we tied eight feet of heavy line. Lures were a couple of monstrous Dowagiac plugs weighted down with gang hooks. The bass found these irresistible, and many a cast, if you plunked your lure into a swirl below a root wad, scored a double.

One morning as we fished a deep hole with minnows, we looked upstream to see a remarkable sight. Down toward us waded a young fellow whose idea seemed to be to give the stream a good switching. He was waving a sort of fairy wand some eight feet long, at the end of which was a small lure. Remarkably often he would tie into a fighting smallmouth. But when it was netted he did a strange thing. Carefully he unhooked his bass and released the fish into the water again,

Abreast of us he stopped, and we observed that his hat was covered with feathered lures. He introduced himself, asked if we could use a fish or two, and told us he had been "fly fishing" this creek for years. His name was Lee Hartwell, he lived in suburban St. Louis, and fifteen years later he and I fly fished not only Mineral Fork, but also many another Missouri stream together.

Lee taught me to tie the bucktail flies that filled my tackle box for forty years. He introduced me to the Granger fly rods and the automatic fly rod reels that sufficed for our bass tackle. Up and down and in and out, I expect we caught more big Ozark stream bass than are hauled into any of the fancy bass boats with 175-horsepower motors that destroy the silence of most of Missouri's flat-water lakes today. We ate the bass if we needed them and turned them loose if we didn't.

Somehow the idea of competitive fishing—or the need for such costly equipment—never entered our heads. The canoe was then and is today the ideal craft for the fly fisherman. As for smaller streams, the roar and dripping gasoline of any motor is a desecration. On the big artificial reservoirs, bass contests are needed to keep up interest. For us the silence of the small stream where the swallows dip and one wild bass rises to our lure is the always-repeated reward of years of fly fishing.

7

Aerial Studies in Music and Motion

Few areas of natural history are more fascinating than the study of birds. Few living creatures attract more friends—or sometimes make more enemies. Avian interest is of many kinds; often aesthetic since most birds are beautiful, sometimes personal and impractical, sometimes scientific, and finally utilitarian. This interest dates to the dawn of history, for we find birds drawn on cave walls by Cro-Magnon man, twenty thousand years ago. Through the centuries, birds have been religious symbols and worshiped as gods. They have been used for ornament and food, killed for sport, and too often persecuted as man's enemies.

Never have more people been interested in birds than today—and this is natural because there are more people. Millions devote leisure and recreational time to bird study and observation. We call these folk birders and classify them into groups. Some are counters striving for the biggest list. Some concentrate on the search for new species. Many go afield with cameras as well as binoculars. Some create summer habitat for nesting species; others build feeders to attract the wintering visitors.

Many naturalists watch birds for science. Charles Darwin was one of these and hit upon the theory of evolution. Rachel Carson's observation alerted us to the dangers of "hard" pesticides. Audubon and other artists built public interest through the beauty of their paintings. The millions spent by sportsmen on guns, ammunition, and the like at least help promote the remaining numbers of the species they want to shoot. Nor should we forget the domestic hens that lay our eggs and the broilers sizzling on a million midsummer barbecues.

Ornithology, whether amateur or professional, is not without controversy. Thus much information came to light recently about the ruthless slaughter of both golden and rare bald eagles by Western sheep ranchers on the unproved theory that twelve-pound eagles fly off with thousands of twenty-pound lambs. No doubt there are rare instances of young sheep, goats, and pigs furnishing a meal for the eagle, but its regular diet consists of ground squirrels, rabbits, prairie dogs, and other mammals generally held to be pests. "Old wives' tales" about eagles carrying off human babies have pretty well died out.

Another point of controversy deals with so-called scientific collecting, generally totally unnecessary today for any scientific reason, of bird specimens. The skins supposedly help identify new subspecies, but they generally end up gathering dust in the drawers of obscure museums, having proved nothing, since the museums already have adequate collections of these species. The total of such skins runs to well over 2 million, yet young science students still receive permits to collect and feel called upon to gather in more unwanted bird skins.

An instance occurred recently in Arizona that stirred up quite a storm. This was the apparently useless (and as it turned out, futile) shooting of an entire family of rare gnatcatchers, the first of their subspecies to be reported north of Mexico, on the off chance that the parent birds were of two different subspecies. They were killed even after the birds had been netted and both parents and three fledglings had been examined, measured, and photographed by qualified ornithologists. Nothing was learned from the killing, the only result was the elimination of a possible new subspecies from Arizona.

The slaughter of the gnatcatchers was observed by some twenty ordinary birdwatchers, and the resulting hullabaloo did no good for the cause of science. Most remarkable is a letter to collecting-permit holders that was issued by the Fish and Wild-life Research Division: "Killing a bird in the presence of uninformed persons who object to killing for any purpose can result in a storm of protest. Take precautions to prevent this and refrain from shooting while unsympathetic eyes are watching." Somehow we doubt this is the answer.

*　　*　　*　　*

One might suppose that the country dweller who spends much time outdoors would have the advantage in recording the largest number of birds during the year. Yet it is really the city-dwelling birders who spend every weekend and every vacation afield, often in groups and always armed with binoculars and cameras, who end up with the longest bird lists.

One reason is that city birders follow the seasons and know the concentration points: the northern migratory routes of song-birds in spring, the southward flight of waterfowl and birds of prey in autumn, the nesting areas of resident species through-out the year. These are the ornithologists, amateur and profes-sional, whose annual lists include three hundred or more spe-cies and grow even longer when they travel far afield.

Our own birding is haphazard and pursued without ambition for the big list; yet there are areas of bird-watching that we have especially enjoyed. The high visibility and dramatic quality of the large water birds as subjects for the movie camera have al-ways attracted us. We have pursued them in Florida and along the Gulf, up and down the West Coast, in Mexico, and here in the Midwest. Thus we have come to know a respectable number of species.

Winter Feeding

Our first big snow often comes just after New Year's, and the thermometer heads downward. There is a line in the second stanza of Will Shakespeare's poem "Spring and Winter" that we see enacted daily when we look out the kitchen window at the first hint of daylight to check the thermometer. "And birds sit brooding in the snow," says the line, proving that birds, at least, haven't changed a whit since 1577. Cardinals, juncos, titmice, chickadees, woodpeckers—all wait for the feeders to be filled.

We're asked every time a cold spell strikes whether it is really a good idea to feed the songbirds in winter. The important thing is that once you start to feed, you must keep the banquet table filled as long as winter weather lasts. There are some competent ornithologists who claim that feeding isn't necessary, that year-round residents can find plenty of food, while insect-eating transients have moved south into milder climes. It seems to us there is room here for discussion.

We think of the robin as primarily an insect eater as we watch him pulling an earthworm from the lawn on a spring morning.

A wintering covey of bobwhite quail in a snow-covered cornfield.

But robin migration is interesting. When autumn comes, our nesting population moves south. Then robins from farther north move into our Ozark forests and winter here in the thousands. This fact has been recorded for a hundred years and would indicate that insect eaters may become seed eaters at certain seasons.

There is no doubt that most resident songbirds, as well as many transient species that winter here, are readily attracted to feeding stations. As to whether winter feeding is a mistake, the most interesting example we have seen was at the busy feeders of the Cornell Ornithological Laboratory in Ithaca, New York. As for Possum Trot, we've fed the winter birds for thirty years and have found that they lift some of the gloom from long winter days.

The old giant sugar maple just west of the house supports two good-size glass-sided grain feeders, a suet feeder, and a large hanging bag of suet. A considerable amount of grain is scattered on the ground and gleaned by such ground-feeding species as the junco, white-crowned and white-throated sparrows, dozens of cardinals, a band of blue jays, and occasional grackles, Brewer's blackbirds, and bobwhites that make a daily visit.

We have been known to feed our guests as much as fifty pounds of chick scratch on a cold winter weekend. Chick scratch is basic, mixed with millet and sunflower seed. Suet comes next—not always easy to come by. A hollow log stuffed with a mixture of peanut butter and cornmeal is a special treat. Some years we have huge sunflower heads to hang from the tree limbs, and many birders attract unusual species with thistle seed. There's no doubt that one reason for feeding is the aesthetic pleasure you will derive from those cheerful winter visitors.

The suet bags attract a variety of birds—some related and some not. There are red-bellied, hairy, and downy woodpeckers; the fairly rare yellow-bellied sapsucker; followed by the nuthatch, titmouse, chickadee, and occasional brown creeper.

Our most resplendent January visitor is the sixteen-inch pileated woodpecker with his brilliant red head. Since he cannot perch but must cling to the tree trunk, he has to hang almost upside down to reach the suet. After thirty years at Possum Trot, we are just beginning to have the opportunity to entertain the pileated at our winter banquet table, for the big bird is generally shy and only seen winging his way from one bit of woodland to another.

An unusual occurrence one February was the appearance of a flock of some thirty big purple grackles shoveling in the scratch feed and sunflower seed at an expensive rate. Never had we known this to happen, since these birds normally move down with cold weather to the swamp and marshlands of the Missouri Bootheel or even farther south.

We see many hundreds of grackles now, each morning and evening, and think they must have stayed with us because a good many farmers are feeding cattle and hogs, which provides more grain than usual for the birds. Because they are on hand every day, the grackles have presented us with some novelties. One has a distinctively mottled white head, another a white throat, and a third has white wing bars touched with crimson. The first two are undoubtedly genetic accidents, but the third could be an immature red-wing or even a tricolor. There are also

Suet bags attract a variety of woodpeckers, among them the red-bellied.

brown-headed cowbirds, an iridescent blackbird that is probably a Brewer's, but, so far, just one starling.

Oddly, although these large birds eat us out of house and home, they seem not to bother the smaller birds. On some of the worst days we've had as many as forty cardinals at the feeders at one time—a beautiful sight. Juncos are plentiful, but a less frequent visitor is the Oregon junco, which usually visits in late winter. Of sparrows we entertain primarily white-crowns and white-throats, song and tree, and on rare occasion the

handsome fox sparrow with bright brown plumage and speck-
led breast or the big Harris' with its black cap and vest.

Other regulars are the Carolina wren, nuthatch, chickadee,
tufted titmouse, towhee, and purple finch. Mockingbirds seem
to prefer the berries and seeds in the hedgerows and seldom
visit the feeders—but the woodpecker family is faithful.

Few things brighten a gray December day like a dozen cardinals bright against the snow, or dispel gloom like the merry
chickadee who never seems to mind the weather. This little
songster, as Aldo Leopold once said, is almost too small to have
enemies. A whimsical fellow named Evolution having shrunk
the dinosaur until he tipped over his toes, said Aldo, tried
shrinking the chickadee until he was just too big to be snapped
up as an insect, but too small to be pursued by big birds of prey.
Lucky chickadee.

Oddest customers at the hanging grain feeder are a pair of
bright brown fox squirrels with huge bushy tails that come

Mockingbirds seem to prefer the berries and seeds in the hedgerows
and seldom visit the feeders.

bouncing in from the woods and clean out the feeder in a hurry. We finally remembered a tubful of two- and three-year-old black walnuts in the garage and are cracking these for an extra ration. The birds get their share, but the squirrels clean up a big bucketful of cracked walnuts in a few hours. It isn't unusual to see two chickadees picking up the bits of walnut that the fox squirrels spill.

We have another open tray for grain under a living-room window and a big glass-sided feeder on a six-foot metal pole under the rough-leaved dogwood. These are favored by all the seed eaters and often lure in the fox sparrow, the Oregon junco sometimes called the "pink-sided," and the big Harris' sparrow.

There are some days when fifteen or more blue jays fly in from the woods where they undoubtedly have acorns stored in the bark of the big oaks. They use their big bills to shovel seed onto the ground where it is appreciated by the ground feeders like the juncos and occasional tree and song sparrows—the former a winter visitor with a rusty cap and dark breast spot. But the big blue bullies give the smaller birds a bad time and we are apt to let Maggie out for a run. This sends them on their way.

Two important winter foods for the songbirds and other field and woodland birds that visit our feeding trays are suet and sunflower seeds. Both appeal to the insect eaters as well as to the seed-eating species, and some of these we are able to provide ourselves. Two or three rows of giant Russian sunflowers in the garden mature a surprising amount of seed, although some is harvested by summer birds while the heads are ripening. When we cut the heads, they are heavy with moisture and must be dried thoroughly before the seed can be shelled out. This is an arduous task, yet we usually manage to fill a couple of five-gallon cans with sunflower seeds.

As for suet, we try to put a supply in the freezer when getting our annual supply of beef, and then beg more from the butcher as winter progresses. The basic bird diet, however, is poultry scratch feed with our sunflower seed added. We find there is less waste when small-size poultry scratch is used. A straight ration of sunflower seed plus the imported seed called thistle will attract large numbers of rare birds like purple finches, pine siskins, and evening grosbeaks, but it makes a costly ration.

Unusual for us, although they have come down from the

north during several winters, is a quartet of handsome evening grosbeaks. They might visit for several days in January, but then their numbers dwindle quickly. Both the blue and rose-breasted grosbeaks summer here, but the evening grosbeak with his yellow forehead and black-and-white wing patches nests farther north.

Signs of Spring

During lunch in late February, we might notice our covey of bobwhites, a hopeful sign of spring, arriving under the bird feeders in the old sugar maple just beyond the kitchen window. We always spread some scratch feed on the ground for the juncos and occasional purple finch, and here the bobwhites were scratching for all the world like a flock of bantam chickens.

Timberdoodles. Often at this time of year we'll have a day warm enough to bring out the honeybees and thus know if our one hive has survived the winter. On such a day in early afternoon we join Maggie for our first round of the woods above the creek—and on our short hike we flush five woodcocks, a good sign for early March.

The woodcock has always been to us something of a bird of mystery. Some years it nests in our woods—and others it arrives some evening in spring then disappears and isn't seen again until autumn. There was a period when it was on the endangered species list, perhaps because of habitat destruction or the widespread use of DDT as an agricultural poison. Woodcocks subsist on earthworms, and we were warned against eating them because of the high concentration of this poison.

Now the danger of extinction seems to be over and the woodcock is making a comeback. Although we've always considered it one of our most beautiful game birds, it is not too widely known, probably because it migrates singly instead of in flocks and is largely nocturnal.

It is somewhat bigger than the bobwhite, with equally handsome plumage, but with an unusually large head and short neck and very large eyes set far back and high. The bill is long and flexible at the end to allow the bird to go fishing in the worm holes that supply most of its food. The birds seem to have

The woodcock is beautifully camouflaged and often sits still in the leafy cover in the woods until you almost step on it.

favorite moist "coverts" or stopping places where earthworms are plentiful—and here one or two birds can generally be found every night of the migratory season.

The woodcock is beautifully camouflaged and often lies still in the leafy cover in the woods until you almost step on it. Then it takes off in its odd erratic flight, managing to put plenty of tree branches between you and it so that it is not an easy target. If we are fortunate enough to have nesting pairs, we may see the "sky dance" of the male bird that takes place at an exact moment each evening that Aldo Leopold told us long ago depended upon a light intensity of exactly 0.05 footcandles.

Spring Migration—Heading North

Somehow no matter how busy the spring day, we manage a short hike with Maggie, out along the wooded path above the creek. At least, it may be a short hike for us, and for the first few hundred yards Maggie stops and turns back to make sure we are going her way. Once convinced of that, she ranges far

The habits of the woodcock have always been something of a mystery. There are years when it nests in our woods—and others when it appears some evening in spring then disappears and isn't seen again until autumn.

and wide. First it is down to the creek, still swollen from the rains. Then it may be a round of the east pasture. Finally, too often for our liking, it is to discover a groundhog den from which she arrives home at suppertime, covered from nose to tail with mud.

At first as we go, we are conscious of the larger birds that are now traveling north. Bands of grackles, blackbirds, and brown-headed cowbirds move through the woods with a rustle of wings and what one observer has called "a good, wheelbarrow chorus." Accompanying this, when mid-April is here, is the jolly "o-ka-lee" of the red-winged blackbirds that flash their colorful epaulets. Some of the males will find nesting sites around the Big Pond and serenade us until autumn.

We sometimes stop to rest on a couple of old wooden benches along the woods path. One is located far out on a rocky point, which makes an ideal place for watching the warblers feeding in the tops of tall trees that tower up from the creek bottom. We realize as we sit there that the spring migration is in full swing, and we wish we were real experts at identifying the birds by their songs. Yet we do manage many with our binoculars.

Some warblers have songs with a melody that can be learned. But others have the exasperating habit of limiting their conversation to "z-zee-e" or "ke-tsee." Sitting on our woodland bench we hear others besides warblers. The tiny blue-gray gnatcatcher, singing beside his mate, has a song so soft we hardly hear it, yet it can scold loudly. We hear our first white-eyed vireo of the season saying "chip-o-wee-o," which one friend translates as "fix my wheel—quick." Its cousin the red-eyed vireo, arriving a few days earlier, has a song often translated as "here I am—can't you see me?," which continues ad infinitum.

On this first sunny day for a week or more, all the birds are exercising their vocal chords. From the pasture the meadowlark has a call that is easily whistled but hard to translate into words. Yet it is altogether cheerful and happy. The cardinal likes a treetop for sending out his ringing "What cheer, what cheer!" And the blue grosbeak who nests in the fencerow along our east pasture has a sweet song that is still to be translated into words.

Black-bellied Plover. But the birds offer other signs of spring. One year in early March we had traveled to nearby Ironton to do the week's shopping. Like everyone else, we stopped to talk to special friends as they came out of the market with their filled shopping bags. Suddenly, I heard a birdcall high overhead and saw the bird circling in the sunny sky. My first thought was that the killdeer were back—but this bird flew higher and its call was a single note. It said, "tee-u-ree," and circled back over flooded Stout's Creek.

The bird must have been a plover, golden or black-bellied, on its way back to its nesting ground in the high Arctic. The golden plover is famous for its migratory flight—from the Arctic east and down the Atlantic Coast past Labrador, New England, the West Indies, the Gulf, and on to Brazil or even farther south. Then like the black-bellied plover, whose southern journey is slightly shorter, it makes a leisurely return up the Mississippi Valley and north again to the Arctic.

We've seen both birds in spring, back in the days when the binoculars went with us as we did the spring plowing. But we

From the pasture, the meadowlark has a call that we can easily whistle but that is hard to translate into words.

decided this was the black-bellied plover because we remembered that single mellow, plaintive, slurred note. That same evening we got out the old *Field Guide to Bird Songs*, which our friends Roger Tory Peterson and Arthur Allen produced some thirty years ago. Sure enough, the call of the black-bellied plover was there and it duplicated the call we'd heard that afternoon. Thus, as my good wife says on every cold dreary February day, "Don't give up hope for spring will surely soon be here."

Goldfinches. After a brief absence, the goldfinches are back in numbers with the adult males taking on their bright yellow summer raiment. So far both the bluebird and Carolina wren are missing—casualties of three hard winters. But the house wren with its fussing and scolding—and the cheerful Bewick's wren whose often-repeated call always sounds to us like "come DRINK your tea" arrived some weeks ago.

Another that we wait for every spring, although it stays only for a day or two so that we sometimes miss it, is the bobolink. Once considered a crop destroyer in the rice fields of the South, its reputation is much better today. It comes in large flocks on migration, generally stops in a high alfalfa field to feed, sings a liquid melody that William Cullen Bryant once put into words, and takes off for nesting grounds to our north.

One problem of spring is to find time enough to watch the migration and then to locate all our nesting birds, but we're afraid that day will never come.

Purple Martins. Every year we hope to play host to our share of purple martins. Although our martin boxes are properly housecleaned and ready early in the season, the occupancy situation is sometimes a big disappointment. This year we watched as a few scouts arrived, circled, and landed on the roofs with their usual cheerful chatter. Then as often happens, they disappeared. Finally a single pair moved in, apparently not disturbed by two early-nesting English sparrows. This pair built its nest and then was joined by a lone bachelor bird, which made for an odd household. We're still hoping for a mate and another pair or two—but even the trio keeps us entertained with their low-pitched warbling as they hunt above the pond.

The phoebe who built for three seasons above the utility-room window came in for a look but decided the old nest needed too much repair and left. Chickadees for the second spring have taken over the wren house that for several seasons sheltered a musical tree frog. Bill Latham, who helps us with a hundred jobs, has a pair of brown thrashers spotted in the multiflora hedge, and when we go walking with Maggie through the woods above the creek, a dozen warblers make spring music. More permanent residents are the red- and white-eyed vireos, towhee, summer tanager, and the shy wood pewee.

Waterbirds

Despite our distance from any body of water larger than the ponds, we manage a small share of shore and waterbirds. In spring we might flush an American bittern from the Big Pond— a handsome brown fellow with a forty-five-inch wingspread and rare with us because it prefers large marshlands. It answers to such odd names as "thunder-pumper," "butterbump," and "stake driver" because of its odd ventriloquial "plunk-a-lunk" in the marsh.

Another that builds its solitary nest in some tall tree near the ponds is the little green heron, long known to every country youngster as "fly-up-the-creek." His harsh alarm note and clumsy appearance as he lands on a slanting branch above the water are misleading, for this fellow is an expert fisherman. No frog, salamander, or minnow is safe from his careful stalk and lightninglike strike. We hope the pair that has been frequenting the little pond near the house decides to take up residence with us.

One May we drove up the highway to the pasture where Gordon's cattle were grazing and there, as I might have suspected, were a dozen cattle egrets unconcernedly catching insects raised by the cows as they moved along. This may not be a first for Washington County, but it was a first in the area for us and carried me back to a day some twenty-five years ago when Ginnie and I were driving past Lake Okeechobee in Florida. There in a pasture we spotted two cattle egrets, reported to be the very first of this species to arrive in North America from Africa via Brazil. They found an open environmental niche in America's pastures and have been busy filling it ever since.

Summer Symphony. It has always seemed to us that the most beautiful song of any bird inhabiting our area is that of the wood thrush, granted it is a simpler melody than the song of the hermit thrush that nests farther north and sings only on its breeding ground. The wood thrush is also the handsomest of the family and, unlike many birds of the deep forest, seems not at all unwilling to live near human habitation. Thus its song is familiar to many. Yet for some unknown reason, the wood thrush has avoided us. Now and then in past seasons we have

It has always seemed to us that the most beautiful song of any bird inhabiting our area is that of the wood thrush.

caught echoes of the song from an extreme distance, but only rarely.

Thus to our great pleasure this spring, we can count three nesting pairs within easy hearing distance and can listen to the music all day long. There have been many interpretations of the song of the wood thrush that is actually a simple two-phrase rising melody but of great clarity and beauty. Some have suggested "Handel's Largo" and Weber's "Invitation to the Dance," but perhaps the most interesting is that it strongly suggests one of the most beautiful themes in Gounod's *Faust*.

Summer Birds

There's a magic about midsummer nights in our Ozark valley. Daylight lasts long and in late afternoon a haze dims the horizon. Then the setting sun is a sphere of fire, sinking slowly and finally disappearing in an instant behind the western cloud bank. Martins circle in evening flight and chatter cheerfully as they come gliding in to their houses.

There is time after supper for a few last chores; a handful of oats for the mares, a box of red raspberries from the garden for tomorrow's breakfast. Now the swifts with their incredibly fast wingbeat dodge like small boys above the fireplace chimney— and out over the hay field, barn swallows harvest their supper.

Nighthawks. One evening we cooked supper down on Saline Creek and were treated to one of the most thrilling sights of the Ozark summer. We had finished our meal and called Maggie in from her hunting and were packing the car for the short trip home. All at once we realized that the air above the pasture was literally alive with dragonflies. These were of the species known as ten-spot with a four-inch wingspread. They hunt at about ten feet, lower than the big "darners," but are great mosquito predators.

Next we realized that above the dragonflies flew hundreds of nighthawks or bullbats with their white striped wings and two-foot wingspread. There was little doubt, for we have watched them each summer for a score of years, that the birds were hunting the dragonflies. These hunters of the summer evenings belong to the family of goatsuckers—along with whip-poor-wills, chuck-will's-widows, and the poor-wills of the far west— all accurately named for their calls.

Nighthawks or bullbats are neither hawks nor bats—but they are valuable insect eaters. Their family name, goatsucker, comes from the fact that European farmers of long ago believed the birds flew low at dusk and lived by sucking milk from the goats. Actually they were hunting the insects around the animals.

Once or twice when driving the back-country roads after dark we have surprised a dozen or more nighthawks performing their mating dance on some level spot in the gravel. But the real thrill is to watch the erratic flight and dive of the birds above

In the evenings the barn swallows can be seen harvesting their suppers.

our valley at dusk. After reaching the desired height, generally at a considerable altitude, the bird suddenly closes its wings and plummets earthward at a rapidly accelerating speed. Finally, just as it seems it must dash into the ground, the wings are suddenly spread to check the dive, and the bird sweeps easily and gracefully upward.

At the very bottom of the dive, when the wings are spread, there is a distinctly loud booming sound. It is very much as if someone had struck a strong chord on a bass violin. It has often been thought that the sound was vocal, but probably it is

Nighthawks have deeply cleft mouths and short, weak bills. They are protectively colored in mottled brown so they are almost impossible to see when at rest.

caused by the rush of air through the spread wings. No one has discovered the purpose of the dive, for often the bird is alone and the dive seems to have nothing to do with the mating season.

The sound, however, must have suggested the scientific name of the nighthawk, which is *Chordeiles*, combining two Greek words: *chord*, a stringed instrument, and *diele*, "evening." Thus the name accurately describes the sound—and since we can establish no definite purpose for the dive, perhaps the nighthawk performs for the sheer joy of it.

The birds of this family have certain common characteristics. They have deeply cleft mouths and short, weak bills, thus undoubtedly they take their insect prey on the wing by holding the mouth open. They are all protectively colored in mottled brown so that they are almost impossible to see when at rest.

Wings are long and feet weak so that the birds oftenest perch lengthwise on a limb and generally can thus escape notice by literally looking like "a bump on a log."

Our Ozarks boasts three members of the family—nighthawk, whip-poor-will, and chuck-will's-widow. The latter pair can keep you awake in your camp bedroll, long after you should be asleep. The great naturalist John Burroughs, who was not given to exaggeration, told of waking one morning at about four o'clock as a whip-poor-will started up and counting a thousand and eighty-two calls before he dropped off to sleep again.

Bachman's Warbler. One of the rarest birds on America's list of endangered species—if, indeed, it still exists—is the Bachman's warbler. It is so rare and so seldom reported and identified that it is not even described in our 1936 edition of T. Gilbert Pearson's *Birds of America*. It will be found, however, in Peterson's *A Field Guide to the Birds* and the Golden Field Guide *Birds of America*.

The great naturalist John Burroughs told of waking one morning at about four o'clock as a whip-poor-will started its call and of counting a thousand and eighty-two calls before he dropped off to sleep again.

The bird was first discovered by Audubon's friend, John Bachman of Charleston, South Carolina, in 1833. Audubon painted it, but it was not reported again until 1886 when a colony was discovered at Lake Pontchartrain in Louisiana—and was promptly wiped out by plume hunters. It is hard to believe that well-dressed women of that era sported the tiny birds atop their Sunday bonnets.

Next sighting was in 1904 or thereabouts by another hunter and bird collector for museums, Arthur Wayne. This was in a lowland forest area north of Charleston known as the Ion Swamp, not far from Bachman's sighting of some seventy years earlier. Wayne's unpublished journal recorded discovery of thirty-two Bachman's nesting sites whose locations he never revealed; but this area has produced reports of the rare warbler by later ornithologists on fairly numerous occasions.

One odd thing about this small warbler with yellow breast, black cap, and black throat is that it has been occasionally recorded over a wide geographic area that includes Alabama, Florida, a single male in Washington, D.C., in 1954—and Missouri. One of these sightings was made at Possum Trot in the spring of 1956 when, with our friends Myron and Muriel Northrop, we identified and watched a pair through an entire weekend. The birds are not hard to identify accurately and had been reported a day or two earlier near Piedmont, where members of St. Louis Audubon Society had gone to search for them. Moreover, on that same weekend the Bachman's was reported from the Crab Orchard area in Illinois by a competent Fish and Wildlife Service ornithologist.

Sightings in 1960, 1962, 1966, 1974, 1975, and 1976 have been reported—all but one or two of them from the Charleston, South Carolina, area and the last one from Ion Swamp, which is in Francis Marion National Forest. Now Jay Shuler, a competent South Carolina naturalist, believes the Forest Service is destroying the last hope for survival of the species by wrecking its nesting habitat. Through commercial logging of the hardwood timber—and especially by clear-cutting—the area where the birds nested is being destroyed.

The Forest Service claims there was logging in the swamp when the warbler was discovered back in 1833. The openings being created, say Forest Supervisor Orr and Biologist Hooper, allow sunny spots that encourage blackberry vines and shrubs like cane where nests were originally found. Shuler wonders about the roar of the chain saw and points to the birds' association with the swamp palmetto and other shade-tolerant species.

Henry Stevenson, the last searcher to find the warbler's nest in 1937, fears the end may be at hand. Only hope is creation of a refuge in Ion Swamp and the fact that other sightings have occurred over such a wide area. The important thing is that the loss of any species that has evolved over millions of years—especially through man's carelessness or ignorance—can be considered an attack on the survival of the human species.

Bobwhite. Somehow despite the vicissitudes of weeds and weather, our garden usually continues to pour out its bounty through the hot weeks of August. One morning we were busy getting the previous day's picking of string beans ready for the freezer when suddenly a cock quail landed in the yard outside the window and gave his cheery, ringing "bobwhite." Surely this is nature's most heartening sound, and we like the old Ozark farmer's translation of "bobwhite" as "more wet, more wet"—foretelling showers when the rains have held off for too many days.

In mid-July the whistling cock may be a bird whose nest was destroyed or who failed to find a mate. But it is still not too late, since July marks the peak of the nesting and hatching seasons. There is an answer to the bobwhite's call, easily whistled but hard to translate into English. We went to the kitchen window and answered our visitor, and at once he whirred in to land on the roof above our heads. Thereafter until we finished our kitchen chore, the quail stayed close by, calling repeatedly so that we felt badly about having deceived him.

These are wonderful days in the country, filled with small adventures like our morning with the lonesome bobwhite.

Mystery of Migration

In November the Ozark streams run full and crystal clear. The water is cold and in our Saline Creek the water cress grows luxuriantly in the swift shallows, although we no longer gather it for salad because we are warned that the creek may be polluted.

Wherever there is a muddy stretch along the bank, however, we find tracks of muskrat, possum, and raccoon—and the sharp footprints of deer.

A few days ago as we hiked down the heavily timbered creek bottom, Maggie bounced out a woodcock that took off in its fluttering, whistling flight. Although we no longer hunt them, this may be the last of these interesting birds we will see until they come north again next spring. The southward flight may take them no farther than Arkansas, and those that return in March may find nesting grounds to their liking in Missouri. Some, however, will continue up the flyway as far as the Canadian border.

Seeing the woodcock set us thinking about this miracle of migration that affects living creatures from plankton, to monarch butterflies, to fishes such as salmon, to sea mammals, to countless bird species and such large land mammals as the barren-land caribou.

Often the term is used loosely; but at least one scientist has classified this movement of populations into three types. *Migration* covers those in which the species returns approximately to the area of its birth, whether seasonally or once in a lifetime. *Emigration* covers movements of a permanent nature, perhaps in search of a new home territory, as in the case of the beaver. *Nomadism* is a kind of wandering, possibly in search of a food supply in which no definite route is followed, as was the case with animals and man who crossed the ice bridge from Asia many centuries ago.

The lengths of migrations vary vastly. Certain planktons in the sea merely rise to the surface at night and sink to the depths at daylight. In contrast is the migratory flight of the arctic tern who nests in the Arctic and winters in the Antarctic for a round trip of more than twenty thousand miles per year. Sea mammals—especially whales—also travel great distances. Richest food areas are the Arctic and Antarctic seas, but most whales travel to warm tropical waters to bear their calves and start them out in life.

While many city-bound folk and a good share of countrymen are unaware of this semiannual wildlife spectacular, migration watching has a steadily increasing number of devotees. Twenty years ago ornithologist Joe Hickey estimated that nearly a million items about migrating birds were published annually in the United States—and the number has doubtless grown, despite the fact that the vast majority of songbirds move south in autumn almost unnoticed.

The journey has a single purpose—to reach a warmer clime where there is plenty of food for the winter months. But most songbirds travel at night, even when their flights carry them to far-off places. They are guided by the constellations or by single stars, by lines of magnetic force, or by instincts as yet unexplained. Their routes remain the same, generation after generation. The old birds often take off earlier; leaving the young to follow unerringly to ancestral wintering grounds in one of migration's greatest mysteries.

Feathered Jewels. There have always been migration mysteries, and many of them we have not solved with all of modern technology. Even when today, traveling on some ordinary errand, we hurtle through space at the speed of sound, our passage is far less wonderful than the flight of the hummingbird on migration. Each autumn after its young are grown, this tiny feathered mite, weighing no more than a quarter-ounce, migrates to the Gulf of Mexico and there launches out on a nonstop flight across six hundred miles of open water to its semitropical wintering ground.

On more than one occasion as I have waded Saline Creek with the fly rod in October, I have had the good fortune to witness the start of this journey. Now along the stream banks, masses of orange and yellow jewelweed or touch-me-not are in full flower. As I move quietly along, suddenly I am dive-bombed by a bejeweled creature no bigger than a hawk moth. It is a ruby-throated hummingbird, attracted by a bright-feathered lure stuck in my fishing hat. Standing still, I realize that dozens—or perhaps hundreds—of hummingbirds are busily harvesting nectar from the jewelweed. Thus they may add that infinitesimal bit of fat that will serve as fuel for their long journey.

Grackles. A two-day downpour in the closing days of October abruptly ended our most colorful autumn in years. Even for several days before the rains came, when we walked the wood-

As we move quietly along the banks of Saline Creek, among the masses of orange and yellow jewelweed, we are suddenly divebombed by a hummingbird, a bejeweled creature no bigger than a hawk moth.

land paths we were conscious of the sunlit air filled with motion. Soon we realized that countless millions of scarlet and golden leaves were releasing their precarious hold on twigs and branches, to drift down to the forest floor. Our first impression was that the leaves fell silently through the still air. Yet when we stood and listened, we caught the whisper of sound.

Two days of bright sunshine followed the rain. On the second afternoon, just before sunset, we had reason to realize that autumn was indeed at hand. The first great band of migrating grackles, red-winged blackbirds, and brown-headed cowbirds came winging its way up our valley. The birds moved from southeast to northwest with a sound like the rustle of silk, pausing in the sugar maples and big oaks or dropping down to feed on insects and grass seed in the meadow.

When the birds were closer at hand we heard the merry "o-ka-lee" of the red-wings, while the grackles increased their music to something sounding for all the world like a rusty farm gate. All these members of the family Icteridae will stay in our territory as long as weather is warm and food holds out. Then they will drift slowly south to winter quarters in the swamplands of our Bootheel and the low-lying lands of Arkansas.

Robins. With the beginning of November came more rain. For three days it alternated between downpour and drizzle, seeming to belie the old adage that "three days' rain will empty any sky." Yet there have been compensations. When we step out onto the east terrace soon after daylight to watch the mist rising from Saline Creek and drifting eastward up the mountain, we are conscious of a new sound. The air is literally alive with the cheerful warble of countless robins. These jolly members of the thrush family—more like common folk than the aristocratic hermit thrush—are everywhere, on the lawn as if it were spring, pausing in the sugar maples, stopping in the rough-leaved dogwoods to harvest the white berries. Farther away, we can see that the woods to the north are full of red-breasts, while many more are moving through the air above us. This habit of the robins to gather in great bands toward the end of the summer has long been noted by birders, both amateurs and professionals.

Robins are not quite as handsome or colorful as their cousins, the bluebirds, nor as musical as the wood and hermit thrushes. Yet their wide distribution throughout the lower forty-eight states and their cheerful tolerance of human society make them perhaps the best known of any American bird and the favorite of many.

One of our most familiar outdoor sights is the robin in spring, tugging away at a worm in the front lawn. This well-known habit must have given rise to the old saying about the early bird catching the worm, and it is true that the earth creatures surfacing during the night make easy prey. As for food, the diet of the robins is about equally divided between animal and vegetable matter.

Our own contention is that many of our summer robins join

Although robins are perhaps best known for their red breasts, the young have spotted breasts, with only a faint wash of the familiar red color.

with the great bands that we see wintering in the Ozarks. The birds must, to some degree, make berries and buds a larger part of their diet. One of the great sights of our Ozarks in early winter is the bands passing overhead when the sun has dipped below our horizon but they are still flying in the light with their breasts like drops of blood in the setting sun.

Waterfowl and Shore Birds

Autumn is a season of many facets. It is the time of harvest—when annual plants die and perennials go to sleep for the winter. It is our most colorful season when forest and fencerow don their raiment of crimson and gold. It is also the season of migration, and while this embraces countless species, it is the flight of waterfowl that has long been of most interest to the outdoorsman.

We have watched this migration, now, for a half-century. When one considers the steadily narrowing width of the great flyways used in the autumnal journey, there is little doubt that with each decade, the waterfowl populations grow smaller. This is not easy for most sportsmen or even many wildlife biologists to recognize, chiefly because their observation is done at concentration points along the flyways and on the wintering grounds where the birds concentrate.

Man's use of land and waterways is responsible for this narrowing of the flight bands available to waterfowl. Wildlife managers have learned to stop the birds at refuges and wildlife management areas. Here the birds feed, are counted, and the harvest is controlled—but at the same time, the concentrations lead to unfounded assumptions of abundance.

Years ago, we discussed this matter with our old friend Ira Gabrielson, who was perhaps the greatest waterfowl authority in the nation. One trouble with both sportsmen and wildlife managers, he said, was that few were alive who had ever observed the vast numbers of our waterfowl before man undertook various measures of gunning and land use that were decimating their numbers.

An ornithologist of early in this century was Edward Forbush, who wrote of an even earlier time: Then, as now, the Mississippi Valley was a highway of bird migration. At times in autumn its sunset sky was darkened by clouds of waterfowl moving in dim strata near and far—crossing, converging, ascending but all trending southward toward waters untouched by frost. Their rushing wings and musical cries filled the air with a chorus of rude harmonies. Above them in the golden light passed flocks of sandhill and whooping cranes—and still higher rode the long, baseless triangles of trumpeter swans, spanning the continent with the speed of wind.

We who have enjoyed the "gunner's dawn" like to believe it is not the gun that has carried many species of waterfowl to the verge of extinction. Yet a quarter-century ago I had the pleasure of representing Missouri in a distinguished volume published by Van Nostrand and titled *Wildfowling in the Mississippi Flyway*. Chapters covered the breeding ground, the Canadian provinces, and the fourteen states that feed waterfowl into the Mississippi flyway on their way south.

The writers who participated in the project were an outstanding group of sportsmen. But many chapters are filled with the feats of market gunners who worked for seventy-five dollars per month and killed three thousand ducks in a season and of sportsmen who sometimes hauled the day's kill home to town in a farm wagon loaded to the guards. Certainly it is useless to claim that the gun—and the lead poisoning that accompanied it—had little to do with today's shrunken waterfowl population. Certainly today's wildfowler must speak in the past tense and strike a nostalgic note when he talks of the great days of wildfowl gunning.

Fewer waterfowl visit us at Possum Trot today than when we came here over thirty years ago. In those days, as autumn approached we could count on the daily arrival of wild ducks at the Big Pond. The earliest included teal and wood ducks. Following them came the main flight—mallards, gadwalls, baldpates, ring-necks, and shovelers. Geese stopped often on the spring migration, and it was not unusual to entertain Canadas, blues, or snow geese in the wheat fields.

Both spring and autumn migrations brought wading birds— resident great blue and green herons, common egrets, and the little blue heron. Of shore birds, the sora rail still nests at our Big Pond, although several sandpipers that visited regularly are now seldom seen. The killdeer is our resident plover, while the upland plover and the black-bellied plover on their long flight from Arctic to Argentina still come through on migration. The bottom fields no longer stay as wet in spring as they did before we seeded them to grass, thus the Wilson's snipe is nowadays a rare visitor.

On the whole, our Conservation Department with the help of

The common egret visits Possum Trot on both its spring and its autumn migration.

its Design for Conservation is building more habitat for migratory and resident waterfowl. In a recent bulletin announcing land acquisitions, we found the thousand-acre Marais Temps Clair area in St. Charles County included. This was originally one of a number of privately owned shooting clubs on the rich flyway area at the junction of the Missouri and Mississippi rivers where wildfowlers of a generation or more ago found great sport at Dardenne, Cuivre, Brevator, Kings Lake, and other clubs. Several had quaint names like the famous St. Francis Literary, Hunting, and Fishing Club down in Stoddard County. The *literary* enabled them to incorporate as "educational and benevolent associations."

That word *literary* might well have been included in the name of Marais Temps Clair—or Fair Weather Marsh—where we had the occasional pleasure of shooting. Here on a November afternoon one might find gathered around the clubhouse stove a group that included Father Russell Wilbur, S.J.; Roy McKenzie, Dean of English at Washington University; world-famous plant pathologist Hermann von Schrenk; and Clark McAdams, and cartoonist Dan Fitzpatrick, both of the *St. Louis Post-Dispatch*.

Our wildlife pleasure today is in creating as much habitat for our resident and transient wildlife as possible—even for the raccoons that raid our patch of sweet corn. We've seen the beaver come back to Saline Creek. The big, handsome fox squirrels are daily visitors in winter to our bird feeders—and this summer by putting out a piece of suet we entertain the whole tribe of woodpeckers.

When a man heads toward the century mark, having racked up his firearms after a fair share of days spent afield with gun, canoe, and camera, he is apt to find himself casting up his outdoor accounts to see what they have profited him. This has been the pleasure of anticipation, and retrospect—yet in the end it is not the clean double on the covey rise, the mallard plummeting into the marsh, or the big bass in the creel. Rather, it is the memory of gunner's dawns, bobwhites whistling on June mornings, comradeship, and the mystery of migration that make the game worthwhile.

Gallinules. We are generally ready and willing to go along with our Conservation Department when it talks about wildlife. However a recent bulletin from headquarters in Jefferson City setting the gunning season for the gallinules and expressing some doubt that such a bird really exists indicates that the Department might do with a few more standard or garden-variety bird-watchers on its staff. Even their library, they say, provides little information on the gallinules.

Our first comment on these interesting members of the Rail family would be that the gunner who hunts them with any weapon more deadly than a badminton racket hardly deserves the name of sportsman. For the gallinule, like his relatives the rails, hates to fly. He or she skitters across the lily pads when disturbed and, as a last resort, takes wing in a feeble and hesitating manner with legs and feet dangling. It reminds us of the little sora rail, which our Irish setter Tiger used to regularly pick out of the air in flight when we were fishing at the Big Pond where it nested.

It is hard to avoid a feeling that to class the gallinules as game birds with a "thirty in possession limit" is pretty much a matter of supplying the gunners with harmless living targets excessively easy to kill and quite useless except as an attractive and curious addition to our marshlands. A bag of thirty gallinules would be beyond the capacity of any gunner to cook and eat in a lifetime. And nowhere do they threaten to overpopulate their preferred habitat.

We have two gallinules, the purple and the Florida, or common; both are present in Missouri during the summer in limited numbers. The purple is so brilliantly colored that it is considered next to the male wood duck in beautiful plumage. The head, neck, and underparts of the bird are a rich purplish blue; back and upper parts are olive green; frontal shield on the head is pale cobalt blue; base of the bill is bright carmine, and the frontal half is yellow. The Florida or common variety is more somber in plumage, somewhat resembling the coot and European moorhen.

Gallinules have long intrigued ornithologists, if not wildlife biologists. From Alexander Wilson to Roger Tory Peterson, men have painted and written about these birds of the marshlands. William Bartram, whose travels among the Cherokee Indians of the Southern Appalachians and the Indians of northern Florida in the 1770s make fascinating reading, was well acquainted with them. He tells of camping in the marsh where he was lulled to sleep by the laughing of these highly vocal birds. Audubon, collecting specimens for his paintings in the Florida Keys, described being lulled to rest by the cacklings of the "beautiful Purple gallinules."

Among modern ornithologists, George Lowery of Louisiana calls the purple gallinule without question one of the most beautiful birds in the United States. So striking is its gaudy colration, says Lowery, that the bird appears unreal and the product of one's imagination. Lowery describes its long-toed habit of walking the lily pads in search of the snails, mollusks, and aquatic insects that are its food. Arthur Allen, who started the great Laboratory of Ornithology at Cornell, describes in detail the way the birds bend the reeds together above the marsh water in order to conceal their eggs. He also tells of the precocity of the infant birds that are able to leave the nest and run about as soon as they hatch.

Rather significantly, Al Day, the former director of the Fish and Wildlife Service, fails even to mention the gallinules in his *North American Waterfowl*. As for us, we had the pleasure some years ago of spending a morning with Allen and the great bird photographer Fred Truslow, deep in the Everglades. They were shooting color stills while we captured the birds on movie film. That night in our camp, we too were lulled to sleep by the laughing and cackling of the purple gallinule.

Trumpeter Swans. One of the saddest stories to come from the Missouri Department of Conservation during recent years tells of the killing, during December, of three trumpeter swans. This was probably a family group and is among America's rarest birds—and the shooting occurred at Thomas Hill Reservoir near Moberly, Missouri. No trace has been found of the killers, but some idea of the status of the trumpeter is given by the fact that the last authenticated record of the big birds having been seen in Missouri was in 1907.

The trumpeter swan is beyond doubt one of the most magnificent of our waterfowl, with a wingspread of a full eight feet. It has been on the verge of extinction for nearly a century, although the open season on the swans was not closed until 1918 in the United States. Since then, through patient wildlife management in Yellowstone Park and the Red Rock Lakes Refuge in Montana, the birds have been brought back to a flock of some six hundred.

A favorite outdoor author of ours is Bruce Leffingwell, whose *Wild Fowl Shooting* was published in 1889. A true gentleman-sportsman of his day, his passage on the trumpeter swan illustrates one reason for the general decline of waterfowl populations, even before the decades of declining habitat. He describes how one spring he and a companion had the good fortune of securing two swans. There was a flock of fifteen, bound for the distant North, and the two they got were separated from the flock. They shot them in the middle of the Mississippi River amongst the floating ice, having trimmed their scull to resemble a drifting cake of ice. Leffingwell concludes that when a hunter has the good fortune to bag a trumpeter, the event will be long remembered with pleasure.

Today Leffingwell would have held his fire and wished the swans good flying as they headed north. Yet the fact that our three Missouri trumpeters were shot and left to rot indicates that the pleasure of killing still exists and that there are still gunners who apparently cannot resist the trigger-pulling impulse. We see this as we drive our smaller highways where every road sign bears the marks of a shotgun blast or two.

As for the trumpeter, it was a victim of man's westward march across the continent. Early settlers reported the birds as plentiful from Maine to Georgia. They were once the prevailing swan of California and were abundant in Oregon and Washington. But in every settled region across the nation when the swans alighted, every man who could lift a gun turned out to shoot them.

The big birds were hunted for sport or for their skins and down, since they are hardly fit for eating. In the almost uninhabited north, the Indians hunted and sold the skins to Hudson's Bay Company, which reported thirteen hundred skins purchased in 1854—but only one hundred twenty by 1877. Even after Franklin Roosevelt created the Red Rock Lakes Refuge in 1935, the big birds had their problems. The army wanted to use the same area as an artillery range.

Hawks

One day in March, while Bill and I were planting our potatoes, we spotted a Cooper's hawk. This fellow is becoming a rare sight in our area, although this may be partly because he hides in dense cover and attacks with incredible swiftness. He is a true predator, yet no longer a threat to domestic fowl since most poultry is kept housed in this modern day. Sadly, the harmless red-tail soaring above the fields is apt to get the load of shot in the belief that he is a chicken hawk—or on the stupid country axiom that "if it's alive, shoot it." Our other two fairly common hawks are the little sparrow hawk, a falcon—and the sharp-shinned hawk, which like the Cooper's is an accipiter.

Fortunately, the habit of shooting all hawks as chicken hawks

The harmless red-tailed hawk is too often shot in the belief that he is a chicken hawk—or on the stupid country axiom, "If it's alive, shoot it."

is slowly dying out. The big broad-wings or soaring hawks called buteos are highly visible as they ride the air currents and are easy targets. Yet as rodent eaters they are highly beneficial to the farmer. Red-tails nest here and are most plentiful, although red-shouldered and rough-legged hawks come during migration. The handsome marsh hawk, a harrier, arrives in autumn and crisscrosses the fields a few feet above the ground as it hunts mice, insects, and small birds.

Two "accipiters," the Cooper's and the sharp-shin, become steadily rarer. These are bird hunters, flying with powerful wing strokes followed by a short glide. They prefer thickets and open woods through which they dart with ease. Too scarce to be a threat to domestic poultry, they are worthy of protection, and we have been fortunate to observe both species in our valley.

Another group has long been favorably regarded by the falconer; yet all are becoming rare. These falcons are "attack" hawks and take their prey in midair by diving at terrific speed and striking with closed talons. Our only resident falcon is the little sparrow hawk or kestrel, oftenest seen hovering above the field with rapidly beating wings and calling "killy, killy, killy" as it hunts.

*　　　*　　　*　　　*

Here at Possum Trot we take our birds as they come, learn a bit about them as the years go by, and enjoy them all in their seasons. Each spring we thrill to the first pair of indigo buntings that takes up residence in our fencerows and the earliest small blue-gray gnatcatchers in the woodland. Each summer we wait anxiously for the song of the wood thrush. In autumn the distant clamor of the first phalanx of southward-trending Canada geese sends the same thrill up our spines. In winter we listen at night for the great horned owl—and invite all local feathered residents to the banquet table we set for them.

It is probably true that these resident birds at Possum Trot have an easier time of it during winter than many songbirds have. There is still fruit on the blackhaw trees in the yard—not to mention the rough-leaved dogwood, coralberry, possum haw, elderberry, and wahoo. Just back of the horse barn the woodland offers acorns, hickory nuts, walnuts, and countless seeds and insects of a hundred kinds under the leaf litter and in the decaying wood of old trees.

For that matter, we should not overlook the woodland borders, fencerows, and open meadow toward the barn. Here pasture grasses, *Sericea lespedeza*, and common ragweed provide food for bobwhites, prairie horned larks, meadowlarks, and many small seed eaters. Yet we enjoy bringing the winter birds in closer where we can watch them. Thus cardinal, chickadee, titmouse, nuthatch, mockingbird, blue jay, and white-crowned and white-throated sparrows are daily visitors, along with downy, hairy, and red-bellied woodpeckers. The red-headed and rare pileated come only now and then.

*　　　*　　　*　　　*

Few aspects of nature have furnished more material and more inspiration to the artist and writer than our friends of the avian world. Perhaps best known are the artists—Mark Catesby and the Bartrams, Alexander Wilson and Audubon, Roger Tory Peterson, and many more. As for writers, our well-thumbed copy

The nuthatch is a daily visitor to the feeders at Possum Trot during the winter months.

of *Bartlett's Familiar Quotations* lists no fewer than a hundred titles and first lines under "Birds." We might start with William Cullen Bryant's "To a Waterfowl" and end with these lines by my good friend, the late Clark McAdams:

> A plover flying by with his plaintive call.
> The first wee prophet of the fall—
> Leading his swift and fledgling band
> Out of the north land—.

8

A Legacy of Wilderness

The idea of preserving any natural resource simply for its own sake is comparatively new in America, and nowhere is this truer than in the preservation of wilderness. The primitive hunters who crossed the land bridge from Asia during the most recent ice age, some thirty thousand years ago, were not exploiters. They were merely a part of the vast wilderness that stretched for thousands of miles to south and east.

Many centuries later, five hundred years before Columbus, the Vikings touched the northeastern shores of our continent to begin a century of exploration. The full extent of this exploration is still a mystery, and by the time of Columbus these early adventurers had long since disappeared and had been forgotten.

During the centuries following Columbus, our population was so small, our space so endless, and our resources so vast that any thought of preservation seldom entered our heads. The aim was to use the wilderness and to exploit the rich resources here for the taking. Thus would we create the good life that had been a primary aim of our new nation; and create it we did in many ways and often with a vengeance.

With the twentieth century, stresses began to appear in the resource fabric of America. Long before this, however, tobacco and cotton had sapped the fertility of our southeastern states. Mountain men with their traps had brought many wildlife species to the edge of extinction. Ruthless logging had stripped the pines and hardwoods of the green woods wilderness. Plowing and overgrazing had turned the grass wilderness into a danger zone of dust bowl and desert, some of it beyond recovery.

Add streams polluted and too often turned into dead-water reservoirs by dams with no real purpose; strip mines worked out and abandoned to leave a "craters of the moon" landscape; irrigation projects turning salt beyond the point of profitable cultivation; marshes and swamplands drained to make plow lands where once waterfowl nested; coastal lands dredged to the destruction of rich fish-hatching areas.

As the demand grows for sprawling suburbs, bigger corn-fields and rice paddies, highways, asphalt-paved shopping and factory centers, and lands for oil exploration and for coal and oil-shale strip mines, one question haunts us with increasing frequency: How can we afford, under these conditions and with these human demands, to set aside *any* wilderness or natural areas? Who really needs marshlands, glades, prairies, unharvested virgin forest? Are the blue whale or the snow leopard or the white-tailed kite really as important as *Homo sapiens*?

The facts forced upon us by the pressures of the human species on all the earth's resources are not easy to face, and the problems presented are even more difficult to solve. Human beings bend environments to suit their primary needs for survival, and these primary needs are food and living space. Already throughout the world, man has exterminated thousands of life forms—both plant and animal. Yet all the knowledge accumulated by every natural science tells us that the ability of our earth to support life depends upon diversity.

We need the millions of plant forms, from giant trees to algae. We need the insects that pollinate the plants. We need the birds of the air, from condor to hummingbird; the life of the sea from blue whale to krill; the creatures of the land and air in all their variety. Whether human life can survive without this diversity is doubtful in the extreme. Yet Hugh Iltis of Wisconsin foresees this diversity threatened with imminent destruction. The crisis for all the living, he says, is here and now. The world of the future promises to be flowerless, animal-less, and lifeless except for masses of people; a nightmare of steel and concrete, algae steaks and yeast pies.

We can't agree with Iltis and have long preached the philosophy of Henry Thoreau: "In wilderness is the preservation of the world." Man's need for wilderness, not always of interest to a very broad public, has still been recognized since the earliest days of our culture. Back in 700 B.C. the prophet Isaiah wrote: "Woe unto them that join the house to house, that lay field to field, till there be no place, that they may be placed alone in the midst of the earth." Three hundred years later the philosopher

Plato mourned the destruction of the great forests that had covered the steep mountainsides of Greece in his grandfather's time.

Henry Thoreau understood man's need for solitude and the need to preserve untouched wild land. In our own time, foresters have been among the first to advocate setting aside wilderness for permanent preservation: for education, for science, for wildlife and the preservation of plant species, and for recreation. Among these foresters, as we have stated, a leader was Aldo Leopold, whose elucidation of the land ethic and of ecology has been invaluable to the conservation movement.

Even ornithologist S. Dillon Ripley, director of the Smithsonian Institution, admits that he became seriously interested in conservation no longer ago than 1950. Until then, he states, he was willing to follow the laboratory scientists who looked on "conservationists" as bird-watchers, and who admired Leopold only for "his lyric writing and devotion to chronicling the cycle of Nature."

Ripley now considers as vastly important the effects of exploding human population and the destruction of ecosystems that make life possible for countless species, each an end product of evolution. As for us, having started life a decade ahead of Ripley, our concern for such matters preceded his by a quarter-century. During those years, in addition to close contact with land both wild and tame, we have accumulated many volumes dealing with those environmental problems that have suddenly become of such concern to mankind.

These books have recently poured from the pens and minds of distinguished scientists in many fields; men like Loren Eiseley, Paul Sears, Rene Dubos, Barry Commoner, Fraser Darling, Paul Ehrlich, Harrison Brown. Yet it has seemed to us that as each reaches the heart of his message, he is saying much what Leopold said back in 1945, in those brief essays that highlight his small masterpiece, *A Sand County Almanac.*

Until today, no one has understood better than Leopold the meaning of and need for wilderness in our mass-minded, machine-minded, technological world. It was he who recognized wilderness as "the raw material out of which man has hammered the artifact called civilization." It was he who pointed out its diversity and the relationship between this and the diverse cultures to which different wilderness types gave birth. It was he who said that wilderness is a natural resource "which can shrink but not grow."

Leopold also called wilderness "the raw stuff" that "gives definition and meaning to all life." We must, he said, save what tag ends we can of our natural areas for the edification of those who may one day wish to see, feel, and study the origins of our cultural inheritance. "Only those able to see the pageant of evolution can be expected to truly value its theater, the wilderness. . . . But if education really educates, . . . youth yet unborn will pole up the Missouri with Lewis and Clark, or climb the Sierras with James Capen Adams, and each generation in turn will ask: Where is the big white bear? It will be a sorry answer to say he went under while conservationists weren't looking."

In listing uses for wilderness, Leopold placed "primitive recreation" as highly important. This includes backpacking, travel by pack train, canoeing, and fishing. A second use is for scientific observation and the study of undisturbed fauna and flora and of land health in a natural state. Third, although not least important, is preservation of wildlife forms that are disappearing from overhunting and habitat destruction. These cannot be restored in any other environment.

Wilderness has two enemies. One is man in numbers so large that he alters its ecology and balance. The other is man's motor, in any numbers whatever. This is today's gravest danger not only to wilderness but also to all our wild lands and waters. The machine includes the snowmobile, the dune buggy, the motorcycle and trail bike, the four-wheel-drive vehicle that leaves the roads, and the outboard motor. None is needed for wilderness travel; all destroy wilderness values. All are polluters, all waste materials and fuels, all are destructive of animal, bird, and plant life. All must be regulated in the near future by stringent laws, or our wilderness and wild lands and waters are doomed.

One reason we need wilderness is that only in wildernsss can we watch natural evolution at work. Only here can we see and understand the origins of our cultural heritage. In wilderness at least a few of us can discard the mechanized recreation that is destroying our woods, streams, and mountains. Wilderness teaches us that infinite species diversity, the opposite of "one-cropping," is the true road to land health. Only here can we preserve our rare wildlife; the pronghorn antelope, bighorn sheep, grizzly bear, wolf, mountain lion, and peregrine falcon.

These may not be all the reasons, but they are enough for a lifetime of study as to how mankind may survive. We have only a handful of years left to determine whether the world's wildlife will be saved or exterminated, and this is largely a matter of creating ample space where these species can live safely and unmolested. Yet there is an even more important reason that writer Roger Caras recently put in an interesting way. Old-time miners, he pointed out, did not take canaries into the mines because they loved music. It was because these tiny birds registered lethal gases more quickly than humans could and so saved many lives. Caras and I agree that wildlife in our environment registers its health or sickness more quickly and accurately than we can.

Once in a long time, men show wisdom in these matters. In the 1930s Franklin Roosevelt, urged by the few conservationists of his day, created five great "wildlife ranges" embracing nearly 5 million acres of what seemed totally worthless desert and high plains land: The Kofa and Cabeza Prieta wildlife ranges in Arizona, the Desert and Sheldon Antelope Range in Nevada and the Charles Russell Game Range in Montana. The primary difficulty in handling these lands was that authority was divided between the Bureau of Land Management and the Fish and Wildlife Service, both in the Department of the Interior. The reason is that the BLM supervises grazing and mining while Fish and Wildlife is responsible for wildlife preservation.

As might be expected, this arrangement created tensions. BLM is primarily a "multiple use" agency interested in commercial exploitation of land. Fish and Wildlife exists to protect and foster all wild creatures. But studies show that most of the game ranges are already overgrazed, while mining interests want wide-open exploration rights. Thus when the secretary of the interior proposed closing certain areas to mineral entry, placing Cabeza Prieta and Kofa solely under Fish and Wildlife and creating inviolate "wilderness areas" in all the game ranges under the Wilderness Act, the department found its own Bureau of Land Management and the grazing and mining interests lined up solidly against any conservation measures.

Considering that BLM is today the sole administrator of nearly a half-billion acres of our public lands, conservationists have long favored making their management more effective and free of exploitive pressures. We believe the five wildlife ranges should be closed to grazing and mineral entry and placed under sole management of the Fish and Wildlife Service. After all, they represent less than 1 percent of the total public domain, and the wildlife species they protect are of far greater value than their other resources.

In the early 1960s Congress became interested in preserving certain federal lands for all time in their natural state. This followed eight years of debate during which some sixty bills for wilderness preservation had been introduced and discussed. There was, as might be expected, controversy between powerful vested interests who made their profits through exploitation of the people's resources, and individuals who represented the public interest.

The Wilderness Act was finally passed in 1964; originally introduced by Hubert Humphrey, sponsored by Clinton Anderson, and shepherded through to passage by Frank Church. As was natural, the primary action for wilderness has been in the western states with large acreages of national forests, national parks, and Bureau of Land Management grazing lands that include mountains, semiarid areas, and desert. Some 10 million acres were immediately designated, with another 40 to 50 million acres anticipated.

Arrival of the 1970s brought realization of the need for wilderness in the densely populated East, which led to passage of the Eastern Wilderness Act. Immediately designated were 270,000 acres, mostly in eastern national forests, with another 125,000 acres under study, certainly not a staggering amount.

There are today some 160 national forests within the boundaries of the United States, and their very names are a record of our history: Shoshone, Custer, Apache, Bitterroot, Shawnee, Sequoia, Medicine Bow; or Custer, DeSoto, Mark Twain, and Coronado. Pete Seeger should have made a song of the names. According to the law of June 4, 1897, the original purpose of the forests was clearly defined. It was to protect the great watersheds that supply our country with water and to furnish in perpetuity a continuous supply of timber for the use and necessities of our citizens.

Since that day, acreage has been added steadily to the national forest system, while its use and purposes have grown apace. The greatest forest acreage is in the West, the ranching and livestock country. Thus livestock grazing has become a primary and often detrimental use of the forests because of local pressures. The forests also contain nonrenewable resources such as minerals and oil so that mining and drilling have become recognized and profitable uses, although they sometimes result in a loss of both material and aesthetic values.

During the past two or three decades the multiple-use concept has been adapted by the U.S. Forest Service, greatly broadening the purposes and objectives of forest management. Although control and suppression of forest fires were early objectives, now we find wildlife treated as a forest resource and a responsibility that is steadily more important. But perhaps the greatest new use of all is recreation as the need for open space and natural areas grows.

There are other forest objectives, however, that could hardly have been thought of in the early days. One of these, and it has become a national objective, is the preservation of wilderness areas within the forests; areas that include not only wild and untouched lands but also lakes and wild and scenic rivers. Other new objectives today include concern for air quality, for natural beauty, for the diversity of forest vegetation including flora in addition to the trees.

A generation ago we could hardly have thought of "wildlife habitat quality" as a primary interest of the forester. Yet today we realize that all wildlife must live where it can find food, shelter, and the space in which to raise its young. Although the suppression of forest fires and good timber management have been in large measure responsible for the return of the white-tailed deer, wild turkey, and other species, the Forest Service still considers the present habitat capability as only about one-third of its potential.

*   *   *   *

The road back for our depleted wildlife species in Missouri

really began with two Forest Service moves, and this statement is made with full recognition of the part also played by our Conservation Department. But the Forest Service led the way in ending the fires that once swept millions of Ozark acres every year. And the Forest Service had the lands that were necessary to create seven federal wildlife refuges. These were closed to hunting and placed under the management of our Conservation Department, and here the return of our deer herd and flocks of wild turkey really began. Eventually all the refuges could again be opened to hunting.

Today the U.S. Forest Service in Missouri has an interest not only in a few huntable wildlife species, but also in the broad spectrum of bird, animal, and fish life that inhabits the 1.3 million acres of federal lands. Here are no less than two hundred resident species of birds, with many more in passage during migration. Ozark forest streams contain sixty-five species of fish. There are seventy kinds of amphibians and reptiles. Our fifty mammals include not only deer but also an occasional bear and large numbers of smaller furbearers. Certainly we who know and enjoy the Ozarks are fortunate, in climate and in soils that make possible the great diversity of plant and animal life.

At no time during our years of interest in wild America have the possibilities for preservation been so favorable. More people daily become interested in nature and convinced that preserving it is important. The reasons for this are diverse and, as one writer recently put it, some are so deeply personal that they can hardly be articulated except in poetry.

As we read that statement, it was impossible not to recall one of the few bits of poetry that have remained with us since high-school days. It was William Cullen Bryant who wrote: "To him who in the love of Nature holds communion with her visible forms, she speaks a various language. For his gayer hours she has a voice of gladness and a smile—and she glides into his darker musings with a mild and healing sympathy that steals away their sharpness ere he is aware."

Many of us today live lives remote from Nature. Yet no day passes without evidence that this contact is essential if we are to develop our full human potential. We must understand the existence and importance of natural communities, the behavior of living organisms and their ability to coexist in relatively stable life systems. To achieve this observation and understanding, the preservation of nature becomes totally essential.

Some time before his election, Jimmy Carter spoke before the National Wildlife Federation. He said, "I am a conservationist, scientist, and nuclear engineer. I am also an outdoorsman." This sounded hopeful, and conservationists found President Carter's message to Congress on the environment in May 1977 even more encouraging. The assault on the pork-barrel water projects, the drive to curb pollution of air and water and the waste of energy, the promised expansion of the National Wilderness Preservation system—these were hopeful beginnings.

In Missouri we have also made a beginning. Few states are richer or more unusual in their natural landscapes. Down in the Bootheel are swamps where bald cypress and tupelo gum are the dominant trees. Flanking our great riverways are fertile bottomlands and prairies. Our Ozark Highland with its ancient granite and outcrops of limestone supports forests of oak and hickory and other hardwoods, as well as of pine and cedar.

It would be wrong to say that we have preserved this landscape in its virgin state. Farming, mining, cities and towns, highways, high dams and reservoirs, channelization and polluted streams are all part of man's attack on the landscape. Yet there is something left. During the years our Conservation Department has managed to accumulate and protect more than a quarter-million acres of public lands. This is a minute part of our 40 million acre total, but it is a beginning.

The land already owned includes, pretty much by accident, a number of high-quality natural areas. Now that our Design for Conservation makes possible the purchase of land for the use of the people, a concentrated effort can be made to include a maximum number of worthwhile natural areas. As we analyze the potential, we realize that climate, geology, water, soils, present and past plant and animal life will determine worthwhile areas for acquisition.

As our best and most important natural areas are found, classified, and designated, plans must be developed for their effective preservation. Of great assistance in this effort will be many agencies and organizations, such as the Forest Service, Prairie Foundation, and the Nature Conservancy, to mention some that already have ongoing programs of natural area preservation. Working together, we can look forward to an effective Natural Area Program.

Certainly no state east of the Great Plains offers finer opportunities for setting aside wild lands than Missouri, with its Ozark Highland. Sadly, when the first eastern land bills were proposed, no movement developed in Missouri with public backing for wilderness. Now the situation has changed. Two areas—the Mingo Swamp in Mingo Wildlife Refuge in the Bootheel and the Herculese Glades in Taney County—have already been designated as wilderness. Four more—Rockpile and Bell mountains in Madison and Iron counties and Piney and Paddy creeks to the west—have also been brought into the wilderness system.

Meanwhile the eighteen-thousand-acre Irish Wilderness in Oregon County has been proposed for immediate designation in a bill recently introduced by Senators Eagleton and Danforth. All harvesting of timber is held in abeyance, pending study action. Also, the U.S. Forest Service held a series of workshops in August 1977, seeking public involvement in identifying and evaluating Forest Service land suitable for wilderness. The workshops were held in Springfield, Potosi, Rolla, and West Plains and were an opportunity for the public to take part in an event that is important to the future of wilderness everywhere.

The time to act is now. If we look back three or four decades we see twice as much wilderness with only half as many people to enjoy it. Try to look forward three or four decades and the picture becomes cloudy. We will have more than 300 million people, bigger cities, more land buried under concrete, huge farms devoted to monoculture. How sad if we have to say, when that day comes, that our wilderness disappeared while we conservationists weren't looking.

Ozark Scenic Rivers

Time slips away from one on the river and the only worry is finding the perfect gravel bar while there is still light. In this matter we follow the adage of an old Chippewa guide whom I once camped with in Wisconsin; that one should pick his campsite while the sun is still a paddle-width above the horizon. This is especially true in autumn when the time between sundown and darkness shortens;

and since we don't like cooking in the dark, we follow the Chippewa rule.

The bar below the mouth of Grassy is a good one; rising a dozen feet above the river and with small gravel, packed hard by the last high water. Willows flank the tent site, making convenient supports for guy ropes. A big drift provides firewood and the sycamores behind camp will shade us in the morning. Meanwhile across the river, the sun has already dropped below the wooded bluff.

Camp is soon made and the tent pitched. Ginnie lays out her supper supplies; mostly provender from the garden at Possum Trot. I had hedged against poor fishing by slipping a sirloin into the icebox and soon this is on the broiler, along with a kettle of Golden Bantam corn bubbling away. Even old Tiger finds his bowl of chow flavored with a bit of suet.

A kingfisher rattles down the long pool above camp. Dusk comes as we pour the last coffee. By the time the dishes are washed and stacked, a moon in the third quarter tops the trees behind camp. A whip-poor-will tunes up; then starts its constantly reiterated call. The fire burns low and we make ready to turn in. Then a barred owl booms from the deep hollow in back of camp.

When this evening was described in September 1957, Missouri conservationists were working for legislation that would preserve on Current River the values we have described. In 1964 President Johnson signed the act creating the Ozark National Scenic Riverways—America's first "national river." The language of the act is important: "for the purpose of conserving and interpreting unique scenic and other natural values and objects of historic interest, including preservation of portions of the Current River and the Jacks Fork River in Missouri as free-flowing streams, preservation of springs and caves, management of wildlife, and provisions for use and enjoyment of the outdoor recreation resources thereof by the people of the United States." Management will be by the National Park Service.

The Eleven Point National Scenic River extends from Thomasville near the headwaters down to State Highway 142 just north of the Arkansas border. Thus the entire forty-four-mile length lies within Oregon County. While it has only one great spring, it is a magnificent float stream and its boundaries will eventually include a quarter-mile on each side for a total of 14,191 acres, of which 3,000 are in the Mark Twain National Forest. Scenic easements will be secured on the rest of the acreage except where federal ownership is essential for access and development.

It is logical that the Forest Service was selected to manage and develop this type of area. Moreover, the service is charged with preservation of the river in its natural and semiwilderness state, and with protection of such scenic and ecological features as beautiful Greer Spring, second largest in Missouri. Commercial development related to tourism and recreation was encouraged outside the area, provided it would be compatible with natural development carried out by the Forest Service.

Development within the area was planned to include restoration, creation of information centers and nature trails, float camps on the river, and one or two more highly developed campsites with automobile access. The Forest Service has had nationwide experience in creating quality recreational facilities, as indicated by their Watercress Campground on the Current at Van Buren and others throughout Missouri.

This plan to preserve the Eleven Point for the people of the nation did not come about overnight. In fact, the first proposal to save the undammed rivers of the southeast Ozarks for recreational use was made in the 1950s. Even before that, conservationists had fought to prevent damming of these streams by the Corps of Engineers. The first *definite* plan, however, was submitted in 1956 following a survey by the National Park Service, State Park Board, Conservation Commission, and Missouri Division of Resources and Development.

This plan took in the entire watersheds of the Current, Jacks Fork, and Eleven Point rivers. It resulted from a recommendation by the Arkansas-White-Red Rivers Basin Inter-Agency Commission that these streams be left free of Army Engineers impoundments for all time, to remain free-flowing and to be used for recreation. It was soon clear, however, that the area included was too large, that it included too much privately owned farm and timber land, and that acquisition, development, and administration would be extremely costly. Thus the plan was abandoned.

Many citizens, however, still believed these streams should be saved and also realized what public recreation could mean to the economy of the region. They urged the Missouri legislature and the Congress to finance a further survey by the proper agencies, and from this request, in due course, came the proposal of the National Park Service for an Ozark Rivers National Monument, including 113,000 acres along the three streams.

The rest is history. Pressure for an army dam at Water Valley in Arkansas brought opposition to the monument from congressmen in southeast Missouri and northeast Arkansas, and so the Ozark National Scenic Riverways plan came into being to include only the Current and Jacks Fork. But pressure built again to save the Eleven Point from the high-dammers, and when the drive for a National Wild and Scenic Rivers System gathered momentum, the Eleven Point was included. Now, as with the Ozark Riverways, the problem is to prevent the overdevelopment and mass use that could turn this area into another Jones Beach or Coney Island. This task is up to the citizens of Missouri.

Not all of the original objectives set out in the Scenic Rivers plan have been achieved, partly because National Park Service management has changed hands too frequently and partly because of a tendency to allow state agencies to dominate policy in some important matters. Most disturbing is that our own Missouri Conservation Department has defined the Ozark Riverways as "the longest farm in Missouri." Those who worked to create the Riverways did not consider it would ever again become a "farm." We are disturbed by reports that a plan is now afoot to bring thousands of acres of abandoned, worn-out bottomland and ridge top fields into cultivation with the objective of increasing their carrying capacity for deer that can be hunted.

It is quite true that the original legislation places the Riverways in the preservation and recreation category, which allows hunting, despite the fact that its narrow width effectively closes it to other public use during hunting seasons. The questions that arise here are whether such a plan can be adopted without a complete public airing of its purposes and extent.

Is "game farming" a legitimate use of a riverway supported by public money, based on the National Park Service obligation to preserve the area and to protect the wildlife? Who decides the areas to be "farmed" and the species to be "cropped"? Can these objectives supersede management of the area for public use—camping, canoeing, hiking, and the like? Perhaps an impact statement is in order here, with hearings to determine how the public's money shall be spent and whether management lies in the hands of the National Park Service or of any state agency, no matter how worthy.

The Scenic Riverways area was the first of national park caliber to be created in Missouri. The fact that *conservation* and *preservation* were the primary objectives of those who worked to save these rivers is made plain by the language of the bills originally passed by the Congress. As too often happens, however, outside forces dominated the final wording on the enabling legislation, without opportunity for public review. In order to open this small area to hunting, which is against all national park practice, the original sentence specifying protection of wildlife was changed to "management of wildlife," while "recreation" rather than "conservation and preservation" was made a primary purpose of the law.

The first action following establishment of every national park unit is creation of a master plan to serve as a guide for present and future management. In the case of the Ozark Riverways, however, more than twelve years passed without any final plan being formulated. Meanwhile there can be little doubt that, as far as the primary reasons for its establishment are concerned, the Riverways has gone steadily downhill.

The legislation provided that an advisory commission would guide the park management for a period of ten years. Members were appointed for two-year terms; one from each county court in the area, one by the governor, and one by the secretary of the interior to serve as chairman. Quarterly meetings were held and pertinent matters discussed. The National Park Service at this time was in a state of flux so that superintendents came and went at a speed that made accomplishment and even planning difficult or impossible.

At every meeting during my four-year term as chairman the advisory commission urged restrictions on river use, especially in matters of firearms and motorized equipment. On the small tributary, Jacks Fork, all motors were to be prohibited; hardly an earth-shaking regulation since the stream is too small for motors. Current River was to be motorless from Montauk at the headwaters to Round Spring; with small motors of five to perhaps seven horsepower from there to Powder Mill and larger motors allowable from there to the Ripley County line, the south boundary of the Riverways. All jet and air boats were to be prohibited.

Except to rule out the jet boat, the advisory commission failed to accomplish any of its goals. If we may credit a statement in the *Federal Register*, there is no master plan and no limitation on visitation or the number or type of boats anywhere on the streams. Nor is there any restriction on the size of motorized equipment including jet boats. Thus the Riverways, except as an area for mass boating, is totally failing its purpose to preserve the stream, its fauna and flora, and its scenery in their natural condition.

As one who was deeply involved in the creation of the Ozark National Scenic Riverways and who served as chairman of its advisory commission at the appointment of Interior Secretary Stewart Udall, I feel that one need not dig too deeply to find reasons for this sorry situation. Nor is this in any sense the fault of its present management. What we have here is simply a national park unit set up with totally opposing reasons for its existence. The first is the conservation and preservation of the Current and Jacks Fork rivers, as specified in the legislation. The second is development of resources for hunting, boating, and every other form of recreation that can be imagined. No logical or practical compromise of these divergent aims has been or is possible.

Only in March 1977 did we receive for comment from the National Park Service a "Statement of Management" for the Ozark Riverways. From a careful reading of the statement and study of the maps and other material accompanying it, there is little doubt that the National Park Service has abandoned all ideas of conservation and preservation as specified in the legislation for the Riverways, in favor of a free-for-all, catch-as-catch-can policy of mass recreation.

The road ahead for Riverways preservation looks as rough and rugged as the Ozark hills through which its rivers run, while the recreational experience is no longer of high quality.

Missouri Wilderness Areas

On recent busy midsummer weekends, recreation-bound motorists driving our Ozark highways were treated to a new experience. At many road junctions leading into the back country, personnel of the Highway Department, Conservation Department, and U.S. Forest Service were posted to warn of overcrowded conditions in most campgrounds. One could only come to the conclusion that Missouri still falls far short of the recreation space needed by our outdoor-loving citizens.

Even in the 14 million acres of the forested Ozarks, many areas are in fact already crowded beyond their recreational capacity. Moreover, this situation is beginning to hold all across America. Yet here in Missouri there is still hope for tomorrow. For one thing, our Conservation Department is steadily increasing its land holdings for outdoor recreation. This has been made possible by our Design for Conservation program.

Here in the Ozarks we once wrote: "Dusk comes as we finish the coffee, then darkness falls and a moon in the third quarter tops the trees behind camp. We spread the bedrolls, throw logs on the fire, and sit back to enjoy the night sounds. A barred owl booms, far down the hollow. The screech owl protests our intrusion of his hunting range. And then from far in the forest comes the somber 'Oot-too-hoo hoo, hoo' of the great horned owl, fierce hunter of the midnight woods. No sound of man intrudes on the silence."

Surely something in man's nature needs wilderness, and here in Missouri we have come dangerously near losing it. Here is no land left that has not felt man's heavy and destructive hand. Yet there are beginning to be areas of significant interest and beauty where Nature has spent several decades rebuilding their wild character.

Conservationists have located several examples of Ozark ecosystems that are worthy of preservation as units of the National Wilderness System. If we can set them aside and continue their rehabilitation, they will serve for scientific research, as seedbeds for propagation of more wildlife than just birds and animals to be hunted, for recovery of the original flora, and for recreation of kinds that put minimum pressure on the land.

One area, the Mingo in the swamplands of Missouri's Bootheel, offers both archaeological interest and a tremendous diversity of plant and animal life. Two areas, Bell and Rockpile, typify the St. Francois Mountains, oldest land on our continent and geological heart of the Ozark Highland. Paddy Creek on the Big Piney drainage demonstrates the north escarpment of the Ozarks.

In southwest Missouri the Hercules Glades are unique in topography and fauna and flora. Piney Creek flanks White River and is heavily forested and embraces a large bird and animal population. Finally the Irish Wilderness, the largest area, borders the Eleven Point River in Oregon County.

Irish Wilderness. A lot of water has flowed down Eleven Point River in the southern Ozarks since we proposed back in 1946 that Missouri create her first national wilderness. The proposal was made in *The Living Wilderness*, magazine of the Wilderness Society, and the area was that section of the Mark Twain Forest known as the Irish Wilderness. As defined today, this includes eighteen thousand forested acres in Oregon County, bordered on the west by the Eleven Point.

The Irish Wilderness has a romantic history dating back to the

In southwest Missouri the Hercules Glades are unique in topography and flora and fauna.

1850s. During those years a young Catholic priest, Father John Hogan, secured a tract of land where he proposed to homestead a group of poor Irish immigrants who had worked as laborers on the rail lines running out of St. Louis. But the Civil War started before the settlement was well established and the area was overrun by outlaws who raided and robbed and killed, eventually driving the settlers from their land. In the end, nothing remained but the name Irish Wilderness and a small post office or two.

We came to know the wilderness well in the days when we floated the Eleven Point River, camped along its banks, visited the Federal Wildlife Refuge, and traveled the Forest Service truck trails with the rangers. The area was and is unique in many ways. Even though most of the virgin growth is gone, it is well timbered with the forest well on the way to recovery.

The Ozark Highland itself is unique; perhaps the oldest land on our continent with much of it above the oceans for most of its 3 billion years. It embraces several distinct ecosystems of which the Irish Wilderness is an excellent example. Unlike the St. Francois range with its Pre-cambrian granites and rhyolites, here we have limestones, dolomites, and sedimentary shales formed beneath oceans and ancient rivers and containing many caves, sinks, and springs. Topographic maps show a rugged terrain of steep ridges and hollows running southwesterly toward the river and drained by White's Creek and deep hollows.

Because of its central location and extreme age, the Irish Wilderness boasts a rich and varied flora. Here are found good stands of oak and pine timber, a rich shrubbery understory, and countless wildflowers. Some of these are natives that evolved here. Others have moved in through the long centuries from north, south, east, and west. Steyermark states that the most diversified flora of the state is found here, due in part to the great variety of plant habitats. As in other parts of the Ozarks, the north slopes hold more moisture and favor the best plant growth.

Missouri conservationists have long urged that the Irish Wilderness be preserved as perhaps our finest example of the Ozarks in a natural state. As with all of our original forest, the area has been logged, but today it is making a fine comeback.

Recently our senators cosponsored a bill designating eighteen thousand acres of the Irish Wilderness as a unit of the National Wilderness Preservation System.

Now the Irish Wilderness Protective Association, a group including most of Missouri's leading conservationists, has been formed to work for passage of the legislation. It is hoped that other conservation groups will join in the effort.

Natural Areas. Another typical project and an interesting one now underway is the effort of our Department of Conservation to identify and preserve Missouri's natural areas on our state-owned lands. These are described as ecological communities, either terrestrial or aquatic, which exist today in a natural or nearly undisturbed state. Once the areas have been designated, they can thereafter be protected against any use incompatible with their natural state except in case of extreme need.

These terrestrial and aquatic "natural communities" in Missouri are too numerous to list here, but already they include the glaciated region north of the Missouri River, the nonglaciated region of the Ozarks, and many aquatic habitats. Already the Conservation Department has designated on its own lands some two dozen natural areas totaling three thousand acres. These include prairies, forest types, glades, headwaters, streams, unique floras, springs, and unusual wildlife features.

The areas range in size from the 1,680-acre Taberville Prairie, perhaps the largest virgin prairie still surviving in Missouri, to a one-acre sinkhole on the Peck Ranch Wildlife Area in Carter County. As the program is explained by Forester John Wylie, it is a continuing one, with new areas constantly being surveyed and added if they warrant it. Typical of those now under study are a tupelo-cypress swamp in the Bootheel and granite glades in the eastern Ozarks quite different in character from the limestone glades of southwest Missouri.

An equally interesting project is a joint program between our Conservation Department and the National Forests to carry out wildlife habitat improvement within the federal forest lands. "In small corners and one bit at a time" is the way the agencies describe the program. Yet already it includes projects endorsed by the state legislature that include pond and small-lake building, improvement of oak stands to increase acorn production, stream management, protection of endangered and unique wildlife species, and research.

The U.S. Forest Service has under way another and somewhat more ambitious project that would provide special management for wild areas that offer unusual opportunities for recreation such as wilderness camping, backpacking, botanical exploration, and the like. One area under consideration is on White's Creek, a small tributary of Eleven Point River, consisting of several thousand acres in the Mark Twain National Forest in Oregon County.

Bell Mountain. A dozen miles west of our farm in the Mark Twain National Forest lies Bell Mountain. Perhaps it is not true wilderness in the sense that it has known the hard hand of man. Yet it is a wild area, going back to wilderness where it lies on the western edge of the St. Francois mountains.

No farms are tilled, or have ever been, on Bell's thin, granitic soils, although mountain people have lived in the narrow creek valleys. Neither does Bell Mountain produce big stands of the oak-hickory combination that is common to much of the Ozark Highland. No highways or power lines disturb its solitude, and the only access is by old logging roads that today are mere dim trails through the forest. Picturesque Shut-In Creek flows south below its eastern crest, which is within a few feet of the Ozarks' highest elevation, while Ottery Creek bounds it on the west.

Through the growing season the treeless glades or barrens of igneous rock that typify Bell Mountain are alive with their unique fauna and flora. Here grow the small rock pink (*Talinum calycinum*), sundrops (*Oenothera linifolia*), and orange grass (*Hypericum gentianoides*), while many lichens carry on the slow process of breaking the granite rock into soil. Pale blue phacelia blooms in early spring, and here the hairy lip fern (*Cheilanthes lanosa*) survives.

Animal life also adapts itself to this hard environment. Here will be seen the hen turkey with her band of poults and the white-tailed doe with her twin fawns. Small furbearers are fairly numerous, and for birds we hear the pileated woodpecker and summer tanager and many more. On one occasion we surprised a collared lizard, or *Crotaphytus collaris*, high on a red granite boulder. Although long called the "Ozark boomer," we know that it is actually voiceless.

Roadless Area Review and Evaluation II. Bell Mountain is just one of a dozen Missouri areas and of 2,686 remote and roadless areas throughout America's national forests that are being reviewed by the U.S. Forest Service to determine whether or not they should be added to the National Wilderness Preservation System established by Congress in 1964. This review, the second Roadless Area Review and Evaluation, or RARE II, involves 62 million acres or 43 percent of the total national forest area.

The U.S. Forest Service, which manages our·1.6 million acre Mark Twain National Forest in Missouri, is today reviewing all of their roadless and undeveloped lands to determine those that would yield a higher return if included as part of the National Wilderness Preservation System. One area of twelve thousand acres known as the Hercules Glades in the National Forest in Taney County has already been designated and made part of the Preservation System, to be used henceforth for nonexploitive recreation.

In conjunction with this and with President Carter's environmental program, the Forest Service conducted an analysis in forests all across the nation to determine what roadless and undeveloped lands might well be included in the Wilderness System. Here in Missouri, the service has already defined ten areas in the Mark Twain Forest in addition to Hercules Glades for intensive study and public hearings.

These areas all have a high wilderness potential, even where they have produced small amounts of timber in the past. They total seventy-six thousand acres, which might seem a large amount of land to lock up in one state as wilderness. Yet the total amounts to less than .5 percent of our 14 million forested acres. Moreover, this land is already federal land, requiring no expense for purchase. Most of it has a low potential for timber or mineral production but does furnish habitat for many forms of wildlife.

The study carried on by the Forest Service included many factors as well as meetings held with citizens of the areas affected. Primary is the possible effect on the environment, and here the study covered the physiographic regions, ecosystems, fish and wildlife, ownership, resource use, and social and economic overview. With all possible information in hand, the Forest Service considered possible alternatives for action. These ranged from Alternative A, which proposed no action, with planning and use continuing as at present, to Alternative J, which recommended all the areas being placed in the National Wilderness Preservation System.

RARE II has been, as might be expected, of great interest to many groups who exploit one or another aspect of the forest resource. These include ranchers who graze livestock on the forest at low cost, the wood products industry, the mining and petroleum people, and recreationists from hunters and skiers to four-wheel-drive clubs and environmentalists who are primarily interested in preservation.

In June 1978, the Forest Service issued a "draft environmental impact" statement that was widely distributed for public comment.Rather than specify areas to be classified as wilderness, it attempted to analyze the effect of putting the various lands into the wilderness system. As many as a million responses were received from the public and weighed. What seems most probable is that the final determination will specify areas about which there is little or no controversy, with the rest to be studied in greater detail. This will at least be a start toward the solution of "how much wilderness America needs."

9

A Land Ethic

Here is an intriguing thought, as we leave our warmly heated homes to drive our warmly heated automobiles to our air-conditioned plants and offices. Our primitive ancestors, who came down out of the trees several million years ago to take their chances in the grasslands, had a considerably better chance for survival as a species than we have today. True enough, those forefathers of ours might run afoul of a saber-toothed tiger or get stepped on in a stampede of mastodons. Yet these dangers can't hold a candle to the ones mankind faces nowadays, despite our vaunted civilization with all its science and technology.

Those far-off ancestors lacked any concept of superiority to the environment in which they lived. Quite to the contrary, they worshiped Nature. Each of her manifestations was a spirit, and this was true of trees and birds and animals, of wind and rain, of sun and fire.

In order to survive, those ancestors of ours instinctively obeyed Nature's laws and, without conscious thought, adapted themselves to their environment. Being few in number, their harvest of food and other raw materials disturbed few natural balances; they upset no processes of soil, plant, or animal growth and life. This attitude began to change when men discovered the uses of fire and tools. Then slowly but surely began man's conquest of Nature, which has culminated in today's overweening belief that we are complete masters of the earth and even of outer space.

Man's high cultures or civilizations have occupied but a brief moment in our history, extending back only a few thousand years. When we examine this period, it becomes plain that, time after time, civilized man has managed to become the temporary master of his environment. Yet this mastery has brought contempt for, rather than understanding of, natural law, so each civilization in turn has gone down to defeat. As one historian put it, "Civilized man has marched across the face of the earth and left a desert in his footprints."

We see the record of dead and dying cultures written in the valley of the Nile where the Aswan Dam, far from rehabilitating a sterile land, may spell its final doom. We see it in Mesopotamia where the Tigris and Euphrates once supported high cultures that are today buried beneath the sand. We see it in lands surrounding the Mediterranean that once supported a virile, forward-moving civilization. Here Syria, Lebanon, Jordan, Tunisia, Algeria, Yugoslavia, Greece, Turkey, Crete, and Sicily today must all be considered backward. The story is the same when we move to the Far East, nor is it different when we cross the oceans to Latin and South America.

All these lands today lack certain basic resources, especially the productive soils that could grow food for their growing populations. It is easy to say, moreover, that the nations that are "on top" in the world today are those with the most arable and productive land, the most water, and the most favorable climates. But we too often forget that some of the other areas we have mentioned were once similarly blessed.

Many of the earth's past civilizations fell not because of invasion, but because of internal troubles, such as impoverishment of their soil or overuse of raw materials to carry on their wars. These nations fell because their governments were no longer sufficiently concerned with the needs of the citizens. In today's terms, these needs are food, clothing, shelter, education, social services, and mutual respect among all sectors of the population.

A generation ago the idea of conservation as a logical part of human behavior seemed to be making progress. Nor was the idea new. Rules for the wise use of resources were laid down by Moses in the Old Testament, by Hesiod in ancient Greece, by Vergil and Horace in Rome, by George Washington and Thomas Jefferson in our own colonial times.

We know that many primitive peoples, through some biological necessity, have instinctively practiced "conservation as behavior." They judge the carrying capacity of their environment and live in harmony with the biota that supports them. Some like the Hunzas of northern India have apparently regulated their populations according to their possible food supply.

Too often, however, as man has advanced in the technology of the machine, he has laid aside this conservation concept and substituted another based upon the exploitation of all available resources. The more "civilized" he becomes, the more greedy and acquisitive he grows, and the more convinced that he is master of the environment that supports him. No longer does he see himself as a cooperating member of the life community, but rather as its conqueror and ruler. No matter what this may mean in material wealth and the so-called good life, it is at this point that the real troubles of the human race begin.

Time and again in history, advancing cultures have brought themselves to the threshold of extinction through this effort to conquer the environment rather than use their knowledge and skills to live with it in peace and harmony. Only the limitations of space and time, of numbers and the distances that separated them, have prevented these localized disasters from becoming holocausts engulfing the entire species of mankind.

Today those limitations of time, space, and numbers no longer exist. Technology is in the saddle. Circling satellites, man's exploration of the moon, planes that annihilate distance, increasing dependence on the machine and the computer, all attest to this fact. To say we become increasingly arrogant with each scientific and technological advance, more convinced that we can live as conquerors rather than as cooperating members of the life community, is to put the case mildly. There is nothing in history or in our store of knowledge to warrant such a view.

A strange fact, yet one that can hardly be denied, is that each step forward toward the unveiling of the ultimate mysteries of the universe also brings us a step closer to the capability of destroying ourselves and all other life on Earth. Put in different terms, we have so upset our life equilibrium with the other forces that make up our environment that only the greatest exercise of the human intellect can reestablish this equilibrium and insure the continued existence of mankind as a species.

One step in this process of restabilization must certainly be to consider "conservation as behavior." It is high time that man examined this idea to see what possibilities it may hold of helping solve some of the ills that trouble us today across our entire planet. Plainly, we must first understand what this concept means.

As we use it, conservation deals with man's attitude toward and use of all resources that supply the things upon which he is ultimately dependent for life. The difficulty here is that each of us applies his own standards. Thus producers of fuels from irreplaceable mineral sources manipulate supplies and governments with an eye on today's annual statement rather than tomorrow's energy supply. The lumberman who talks "wise use" may interpret this as cutting the people's national forests for the quickest profit. Thus we come to "behavior," which is a matter of ethics and morals.

In discussing the matter of behavior in relation to our environment, many of us have run into the word *ecology* only in the past two decades. The term may seem so new that many of us feel it must have just been invented to help understand a world suddenly complex beyond comprehension. Yet ecology is an old concept, deriving from the Greek word *oikos*, which means house, habitat, or environment. In the biological sense dealing with living things, which is the way we use it, ecology has to do with the relationships between organisms and between these organisms and their environments.

This plainly brings us to another word that can be a stumbling block. Yet this one shouldn't be too difficult, either, for the word *environment* simply means the sum total of all the external conditions and influences that affect the life and development of an organism. This is true whether the organism is a human being, an elephant, a giant sequoia tree, or a single cell seen floating on the slide under the microscope.

The eminent microbiologist and philosopher Rene Dubos has described the ultimate environment as the cosmos; a gigantic organism evolving according to laws that are valid everywhere and that therefore generate a universal harmony. Barry Commoner and other workers in the field have pointed out that the fundamental law of ecology is really quite simple. It is that everything is relevant and related to everything else.

The trouble with all these definitions is that, being ordinary mortals, we can understand them only if they are reduced to fairly simple terms. Realizing this fact as long ago as the 1880s,

Overgrazed and overcut areas of the Ozarks represent places where forests have been used for quickest profit.

the American entomologist Stephen Forbes literally invented what he called the *microcosm*, which we now translate as the *ecosystem*. As Forbes put it, a lake can be said to form a little world within itself—a microcosm within which all the elemental forces are at work and the play of life goes on in the full, but on so small a scale as to bring it within our mental grasp. If we are willing to think of ecology and environment in these terms, they become readily understandable.

We create ecosystems out of our minds and interests. Thus when we find the nest of a cottontail rabbit in a neglected corner of the yard, we begin to consider what is involved in the life of this cottontail. Does its nest have sufficient cover to hide it from possible predators? How many dogs or cats or hawks live and hunt within this ecosystem? What possibilities are there for food as the young start to grow? Is there room for them to spread out and occupy new worlds or ecosystems of their own? Will someone spray this corner with a poisonous pesticide or touch a match to the dry grass?

Ecosystems are endless. The bird's-foot violets blooming in April along every Ozark roadside offer an interesting opportunity for ecological study. We bring a few plants in for our wildflower garden from some spot where they won't be missed. They linger for a season, then die out. Why should this violet prefer raw, recently disturbed roadside clay to the humus-rich wildflower garden? Can it be that *Viola pedata* dislikes intensive competition?

Thus an ecosystem can be a rabbit's world, a colony of wildflowers, a village or city, an ocean, a continent, or the universe. Each offers infinite opportunity for study.

*   *   *   *

Few days pass in these times without our seeing, hearing, or reading discussions of man's chances for survival on an endangered planet. After almost complete neglect of this subject we now find expressions of concern for the future of the human race from some of the best minds in many disciplines.

These discussions cover many subjects: overpopulation and approaches to its control; means for increasing food production from land and sea; environmental pollution in its many forms; threatened exhaustion of essential resources. The discussions are generally informed, intelligent, and otherwise valuable. Yet it is our feeling that this concern for tomorrow has somehow failed to penetrate deeply into the consciousness of the world's people who must implement and carry out the solutions for these problems.

As far as those underdeveloped and undeveloped areas that we call the Third World are concerned, this lack of interest is easy to understand. When the people of these areas look at the prosperous, highly developed nations of the West, their own environmental problems appear far less important than does catching up in matters of technology and thus achieving the so-called good life and apparent prosperity that the people of the West enjoy.

Another matter may help explain our lukewarm environmental interest. Those who are most concerned about the problems ahead seem unable to present a united front, and this we find confusing. Just what is the total, overall environmental issue? Years ago Rachel Carson in *Silent Spring* wrote of the dangers of overuse of poison pesticides and herbicides, yet alleged experts still deny these dangers. Biologist Paul Ehrlich concentrates on the disasters certain to result from a continuing population explosion, but others claim a vastly greater carrying capacity for our earth.

Plant geneticist Georg Borgstrom counts on a Green Revolution to feed a burgeoning population, while others point out the dangers of plant disease and insect epidemics in a monoculture agriculture. John Calhoun demonstrates the breakdown in a society of laboratory rats under conditions of severe overcrowding. Barry Commoner, attacking the problem of environmental danger on a broader front, points out the deadly forces unleashed by an unexamined technology.

Historian Lynn White of California has made an excellent case for his belief that the Judeo-Christian tradition is largely responsible for the desecration of nature in our modern world and suggests a philosophical return to the teaching of St. Francis of Assisi. But bacteriologist Rene Dubos, who sees no danger in a world of nature improved upon by man, believes we would do better to follow the working Benedictines whom he feels created new and ecologically viable environments in their management and use of the land and landscape.

We Americans have tough environmental lessons to learn in the critical days ahead. Nor will the task be made easier by the fact that our neighbors in the developing countries have barely started to kindergarten in these matters. First and most important, we must learn that all of the resources that make human life on earth possible, possibly with the single exception of sunlight, are finite. All have definite limits and many are in large measure nonrenewable. We suddenly find that in many areas resources are running low, or can only be enjoyed at prohibitive cost, or have even become illegal.

Today sidewalks and highways insulate our feet from the soil. Two tons of metal powered by fossil fuel is our substitute for shoe leather. Even those who work directly with the land seem only dimly aware that recent decades have concerned themselves with improving the exploitive pump, rather than with maintaining the well from which our resources flow. As the urban dweller searches for the easier life, the countryman asks for more fertilizer, more deadly pesticides, miracle crops that can bypass the true productivity of the land. Yet only in Nature can we read and understand the laws that Nature has written; laws that must be obeyed as the price of survival.

The Land as a Resource

Recently we have heard much of depletion allowances for industries that exploit such irreplaceable resources as our fossil fuels, oil, and coal in order to produce the energy to keep our country running. These depletion allowances, in the form of tax benefits, have a certain logic; their purpose is to pay the costs of finding and developing new sources of irreplaceable fossil fuels to keep the energy circuit flowing—at a profit to the producer. If he pockets the allowance instead of using it as intended, he eventually finds himself out of business.

Energy is the essence of existence, and certainly no humans on our planet have ever used it as lavishly as we Americans to furnish ourselves with the good things of life. Yet few industries use as much energy per ton of produce as does American agriculture. Farmers represent the biggest market for steel in the machinery and equipment they buy. They are one of the largest users of fuel and power. With this energy, and with the fertility of their soil, which we are apt to forget, they feed America. They also produce a surplus that is sold abroad, although not always wisely. In many ways the farmer is little different from other exploiters of our natural resources, except for one thing. The resource that he exploits, and the essence of what he sells, is neither grain nor meat. It is the fertility that has been stored in his land through literally hundreds of thousands of years. Here are basic elements such as calcium, phosphate, and potash, as well as nitrogen, a dozen trace minerals, and countless billions of bacteria and other life forms that feed essential elements into the plants grown by the farmer.

In parts of agricultural Europe, for example, France, there are lands that have been farmed for a thousand years and are as rich today as when primitive man plowed his first furrow with a crooked stick. The same is true in North Germany and in parts of Britain. One reason is that Europe has few torrential rains that wash away topsoil. In early times, Americans created problems by trying to adapt British methods of tillage totally unsuited to our soils and climate.

But primarily, here in America we didn't care, and the truth is that we still don't care enough. At first there was always more land to the west, good, cheap land rich in organic matter and minerals. So we moved west until we came up against the Pacific Ocean and had to stop. Meanwhile we had destroyed millions of acres, in the east by overcropping, on the prairies by erosion, in the Great Plains by overgrazing and plowing the semiarid lands. But always there was a new frontier and a farmer might boast that he had worn out four farms in his westward trek.

Today we believe we know better than that. Yet we destroy the ten-thousand-year history of our farm soils in a different way. We destroy its organic and chemical diversity by monoculture, planting single crops to replace the hundreds once there, and by using herbicides to kill those that survive. And we believe we can maintain fertility with huge quantities of fertilizers that produce steadily smaller gains for each hundred pounds applied, at higher cost to the farmer.

The Dust Bowl—Again? In 1890 or thereabouts Mark Twain described the basin of the Mississippi River as the body of the nation; all other parts being but members. A half-century later, writer and photographer Pare Lorentz made a film called *The River* that told what was happening to the Mississippi. The narration begins: From as far west as Idaho, down the glacier peaks of the Rockies, from as far east as New York, down the turkey ridges of the Alleghenies. Down from Minnesota, twenty-five hundred miles, the Mississippi runs to the Gulf. Carrying every brook and rill, rivulet and creek, and all the streams that run down two-thirds of the continent—the Mississippi River runs to the Gulf of Mexico.

In the century that had passed, we had plowed the black lands of Arkansas, Louisiana, Mississippi, Alabama, and east Texas and Oklahoma and had planted them to cotton. We had turned under the big bluestem to plant wheat in Kansas and Nebraska and the Dakotas—and corn in Iowa, Missouri, Illinois, and Indiana. In Wisconsin, Michigan, and Minnesota, we had cut the tall pine to farm the sandy soil. And we had killed the last buffalo so we could overgraze the short-grass prairie of Montana, Idaho, Wyoming, Colorado, West Texas, and Oklahoma.

In the spring of 1935, Hugh Bennett of the newly created Soil Conservation Service stood on the St. Louis levee and estimated that every sixty seconds the topsoil from 640 acres of good American farmland was riding the brown Mississippi flood past the point where he stood—headed for the Gulf. Later, as he was asking Congress for funds to fight erosion, he spoke to a group of senators of the phenomenon of dust from the heartland east of the Rockies blowing two thousand miles east to the Atlantic and then covering the decks of ships far out at sea.

As Bennett talked, the Senate hearing room grew dark as night and the lights were turned on. A fourth dust storm had swept eastward into Washington, and Bennett got his appropriation. He also nailed to the masthead of his newborn agency the credo of the organization: "Hold the rain on the land where it falls. Use the land according to its true capabilities—with the knowledge of its utility, its beauty, its physical qualities, its weaknesses and its strength."

On our first drive through Arizona, New Mexico, and Texas in the 1940s, we witnessed the aftermath of drought and years of dangerously bad farming. During those times, a single dust storm could pick up millions of tons of fertile topsoil and blow them east until they reached the Atlantic. In many places on that long-ago trip we saw desert shrubs—mesquite, creosote bush, and catclaw—standing on earthen mounds four feet above the surrounding surface. Everything between had been blown away.

In the 1970s we followed a similar road. Since we traveled on a four-lane interstate, it was faster than the trip back in the forties. The road still traversed low-rainfall country that on that first journey was just recovering from the Dust Bowl, when we were beginning to believe that, with the help of the Soil Conservation Service, the problem could be conquered.

Thus we were alarmed to look out across the countryside and see the dust rolling. Often a cloud covering hundreds of acres originated with a single tractor pushing across the distant landscape. And there were still areas where mesquite bushes and scrub cedars grew atop small islands of earth. We couldn't help but remember that Hugh Bennett had warned Congress that those dust storms would come again, unless farmers were careful to behave themselves.

The tragedy is that our agricultural agencies, whose task it is to guide farmers, are the leaders in urging farmers to misbehave. In California, Arizona, New Mexico, and Oklahoma, as well as in the heartland of Iowa, Kansas, and North and South Dakota, farmers are again in deep trouble.

Millions of the world's hungry people depend on North America for food. Recent estimates show that 2.5 billion of the nearly 4 billion people now living on Earth are short of all of life's necessities. Two-thirds of these people live in food-deficient countries where both land and the means for production are lacking. Thus every ton of food raised can find a market. But most of it will undoubtedly be sold to countries who bid the highest for it, even though some of these countries may then sell or trade part of it to promote their own national interests.

Here in America we have embarked on a dangerous course. We have urged every farmer to plow every acre that can be plowed and put into exportable crops. Much of this new land is marginal because of lack of water or natural fertility or other causes. Often production depends on irrigation that can destroy the land through accumulation of chemical salts, or on heavy application of costly chemical fertilizers that are themselves nonrenewable resources.

To one who has practiced conservation and still done his share of plowing but is no economist, a basic question arises. How is it that the world's richest and most powerful nation, with the greatest technology and industry and a population that does not yet strain its resources, depends on selling its most precious resource, its soil fertility, to maintain a favorable trade balance?

Floods. In a flood year, and 1973 was a devastating flood year for this part of the country, man is taught once again that he is not the master of Nature. The power, immensity, and tragedy of a big flood are hard to realize when you live in a hill country, until you have spent nights filling sandbags on a levee where the brown tide creeps higher or have seen helpless livestock stranded on a disappearing island or a family of raccoons clinging to a treetop being swept past, or have flown at low altitude over valleys where farmsteads and villages are inundated and water stretches away into the distance.

It has taken years to estimate the total cost of the 1973 flood. Topsoil from thousands of farms was swept down to the Gulf or lies at the bottom of reservoirs built to prevent such disasters. Thousands of homes must be rebuilt; in many cases whole farmsteads with outbuildings, livestock, and machinery. On millions of our richest acres, no crops grew that year, and many more years would be needed to bring them back to high productivity.

In times of inflation there can be little doubt of the effect this had on food prices. And in a flood year, few surpluses exist to help feed a hungry world.

It takes courage to even suggest solutions for problems that are monumental in size and scope. Yet they must be faced, and one is whether the time has not arrived for proper use of our floodplains, lakefronts, and seashores. We can't stop farming river lands that flood, because they are our richest lands. But we can consider whether residential and industrial development of these lands is profitable or desirable. All across the nation, mobile-home developments wash away; homes on unstable oceanfront lands slide into the sea; lakefront developments are battered by waves and destroyed by shifting shorelines. There is an answer here, and the answer is zoning.

Next problem is tougher because it is backed by one of the nation's most powerful lobbies. This is the dam-building program of the Army Corps of Engineers and the Bureau of Reclamation. How many of their reservoirs are today silted to the tops of their dams so they hold no surplus water whatever?

How many dams built before the day of the "impact statement" are useless or harmful? How many acres of irrigated land go out of production each year compared with land brought under irrigation, and what is the per-acre cost to taxpayers? The investment here creeps toward, or may have passed, the trillion-dollar mark, and all the answer aren't in.

The Soil Conservation Service of the United States was created to stop erosion. Its philosophy was sound—to start at the headwaters and hold water on the land to feed the crops and prevent floods. Now the shift of farming toward monoculture has helped create a new SCS program. This is "channelization" of streams into ditches that rush the water off the land at high speed. Thus its use is lost, and the farther it goes, the greater its potential for flood damage. The program needs, and indeed, is getting, analysis, but hardly by the Soil Conservation Service.

Something has happened in America during the years of exploding technology that was well put by Aldo Leopold in *Sand County Almanac*: "By and large," he said, "our problem is one of attitudes and implements. We are remodeling the Alhambra with a steamshovel, and we are proud of our yardage. We shall hardly relinquish the shovel, which after all has many good points, but we are in need of gentler and more objective criteria for its successful use."

Here at Possum Trot we are rounding out a lifetime of interest in and concern for the land. To us, unlike the economist, the land is not merely a resource to be exploited to boost the thing called gross national product. Moreover, each year strengthens our belief that economics, at least as it relates to feeding mankind, is not the exact science its practitioners like to imagine. Certainly, if it were, farming would operate on an evener keel while society as a whole would not bumble along with as many technological headaches as triumphs.

Most economists are intellectual urbanites, knowing little of the land and seeing it merely as expendable income, instead of as irreplaceable capital. Such thinking translated into farm policy inevitably favors monoculture that has, in times past, marked the end of civilizations. As for the physical work demanded by the small farm, it is regarded as a hardship to be done away with. Yet working with the land and livestock can be a creative and satisfying occupation, providing a rich reward in health, happiness, and permanence.

In Missouri, we are more fortunate than most of the world in the proportion of our land suitable for production of crops and forest. Yet one thing is clear: We need to set aside, before it is too late, more land for recreational, aesthetic, and scientific uses. These lands falls into two categories. The first we might class as countryside, and the second as wilderness.

Probably no better analysis has been made of the general character of these lands than by Steyermark in his *Vegetational History of the Ozark Forest*. In this work he shows clearly that the same types of forest cover exist here today as were present in the early years of the nineteenth century, granted they are not in the same virgin state or total acreage.

Few land areas of similar size in the nation have been subjected to harder use than our Ozark Highland. The area was always sparsely settled because of the scarcity of good farmland; thus the timber and wildlife and eventually the minerals became the resources on which the Ozark people depended. Often the result was a subsistence livelihood with considerable waste through lack of knowledge.

One of the earliest uses of Ozark timber was for the smelting of lead and iron. Here the custom was to clear-cut everything that could go into the charcoal kiln. Some areas, like the famous "Sligo Choppings" that denuded much of Dent, Iron, and Reynolds counties, are only now beginning to recover after nearly a century. Also, not long after the Civil War, commercial logging started, and here the practice was to buy the land for perhaps a dollar an acre, strip it, and then let it go for taxes.

First target of the big loggers was the virgin pine, and by 1890 sawmills operated throughout the eastern Ozarks. The largest mills in the country were built along the Current River at Grandin, West Eminence, and Winona, and later at Bunker, Ellsinore, Williamsville, and Poplar Bluff. These cut the virgin oak as the demand grew for railroad ties, whiskey barrel staves, wagon hubs, tool handles, and oak flooring.

The common practice was "high-grading," which is to say, cutting the best trees and gradually going down the line. This pretty well cleared out the virgin oak by the early 1920s. It also built the practice known as "grandmaw-ing," which became the source of livelihood for many an Ozark mountaineer. The practice was simply to slip in on the company land whenever a tree got big enough for a saw log and haul it to the mill. Then, since the mill was supposed to know from where the logs came, the logger simply said he had "cut'em down on grandma's place."

During three-quarters of a century the quality of yield from our Missouri forests went steadily downhill. The cutover land became "open range" for the livestock of the hill people who set fires each spring to "kill the ticks and make the grass grow." The result was a steady loss of soil fertility, the disappearance of wildlife, and runoff that carried millions of tons of gravel down into the streams and prevented the regeneration of the forest. Thus establishment of our Clark and Mark Twain national forests in 1931 came none too soon. Now the practices of timber stand improvement, reforestation, and selective and balanced harvest of the forest trees have begun to spread to private lands throughout the state.

The problems we face in utilizing both types of land for the public good are those of planning, classification, zoning, acquisition, restoration, and preservation. In the years ahead, with advances in agricultural techniques, considerable acreages of submarginal farmlands will go out of crop production to return to their natural state. Some of this land will be near centers of population and thus subject to heavy use for picnicking, hiking, and similar activities. Little thought has been given to such lands except for city and county parks; yet if we do not start soon, they will be lost to unplanned development and eventual urban sprawl.

Wild lands are different. In Missouri, for example, we have 14 million forested acres, most of it in the Ozarks and most supporting poor stands of cutover timber. Although the potential is good in stands of oak–hickory, oak–pine, and hardwoods in the stream bottoms, their present condition reflects little credit on the timber industry or on farm woodlot owners.

Missourians would not be proud of the analysis of the Ozark country made a few years ago by British ecologist Fraser Darling. More than any scientist we know, Darling has the broad knowledge to look at a land area and then tell us what it was originally, where it stands today, and in what direction it is heading. He defined the Ozarks as an area subjected to tragically bad land use by its residents and outside exploiters. Yet he valued the determination of the Ozark people to live life as they liked it—to own a good coon hound and to value the music of a fox chase more than a big corn crop.

Despite this grim picture, even badly used land comes back if we quit abusing it, as is happening here and there throughout our Missouri forests. The Forest Service and the Conservation Department are working together to improve habitats for wildlife. The Conservation Department has initiated a program to develop outstanding natural areas. Citizens' organizations are helping. The Conservation Federation supports the work of the Department. The Nature Conservancy and Sierra Club have their own natural area programs.

Our Forest Resource. Perhaps we should all have a special respect for the majesty of the stands of trees that can be found in unexpected places in our own Ozarks. A profound ecological statement that is a sign of such respect was made to us by an old German farmer who was a good conservationist. We hiked through his woodlot, eighty magnificent acres of tulip poplars (*Liriodendron tulipifera*), mixed with other Ozark species. The tulip poplars are one of our largest and most valuable trees, and these towered to 180 feet. Many were, moreover, clear of branches up to 60 feet or more.

Someone asked whether the trees should not be harvested, since they were mature and might soon start to deteriorate. The old man agreed that many lumbermen were urging him to sell and let them bring in a sawmill. "Why not?" we asked. "The lumber would certainly take care of your old age." Since he was well along in his eighties and in no danger of starving, I felt sure I captured a twinkle in the old man's eye as he answered. "We've been through a lot of years together," he said. "And by Gott I think there should be some trees die of old age."

*　　*　　*　　*

We have had occasion recently, as the energy crisis deepens, to consider the use of wood as fuel for cooking and heating—and even for producing some kinds of industrial power. Moreover, many other uses of wood have affected the world supply throughout the centuries. This supply plainly depends on the size of the forest resource and the uses to which the wood is put.

Here in America and in many other highly developed countries of the temperate zone, two demands for wood probably exceed all others, its use as a building material and its use as pulp to manufacture paper. Shortages loom for the future as population mounts, yet most of the developed countries are learning to husband their forests. It is mainly the ones with minimal space and growing population such as Japan that are in danger of severe timber shortage.

Man's use of the forest began early in history. Thus it has affected not only his cultures and his physical well-being, but even his climate. Far back in the time when primitive man was a hunter, he learned to use fire to drive game animals into areas where they could be more easily killed for food. This practice, moreover, may have contributed to creating grasslands and even deserts.

Thinly populated continents, such as America was before the white man came, suffered least from such practices. Yet even here, fire was used to drive game and also to prevent the incursion of trees and brush into the grasslands. In densely populated countries, the use of wood created problems. As the cities of ancient China grew, for example, so did the need for wood as fuel and as charcoal to fire the kilns used in baking pottery and ceramics. As forests were stripped from the highlands, annual floods poured down the rivers, and historians tell of smog from wood smoke hanging over the cities.

In our own travels through Mexico and Central America where wood is still almost universally used for cooking and heating, we have observed severe fuel shortages. Most Mexican cities are built in the healthy temperate highlands that once supported fine forests of pine and oak. Today the forests are gone and the peasants must travel long distances for cooking wood. Bundles transported long distances on burro-back sell at high prices in the markets, and out in the country most trees are trimmed of their branches for many feet above the ground. Yet this condition had already begun to be noted by the end of the Spanish conquest.

This shortage of wood for cooking fuel today affects hundreds of millions of people in Asia, Africa, and Latin America, especially those of the Indian subcontinent and the borders of the Sahara. Many of these people have long been forced to burn animal manure for cooking when it should have been returned to the land to enrich it.

Equally dangerous is the large-scale logging underway today in the lower reaches of the Himalayas and throughout Central America and Brazil, especially during the construction of highways. Recently we have read of a land-clearing project in the Amazon Valley where 6 million acres owned by North American interests are being cleared of native timber to be replaced by a plantation forest of exotic trees for lumber from which to manufacture paper. The only tragedy is that the existing population on this 6 million acres is being forced to move out and up onto the mountainsides. Here the old slash-and-burn agriculture will begin again, followed by floods and a second move by the peasants into the cities.

That brings us back to America's problems. She is facing many problems of conservation of energy resources, and few are receiving more attention than the rapidly growing demand for energy from wood. As a renewable resource, our forests can contribute greatly to our energy needs, perhaps 20 percent of the total. The big question is whether we can secure this energy without permanent damage to the forest resource.

Some foresters make a good case for the possibility that we can, through expert management, secure this energy while at the same time improving the forest. They point out that scientific tree harvest with its resulting contribution to our total BTU might actually double today's growth capacity of our woodlands. On the other hand, some danger signs are already on the horizon. Clear-cutting, high-grading, and charcoaling can, as we have learned, destroy a forest forever.

If we are to develop means of securing maximum energy from wood, sound policies and programs are needed on a national basis. Already we read of the complete use of cull trees and inferior species in forest stands. Much attention is given to use of the entire tree by means of wood chippers and similar machinery that can utilize every branch of every tree that is felled and also trees of smaller diameter than those used today.

Our own interest in the forest and the use of all its products goes back over the past half-century, and from this certain facts stand out. First is the broad but shortsighted forestry interest in turning trees into cash. Another is that wisdom directs us to use at least our national forest holdings to provide timber for the future and to use these forests for watershed protection, for recreation, and for purely aesthetic values.

Professional foresters preach that trees are a crop like any other crop, although generally planted by nature rather than by man. This means that the trees through photosynthesis combine sunlight, air, water, and soil minerals, turning these things into wood. A second fact is that the forest flora is almost always complex, consisting of many plant species including other trees, shrubs, grasses, and forbs.

When a tree is harvested in the old way, only that portion large enough to make a saw log is removed. Leaves, branches, and the remainder of the trunk are left to decay and, in the course of time, to return their nutrients to the soil to nourish future trees. The saw log removed may represent no more than 15 percent of the tree, and even this is replaced by gradual weathering of the soil.

What we do not hear about is that intensive utilization and removal of all parts of the harvested tree may so deplete the fertility of the soil that the succeeding tree will be starved for food and thus an inferior specimen. This has happened on many forest acres, and even the removal of cull trees and species of little value as lumber can cut the productivity of the forest. On the other hand, the practice known as "timber stand improvement" or TSI, where the culls and damaged or inferior trees are cut down and left to decay, will greatly promote better growth for the remaining forest.

Wood for energy is an important issue of the day. But it can be seen even from this brief comment that there are many complexities. What will happen to the watershed under more intensive use? Will we improve or destroy the habitat for desirable wildlife? Have both public and private forestry learned the lessons of history and of earlier forest destruction? As the head of the American Forestry Association has said, wood is a critical element in our energy future, but let's not fail to examine the trade-offs in our burst of enthusiasm.

The use of wood for fuel and of pulp for papermaking is perhaps the most visible reason for conserving our forest resources. But our forest helps provide us with another essential element, even if that is more easily taken for granted.

Fifty years or more ago the great Arctic explorer Knud Rasmussen was discussing with an elderly Eskimo holy man the things that create the real problems in life. The old Eskimo's statement seems so basic to our continued existence on this planet that it is well worth thinking about and remembering. "We fear the cold," said the ancient Eskimo, "and the things we do not understand. But most of all we fear the doings of the heedless ones among us."

Today in our temperate America, we have little fear for the cold. Yet when the day comes that energy sources run out, as they already are in many areas, we too will fear the cold. But an even greater danger lies, as the old man said, in the doings of the heedless ones among us. Examples of this heedlessness are all around us and, as we fail to find ways to check and overcome them, the day of disaster draws steadily closer.

Let us take the matter of air, a priceless asset without which human life, or any life, cannot exist. Man depends on oxygen for air to breathe, and this oxygen depends on the green plants that manufacture and release it. Few if any city today produces enough oxygen for its citizens. Streets, sidewalks, buildings of brick and concrete, shopping centers with large parking areas paved with asphalt. These produce little or no oxygen. Yet a city needs far more air than just the amount its people breathe. The countless processes of industry, combustion, and the heedless horseless carriage that jams the city streets—all these use oxygen in vast amounts.

Here in Missouri before the white man came, oxygen was no problem. We had millions of acres of virgin forest, each acre manufacturing quantities of this essential material. Today we have reduced this acreage to 14 million, about one-third of the original amount. Since trees are probably the most efficient and prolific oxygen producers and our primary oxygen source, this is still a huge volume. But there are heedless ones among us who think of air as something that endlessly and automatically renews itself, and of trees in terms of dollars rather than as the source of life.

Not long ago our forester friend John Wylie set down some interesting figures about trees and the air we breathe. He started with an acre of forest and found it could produce enough oxygen to supply four people and two small dogs. This was, of course, for breathing and didn't include oxygen consumed by their 300-horsepower car, furnace, air conditioner, and other gadgets deemed necessary for the good life.

Actually Missouri's 14 million forested acres, according to John's calculations, grow at the rate of 16 million tons of wood per year, which creates enough oxygen to support 72 million people if none is used for anything else. This sounds just dandy, but remember that we are logging off many acres of forest for lumber each year. What is worse, we spray and clear more acres to turn into agricultural land. We are, in other words, losing approximately one hundred thousand acres of forest every ten years.

Thus, with every 640-acre section of forest that is cleared, we lose the potential oxygen for twenty-five hundred human beings. At fifteen hundred sections per year, that is the oxygen for a city of more than 3 million inhabitants with, as John says, their dogs, cats, and canaries. It is vitally important for the heedless to remember that no city any longer produces all of its own oxygen supply, but depends on country air. Little wonder that the President's Commission on Materials Policy urges that "fragile forest areas" be permanently withdrawn from lumbering and that environmental standards be made a condition of timber harvest even on privately owned land.

Philosophers of the Environment

A concern for the world of nature and a basic feeling for ecology can be traced throughout history. Plato wrote, nearly five centuries before the Christian era, of the tragedy resulting from deforestation and erosion on the steep hills of the Greek peninsula. Our own Old Testament, too often cited as proof that all nature exists to serve and to be dominated by man, offers evidence to the contrary. "Be fruitful and multiply" was in fact an admonition only given to Adam and Eve when they constituted a world population of two. And if we read our New Testament correctly, there are warnings against a plundered planet and of the punishment that will surely follow the waste and defilement of the earth's resources of which we are custodians.

Regardless of such warnings and the fact that many scriptural passages are read out of context in our materialist society, it seems inevitable that in the swift growth of this industrial age, man has come to regard resources as property to be exploited for maximum profit, rather than as blessings from his Creator to be treasured and used wisely. We have always, here in America, credited our material success to some special genius in our Yankee makeup. Yet it might have been better to realize that for most of our four-hundred-year history we have been only a handful of people with skills inherited from our European forebears, placed in a land blessed with unparalleled resources. These have provided material wealth, well-being, leisure for education, time to perfect the methods of exploitation.

Through three hundred years of this history, the rich environment absorbed the impact of our exploitation with hardly a ripple. Yet even during those years our destructive proclivities did not go unnoticed. Audubon, often blamed for the number of wild creatures he collected for food and as models and scientific specimens, commented on these matters. In his journals he described the needless slaughter of passenger pigeon, golden plover, Labrador waterfowl, and buffalo of the western plains. For all of these he predicted, quite correctly, eventual extermination.

George Perkins Marsh, a scholar with far more education than Audubon, published his *Man and Nature* in 1865. In it he states that America's attack on her resource base was of such ferocity as to threaten, through barbarism and depravity, the extinction of the human species. And there were others of that era—Thoreau, Emerson, Whitman, and Melville—who were measuring, to quote Professor Leo Marx of MIT, the quality of American life against an ecological idea.

Premonitions of big disaster coincided with the Dust Bowl and the Depression years of the 1930s. This was when scientists Whyte and Jacks published their prophetic *Vanishing Lands*, which was followed by Hugh Bennett's *Soil Conservation* and Paul Sears's *Deserts on the March*. These dealt with the disastrous effects of erosion on past civilizations that were now showing up in America.

Problems of burgeoning population crept into conservation literature in the 1940s, along with the beginnings of ecological thought; the conviction that man was not master, but only one creature in the vast chain of life on our earth. Ed Graham of the Soil Conservation Service wrote *Natural Principles of Land Use*; then came Leopold's epoch-making *A Sand County Almanac*, which is still the foundation for sound thinking about the importance of wildlife and wilderness in our culture and the necessity for a new and sound land ethic. Fairfield Osborn followed with *Our Plundered Planet*; Edward Faulkner in *Plowman's Folly* set forth principles of organic farming; Bill Vogt in *Road to Survival* tackled the population problem. Then came studies of the pressure of people on land in Ward Shepard's *Food or Famine* and in *Tomorrow's Food* by Philip Norman and James Rorty.

In the 1950s, geochemist Harrison Brown wrote *The Challenge of Man's Future* and biologist Marston Bates followed with *The Prevalence of People*—two profoundly disturbing studies of the human condition. Sam Ordway examined our raw material limitations in *Resources and the American Dream*. L. Dudley Stamp wrote *Land for Tomorrow*, and Tom Dale and Vernon Gill Carter set down the story of lost cultures in *Topsoil and Civilization*.

There are many who have contributed to our understanding and sometimes misunderstanding of the environment and who deserve more than a mere mention.

George Perkins Marsh. "The earth is fast becoming an unfit home for its noblest inhabitant, and another era of equal human crime and human improvidence . . . would reduce it to such a condition . . . as to threaten the depravation, barbarism, and perhaps even extinction of the species."

It is easy to assume that today's problems began with Watergate and Vietnam; yet the above paragraph was written in 1864 by an American named George Perkins Marsh and published in his epochal book *Man and Nature*—America's first great work on conservation and based on a remarkably broad ecological point of view. Marsh's concern for the morality of his day did not cure all its ills—but plainly he saw the problems for resource conservation that lay ahead in America.

Rosalie Edge. An interesting controversy occurred between Rosalie Edge, a New York banker's wife, and the Audubon So-

This spot on Long's Creek could be one of George Perkins Marsh's "schools for instruction of the student, gardens of recreation for the nature lover."

ciety, whom she justly accused of a highly biased conservation attitude. This was when the Audubon Society, in a mistaken belief that furbearers were destroying wild goose habitat in the Rainey Sanctuary in the Gulf, profited $100,000 from trappers who harvested 289,000 pelts of mink, muskrat, and raccoons in three years.

Mrs. Edge had actually hit on one of the real villains of wildlife management—the predator control programs that are still deeply rooted in the policy of many state and federal bureaus. The policy continues even after research has shown the programs are in no way helpful to the species they supposedly protect.

Bureaus move slowly, developing blind faith in science and technology, worshiping bigness and developing arrogance toward the landscape. Such expressions as "multiple use," "conservation is wise use," "the greatest good for the greatest number" become imbedded in bureaucratic thinking, establishing a cloak of conformity behind which we in the conservation movement cannot afford to hide.

Aldo Leopold. Leopold, whom we counted as a friend, died fighting a brush fire on his Wisconsin farm in 1948. This was a year before publication of *A Sand County Almanac*, which has probably been more widely read than any book in its field. Beyond doubt Leopold stands today as one of our great ecologists and conservationists, with influence that continues to grow. *Almanac* is a powerful expression of the ecological attitude toward man, wildlife, and the land.

Susan Flader has written a study of the development of Leopold's philosophy, titled *Thinking Like a Mountain*. This title is from an essay included in the *Almanac* and is explained by the subtitle: *Aldo Leopold and the Evolution of an Ecological Attitude Toward Deer, Wolves, and Forests.*

Leopold's essay, which we have read more than once, seems to us to mark his growth from forester and hunter to game manager and naturalist in somewhat the Thoreau tradition—into a master of ecological science, understanding not only the deer, wolf, and forest relationships, but also man's relationship to his entire environment.

If you happened to cut your conservation eyeteeth on the writings of Leopold, one question might remain in your mind. At what point in Leopold's career did he outgrow being a hunter—full of "trigger itch," to use his own expression—and grow to manhood with a man's horizons? To find out, go back on some winter evening to spend some time with *A Sand County Almanac* and read the essay "Thinking Like a Mountain." You can read it twice and still have time for a bit of thinking before the fire dies down.

Norman Borlaug. Back in 1950, Anthony Standen wrote a book called *Science Is a Sacred Cow*, which begins with the idea that when a white-coated scientist, looking up from his microscope, makes a pronouncement for the public, he may not be understood, but is certain to be believed. No one doubts a scientist.

The book then goes on to prove that such unquestioning belief can be dangerous.

The sentence came to mind when we read recent statements by plant breeder and Nobel Prize winner Norman Borlaug. Called "Father of the Green Revolution" for his development of high-yielding wheat, Borlaug has attacked what he called hysterical conservationist efforts to ban DDT. Borlaug makes four points: (1) in 1970 we needed 260 million acres to produce the next year's food for ourselves and other nations; (2) the same total yields thirty years ago, when he says most of today's pesticides and fertilizers were nonexistent, would have required 600 million acres; (3) this would have meant sacrificing forest and grassland for crops, crowding some animals to extinction; and (4) pesticides have therefore helped prevent decline of wildlife species.

Now even a nonscientific generalist cannot help wishing that Borlaug had done more pesticide research before making these statements. The first thing we find is that if present birth rates continue unchecked in the Orient, Near East, and Central and South America, then chaos and starvation are inevitable regardless of the Green Revolution plus DDT and other pesticides. Moreover, in the absence of population controls abroad, no sharing of America's food at the cost of the inevitable destruction of our farmlands can prevent a world of misery and semi-starvation that may eventually drag our own country down to ruin.

We must also question Borlaug's second point. It is simply not a fact that "most of today's pesticides and fertilizers were nonexistent thirty years ago." In our earliest years at Possum Trot we mistakenly sprayed our beef herd with DDT. When flies soon became DDT-resistant, we added dieldrin, malathion, methoxychlor, BHC, and other poisons to the mix, although we have since learned better. Weed killers were also available and widely used. Fertilizer analyses may vary today, yet yesterday's ingredients were the same: nitrogen, phosphate, potash, calcium, and an array of trace minerals. Does Borlaug infer that there are others today?

Today's record crop yields have resulted from tremendous increases in chemical fertilizer use, plus pesticides and herbicides.

They are also due to the one-crop farming we now practice while allowing our soils to deteriorate in organic richness and complexity and from erosion. Yet no sensible scientist would advocate abolishing fertilizers or all insect and weed controls. Neither would he urge abolishing the use of DDT in developing countries where malaria control is a factor.

On the other hand, poisons such as DDT and 2-45T do kill birds, fish, and small mammals and build up in the food chains to render the birds of prey sterile. Continued use of these poisons for insect and weed control may end by poisoning man and could actually destroy the Green Revolution that Borlaug has worked so brilliantly to produce. Charles Wurster, noted environmental scientist, points out that in Mexico, quite near Borlaug's own laboratories, insect problems *created* by pesticides forced abandonment of cotton-growing and caused the collapse of the dependent economies. Perhaps, as Wurster suggests, Borlaug's concentration on high-yielding grains has prevented his expertise in the matter of environmental damage by pesticides.

Raymond Dasmann. A book has come to our attention that may have almost as profound an effect on ecological thinking as Leopold's *Almanac*. This is *The Conservation Alternative* by Raymond Dasmann. Dasmann is a native of California with so diverse a career that we must touch on its highlights. Often called an ecological statesman, Dasmann took his doctorate at Berkeley, then taught briefly at Humboldt College. Teaching couldn't hold him, however, and he spent three years as biologist at the Natural History Museum of Rhodesia, lectured on zoology at Berkeley, served as ecologist for the Conservation Foundation, in 1970 joined the International Union for Conservation of Nature in Morges, Switzerland, as senior ecologist, and in 1977 returned to teach at the University of California at Santa Cruz.

Not content with teaching and research, Dasmann has written constantly, on California wildlife, African game farming, and the ecological destruction of California. Two recent books have provocative titles: *A Different Kind of Country* and *No Further Retreat*. A third book, *The Conservation Alternative*, is a short 164 pages in which be extends his area of inquiry into works of social criticism, economic and political commentary, religious and cultural matters because he finds them all central to conservation.

Dasmann ends with six statements that challenge us all: (1) Civilization today uses a high percentage of its energy and resources to prepare for total war; (2) Western civilization has brought great wealth to a few, while leaving the world's majority in desperate poverty; (3) since no world incentive for limiting population exists, how will we avoid eventual death by disease and starvation for hundreds of millions?; (4) technology, out of human control, is oriented toward an economy of consumption and waste; (5) pollution of the total environment is reaching ever higher and more dangerous levels; (6) destruction of the life-support systems of the biosphere, based on plant and animal life and the soils and waters that support them, constantly accelerates.

Only One Earth. How to chart a course to maintain a livable and navigable spaceship Earth was at least partially spelled out at the United Nations Conference on Human Settlements and Habitat, held in June 1976 in Vancouver. This was the fourth of such meetings, which began in 1972 in Stockholm with the Conference on the Human Environment. Other meetings followed on population, food, and the place of women in our world.

The problems set before that first meeting were well expressed by two leaders of the Western world, economist Barbara Ward and ecologist Rene Dubos, who headed a committee of intellectual leaders from fifty-eight nations. Their report was a book called *Only One Earth: The Care and Maintenance of a Small Planet.* The book achieved a global view of social, economic, and political perspectives and covered such matters as pollution, population, resource misuse, the impact of technology, and the worldwide problem of urbanization.

At this fourth Environmental Conference, 4 billion human beings were, literally, being asked to draft a land-use plan for an entire planet. This plan must show us how to pool our knowledge and husband our resources to preserve our global biosphere. More than that, the rich and industrialized nations are asked to take the lead in this gigantic operation. At the same time, the Third and Fourth World countries who are still struggling with problems of nationalism, colonization, and population are asked to avoid the mistakes of greed and overdevelopment by which the industrialized world has brought our planet to the edge of disaster.

The quality of leadership and amount of discipline needed to achieve such ends seem almost beyond the bounds of human capability. Yet, if the cooperation of nations and continents is not somehow achieved, coming generations will surely find themselves condemned to life on a "Spaceship Earth" that is no longer navigable.

The Limits to Growth. In 1972, the prestigious Club of Rome published its report, *The Limits to Growth*, the result of its survey of the condition of Earth's resources in relation to consumption. Some economists scoffed at the warning that we must slow down both industrial and population growth, yet the book has been translated into thirty languages and has sold 4 million copies.

We have come to believe, because the wordmakers have said it is so, that our profligate use of the world's resources to create "the richest and most powerful nation on earth" is all to the good. Yet do we, who are one-sixth of the planet's people, have the right to consume one-half of its energy and an even larger portion of its other resources? Today it appears we have decided by a large majority that this position is morally wrong; that our action has hurt the well-being of much of mankind and has turned many against us. Eighty percent of our citizens now agree, say the pollsters, that such high consumption of world resources also results in the pollution of our own air and waters. The energy shortages that loom and have already skyrocketed costs, or the rising inflation, these are seen by the majority as in large measure the result of reckless overconsumption.

Perhaps the time has come for a new national purpose based not on gross national product but on a new attitude as to what constitutes the good life. Nor can we do better than to look back at 1776 when the founders of the Republic spoke not just for the new America but for all mankind. There is a need for greatness in meeting today's problems, just as there was two hundred years ago. And how achieve this greatness better than by emulating those plain men who fought the Revolution and, through the Constitution they drafted, created here a new kind of nation, men such as Ben Franklin, Thomas Jefferson, George Washington, Patrick Henry, and Daniel Webster.

Did these men live in a greater time than ours? This hardly seems possible in a day before the industrial revolution and the great forward march of science. Yet they had a conviction that we lost in the trauma of Vietnam and the shabbiness of Watergate. Nor can we think of a better resolve for the future than this from the pen of Oliver Wendell Holmes: "I think that, as life is action and passion, it is required of a man that he should share the passion and action of his time at peril of being judged not to have lived."

10

"Things Wild and Free"

A comment often heard in these days of environmental crisis runs like this: "Why should we worry about the disappearance of bald eagles, Indiana bats, whooping cranes, sea otters, or blue whales? Aren't men more important than animals? Haven't whole orders of birds, mammals, reptiles, and fishes been disappearing since history began. Won't other species come along to take their places? Look at the dinosaurs; aren't we lucky they aren't here today?"

Certainly the disappearance of plant and animal species and the appearance of new ones is part of the slow but universal process of evolution. The fossil record tells us that most organisms that have lived on earth during the past 6 billion years are no longer here. Thus we can surmise that the eventual fate of every species is extinction.

What we fail to remember is that these disappearances have taken place slowly—mostly in geological time, which is to say thousands or even millions of years. Climatic change, periods of glaciation, development of predators or competitors, disappearance of essential food sources; when a species cannot adapt to such changes, it is doomed. On the other hand, although such species may eventually be replaced by others, the process involves long periods of time.

Before man appeared in the biosphere, plant and animal extinctions resulted from natural changes in the environment. There is little doubt, however, that man's arrival started a whole new ball game. New and rapid stresses affected the environment and its plant and animal inhabitants. Consider how farming or forestry, for example, can change or destroy whole ecosystems. Hunting for food or sport, mining, water pollution, use of poison pesticides—all these can eliminate plant and animal species.

243

The important thing here is not so much man's natural aesthetic commitment to nature, but rather the tremendously complex interrelationship between all life forms in a given ecosystem. The elimination of a forest or of a single animal species can disrupt an entire ecological community and even cause it to die. When we consider that our biosphere has taken billions of years to develop, the swift disappearance of species caused by man can disrupt the system in ways that evolution cannot repair.

Several theories attempt to explain causes of species extinction, and the appearance of man on the scene seems a most probable one. Even early man was a superpredator, sharply increasing the rate of overkill. The use of fire and the development of effective weapons and hunting techniques as long as fifty thousand years ago seem to account for the disappearance of many large mammals and ground-nesting birds. Thus man's skills created a predatory ability greater than the ability of the prey to recover or adapt. The slaughter of the whales is a present-day example of overkill.

The outstanding quality noted in any healthy life community is diversity. Perhaps the simplest example of this is the ecologist's biotic pyramid. Here we see the soil layer made up of minerals and organic matter and above this a plant layer. Next are layers representing insects, birds, and rodents that feed on them, and so on up through many life forms to the carnivores at the top. Each layer is less numerous than the one below it and each performs services, such as providing food, for the layers above. Moreover, the diversity of each layer grows through evolution and thus creates the stability of our universe.

Aldo Leopold used the food chain to illustrate the need to preserve this diversity. A simple example of the food chain consisted of soil, oak, deer, Indian. Of course, oak is not the only plant produced in the soil, the deer eats many more foods besides the acorn, and the Indian uses many plants and many animals besides deer. Yet eliminate any one of them and the life pyramid can collapse. So those who would preserve life must ask: "Who knows what ultimate purpose may be served by whales, whooping cranes, mountain lions, or prairie wildflowers?"

This sets us thinking about all the living things within the boundaries of our small Possum Trot world that depend on the farm for their sustenance. And we recall a distinguished soil scientist who, when he was near retirement, was asked what was the most important thing he had learned during his years. The answer came quickly. "When I was a youngster fresh from the university," he said, "we used our microscopes and estimated there must be 10 million living organisms within a cubic foot of soil. Now that I am about to put the microscope away, we know the count to be closer to a billion organisms."

Returning to Possum Trot and its population, we estimate that the number of resident species of considerable size might easily run to ten thousand, while a count of individuals would be the work of weeks for a corps of zoologists. Even to list the orders and families would be a tremendous task, for we would have to start with the protozoa of which some fifteen thousand species are known, and then work our way up through all the members of the animal kingdom.

First would come the soil fauna; the many orders and species of small creatures that live within the earth. Next would come mollusks, such as snails and shellfish; then the arthropods that include crayfish, millipedes, spiders, and countless insects. The ponds and creeks provide homes for fishes, turtles, and frogs, and there are land and water reptiles.

Not all our birds use Possum Trot as their year-round residence. But many nest here and others pass through on migration and still others come for the winter. Thus there have been days during migration when we could list a hundred species, and among these are the wild turkeys that harvest our acorns, several kinds of owls, the hawks that nest in the deep woods, and water birds like the green heron.

Finally there are mammals, both wild and domestic. The wild ones range from white-footed mice to furry-tailed wood rats, cottontail rabbits, gray and fox squirrels, chipmunks, groundhogs, opossums, raccoons, muskrats, skunks, red and gray foxes, coyotes on the hunt, and deer whose tracks we mark daily. There is even a colony of beavers here.

Habitat

The chief enemy of habitat—whether for wildlife or plants or any living thing—is people. We often have an urge to ask, "Why

Many wild mammals make their homes in the forested refuge of
Possum Trot.

do we care about habitat—the place where things live?" Is it
because we are interested in the whole community of life—or
because we want more cottontails or bobwhites or deer or smallmouth bass to harvest when the hunting and fishing seasons
roll around? Are we really as interested in creating habitat for a
rare wildflower or a Bachman's warbler as for some creature that
we can, to use the wildlife manager's expression, "reduce to
possession" and carry home in our creel or game bag?

But this is not quite fair, according to our experience with folk
who love the out-of-doors, and certainly we've done our share
of hunting and fishing. Often man is the enemy of habitat just
because there are too many of him. This we have found especially true in Latin American countries that still have birthrates
of 3.5 percent per year or even higher; and this without enough
arable land to feed their present populations. Such countries are
doubling their human numbers every thirty years or less, a condition that leaves little habitat for wildlife.

We have long felt that one serious enemy of our wildlife, both

game and nongame, can be the American farmer. This is because each year sees greater destruction on farmlands of the
habitat that lets wild creatures live, reproduce, and raise their
young to adulthood. Some of this habitat destruction could be
avoided, although the trend of today's farming is not in this
direction.

Enemies of wildlife on farmlands start with the one-crop
farming that we call monoculture, plus the drive to plow even
the marginal acres for crop production. Equally damaging is the
tremendous increase in use of poisonous herbicides for weed
control and land clearing—and of poisonous pesticides for insect control. Yet some hope may lie in the fact that as the production costs of today's agriculture skyrocket and as continued
overproduction forces prices down, we may come to saner
methods of land use.

Gradually we are learning that a casual attitude toward living
things must change. We begin to realize that diversity in nature
is all-important and that diversity really means the immense
and unending chain of interconnected living plants and creatures. We know that every living organism has developed
through evolution and is in some way essential to the health of
the whole life community.

When we look at this vast life complex with its millions of
species, we begin to understand the meaning of the word *habitat*, which we see increasingly often. Habitat, we believe, can be
defined as "place"—whether it be forest, farmland, desert, lake,
or mountaintop—where the species in question can find adequate food and shelter and where it can reproduce and raise its
young in safety. Thus we see that all wildlife populations, be
they grizzly bears or earthworms, are limited by habitat.

All creatures need certain things to make life possible, and
Possum Trot tries to provide these things for those that live
here. On a farm, you can have wild things or not, as you are
willing to encourage them or wish to ignore them. Along with
food and water, wildlife must have cover. Cover is of many
kinds; deep grass for nesting, hollow trees or creek banks for
making dens and burrows, brush piles, and a dense understory
in the woods to provide browse and shelter.

Here in our Ozark cattle-raising hill country with its grass
pastures, small fields, clear streams, and bits of woodland, we

still manage to avoid many of the "big farm" problems. Many woodlands are protected from grazing, while land in grass prevents erosion unless overgrazed. Stream banks and small wildland areas can be planted to encourage wildlife.

Last week when we went out on a fence-patching job we realized how the small farm can promote wildlife through creating habitat. A giant bur oak at the fence corner supported a colony of honeybees. Twice we stopped to remove box turtles from the tractor path. At the creek a pair of green herons took wing, and a red-tailed hawk cruised above the meadow. At the pond rim we found tracks of deer, raccoon, and muskrat. Near the woods a young coyote stood and watched for seconds before loping off toward the mountain. Thus from butterflies to wild turkeys and from bullfrogs to white-tailed deer, we've managed to build a home for a goodly number of our wild creatures.

Some years ago we made a study of land use in our United States and learned, rather to our astonishment, that the bulk of our land is still privately owned. In other words, 68.6 percent, or more than a billion acres, is in farms and privately owned forests. The remaining 31.4 percent is divided between public grazing and Indian lands, national and state parks, and forests

At the rim of our pond, we find deer tracks.

and wildlife refuges, and such uses as highways, cities, and the like.

What this means for the years ahead is that we will depend more and more on our private lands to furnish the habitat for a large percentage of our wildlife. Only the big game and large predators, migratory waterfowl, and water-dwelling mammals dominate public lands. Yet once we get away from species that may return a profit, such as the small furbearers, we begin to face problems. As human population grows and the pressure on land for food increases, acreage for wildlife habitat seems certain to shrink.

One might think we Americans were too civilized—and too prosperous even in hard times—to let these things happen. Yet the whole environmental movement that is essential to America's survival as a strong and healthy nation is under attack as never before. We can't afford, say many powerful industries and politicians, the restraints that environmentalists believe are necessary for tomorrow. Thus in 1974 the land-use bill that all conservationists had worked for went down to defeat. Wildlife felt the pressure of recession and inflation on many fronts, as it does again today.

The number of endangered species increased. Many new wildlife refuges were created but left without funds. Forest acreage declined—in our own state of Missouri by more than 1.5 million acres in the last twenty years. Here and there we find bright spots in the picture; yet the experts who chart the resource situation show a decline in wildlife potential from an overall level of sixty down to forty-seven in the past six years. We're going to have to do better than that.

Hunting

November is the Hunting Moon, and the autumn thoughts that follow here are those of an individual who, almost like Henry Thoreau, "shouldered a fowling-piece between the ages of ten and fourteen; and [whose] hunting and fishing grounds were not limited, like the preserves of an English nobleman, but were more boundless even than those of a savage." There can be no better introduction to nature than this. Yet, in the end, if we may again quote our old friend Henry, we must conclude that the hunter, "if he has the seeds of a better life in him, . . . distinguishes his proper objects, as a poet or naturalist it may be, and leaves the gun and fish-pole behind."

Thoreau pitied the boy who had never fired a gun, feeling that he was no more humane, while his education was being sadly neglected. But he also concluded that no human being past the thoughtless age of boyhood can wantonly murder any creature that holds its life by the same tenure that he does.

Fraser Darling reached the same conclusion when he said that if we accept the philosophy of respect for life, with its view that all organisms exist in their own right as fellow members with us in the world community of living things, then we must be guided by the discipline of ecological observation or become rather silly. There can be no room for "preciousness." Man is a carnivore, says Darling, and even the vegetarian must realize that he swallows countless lowly living organisms on every lettuce leaf. We tread and eat and live as men, prepared to kill if the necessity or inevitability is there, but not for fun.

It has become the fashion lately for the hunting fraternity to claim that they and they alone are responsible for all conservation effort and especially for the preservation of wildlife and wildlife habitat. The claim is made that hunting is the primary reason for game species' survival. One distinguished wildlife scientist ends a dissertation on "the morals of hunting and the ethics of hunters" by stating that even when we fail to make a clean kill and the wounded animal staggers off to die a lingering death, we have at least "saved it from a toothless old age." He quotes Xenophon that "all men who love hunting are good" and an obscure German writer to the effect that "only the mature can appreciate the joys of the kill." The good professor bemoans today's "mass participation" and admits that some hunters debase the sport. But these are few, he says, and are eager to learn sportsmanship.

But this is a controversial subject, when nonhunters stand with Albert Schweitzer, Thoreau, and Fraser Darling, while hunters and wildlife managers sneer at the nonhunters as "preservationists" and "little old ladies in tennis shoes." Teddy Roosevelt unlimbered the hunter's guns against Reverend William J. Long, whose nature books had gained great popularity.

Roosevelt called Long a nature faker and said, "I don't believe he knows the heart of wild things." To which Long replied, with justification, that "every time Mr. Roosevelt gets near the heart of a wild thing, he invariably puts a bullet into it."

As a lifelong outdoorsman, an avid angler for sixty years, and a hunter for almost a half-century, I would contest the claim that only hunters preserve wildlife and are alone responsible for wildlife survival. Good forest management in our national forests, plus fire control by state foresters on private and state lands, is largely responsible for the return of populations of deer, wild turkey, and small furbearers. Soil conservation plus the effort of farmers and private landowners helps maintain our quail and small game populations.

Even with claims such as this, we must remind ourselves that not all hunters are ethical or sportsmen, as note the number of endangered game species in America. Polar bears are shot by license-holding sportsmen from airplanes. Waterfowl in Canada and south of our border are killed by American sportsmen in large numbers. Sportsmen are hired to shoot eagles illegally from planes. Sportsmen illegally kill antelope and deer that are then stuffed with poison to kill golden eagles plus numberless coyotes, kit foxes, hawks, and other harmless creatures. And nonhunters make the fight to preserve our few remaining mountain lions, to set aside inviolate wildlife refuges with no hunting for endangered species, and to end the vicious poisoning programs carried on by the Fish and Wildlife Service. Not all the medals for conservation can go to the hunters.

In Missouri, for example, the illegal kill of white-tailed deer in and out of season probably exceeds the legal kill. Some gunners pay no attention to seasons or bag limits when there is little danger of apprehension. Others blast away at nongame and protected species such as eagles, hawks, owls, and even songbirds. In the Ozarks, a matter of status for the pickup truck driver is to display a gun or two hanging in the window behind the driver—doubtless to ward off the attack of vicious squirrels and cottontail rabbits.

Recently we read a shocking account of a sporting event carried on by one state that has a large pronghorn antelope population. Each year this state invites all fifty governors to come with their high-powered weapons to compete in their infamous

"One-Shot Antelope Killing Contest," complete with trophies. The governors are driven out into antelope country accompanied by guides who are expert hunters.

In the hunt, animals that are wounded by a governor's shot but not immediately killed are not promptly dispatched by a second "mercy shot." Instead, the wounded animals are allowed to stand, travel, or lie bleeding for hours in the hope they will die and thus qualify for the "One-Shot" trophy. Governors participating in the hunt seem to us to have a sense of sportsmanship that bodes ill for the voters as well as for wildlife.

Wildlife Managers

A sage bit of advice uttered by Will Rogers was to "buy land—because they ain't making it any more." As an investment adviser, old Will wasn't far off base. But as a practical matter, we can't always follow his advice.

Fortunately there are other ways to share in the land—at least, for recreational use—without acquiring deeds to vast acreages. One method used to excellent effect here in America has been to acquire for public ownership such properties as state and national parks, state and national forests, wildlife refuges, wilderness areas, and public waters, and to entrust their management to capable agencies.

One such agency that has the reputation of equaling any in the nation is our own Missouri Conservation Department. It was created back in 1936 when our outdoor resources were literally scraping bottom. Soil erosion, forest fires, flood and drought, overcutting and overgrazing of the timber—these had all but wiped out most species of wildlife. Many grown men had never seen a wild deer in Missouri—and wildlife experts predicted that the wild turkey was extinct as a huntable species.

All of us interested in the outdoors know that today the deer herd in Missouri probably exceeds its numbers in pre-white-man times. Back in the 1930s, we also created our Missouri national forests, where good timber management and the well-being of wildlife were part of the program. Forest fires became almost a thing of the past, and the wild turkey responded by greatly increasing in numbers. At the same time conditions improved on many of Missouri's streams.

The wild turkey has returned to Missouri in huntable numbers;
wildlife experts had predicted its extinction earlier in the century.

We would need a volume to detail the accomplishments of
our Conservation Department. But today stream fishing is starting up again. Trout hatcheries and lakes offer rich rewards to
the angler—and provide havens for many species of waterfowl.
Hiking trails, campgrounds, and stream access sites are part of
the program. Land has been acquired for upland wildlife as well
as for waterfowl and for forests and natural areas.

But the pressure of people never stops. Towns and cities
grow, highways and shopping centers cover once-good wildlife
habitat, timberland is cleared for pasture, farms grow bigger
and fencerows narrower. Yet all the time the demand for outdoor space proliferates. In the late sixties Missouri surveyed this
situation, the conservation job we were doing, and the possibilities that lay ahead. Out of this survey came a Design for Conservation and a solid plan to expand our efforts over a wide field.

The plan that was drawn up included acquisition of more
land for recreational use, for upland wildlife and for waterfowl,
for forest wildlife and for natural areas. It included plans for

lake development, for more access to Missouri's streams, for development of cold spring waters for trout. It included services to the public in many areas; in land and water and wildlife management, forest management, education, information, research, fire control.

Since all this is planned for all the people, it must be financed by all the people, not just by hunters or birders or wildlife photographers. The cost per individual is infinitesimal, but the results will probably insure that our children and their children will know something of Missouri as she was in her past.

*　　*　　*　　*

It is probably accurate to say that in our United States we have fifty departments of wildlife conservation. It is equally accurate to say that all these agencies claim, regardless of who owns title to the land, that the wildlife thereon belongs to the state.

This claim is subject to reservations, yet on the whole our citizens create the agencies and empower them to execute certain duties. These include the right to own land as state forests, wildlife refuges, and management areas; to regulate and enforce hunting and fishing regulations; to carry on wildlife research; and to develop programs for public education and information in matters relating to wildlife and natural resources.

As for the statement "the state owns the wildlife," it is convenient but tenuous. Many wild birds and animals make their homes on privately owned lands; yet there is no way the state agency can dictate how these lands should be used to encourage or eliminate wildlife habitat. Thus one owner works hard to raise game birds and animals, while another clearcuts his timber or plows his fields to the fencerow and produces no wildlife whatever. Here, obviously, wildlife is in the hands of the landowner.

However, on federal lands existing within the states, such as national parks and forests, Indian lands, and those administered by bureaus of land management and reclamation, this matter of control has never been finally determined. Thus a case that arose in New Mexico may have an important impact on the future of wildlife management by the states.

Several years ago the Wild and Free-Roaming Horse and

Burro Act was passed by Congress to manage these animals on public lands. New Mexico violated the act by rounding up and selling burros captured on public land. The federal management agency demanded release of the burros, and New Mexico sued to have the law struck down. The U.S. District Court supported the claim and declared the act unconstitutional.

This shocked conservationists because the act is clearly founded on Article IV, Section 3 of the Constitution, known as the Property Clause. This states, "The Congress shall have Power to dispose of and make needful Rules and Regulations respecting the Territory or other Property belonging to the United States." The decision was appealed to the Supreme Court, which reversed the District Court, stating, "We hold today that the Property Clause also gives Congress the right to protect wildlife on public lands, state laws not withstanding."

In other words, our public lands are held for all Americans, not for one or another special interest group; and nonexploitive values shall be preeminent over private-profit values. To be considered here are matters such as management of federal wildlife refuges often opened to hunting through state pressure, and lands along our national riverways such as the Ozark National Scenic Riverways. Here it is plain the Supreme Court specifies that "wildlife belongs to all the people."

A serious controversy between state and federal governments as to the management of fish and wildlife on federal lands involves demands made by state game authorities that National Park Service personnel and other Interior Department agencies must obtain state permits before carrying out scientific wildlife research or reduction of surplus or harmful wildlife populations in national parks and other federal areas.

A specific instance was the taking by park rangers of a number of deer in a national park to make stomach examinations of food consumed and to analyze problems of parasitism and overbrowsing. The study was expected to result in a healthier wildlife population in balance with the carrying capacity of its range. The state involved arrested the national park rangers, and the case soon attracted nationwide attention.

The actual point at issue here is the old claim, "The game belongs to the state." This concept has no sound legal foundation, even though the states manage wildlife use to a very considerable extent. The organic law creating our national parks specifically designates as one objective the preservation of wildlife unimpaired, for the enjoyment of the people. National parks are one of the few places where we can still observe wildlife in its natural habitat, unpursued by any but its natural predators. In the present controversy, however, the interests of the powerful International Association of Game, Fish, and Conservation Commissioners soon became apparent, although never specifically stated.

There has long been pressure from sportsmen to open national parks to hunting. Already our federal wildlife refuges, created as safe sanctuaries, have in too many cases become mere concentration points where waterfowl and other species may be easily killed. Thus the present national park case becomes a "foot in the door" to provide more hunting space and more revenue for the state game departments. No true legal concept is at stake here. In fact, the courts have long held that states cannot impose license requirements on federal rangers carrying out duties on federal lands.

Efforts to extend the wildlife authority of the states to include federal lands through the Congress have so far been unsuccessful. It now appears that lobbying by state game agencies has reached the top. The secretary of the interior is now promulgating a "Proposed Policy Statement on Inter-Governmental Cooperation in Respect to the Preservation, Use, and Management of Federal Wildlife Resources." This foot-in-the-door regulation, if put into effect, would literally give the states the power to control wildlife research and reduction of surplus or harmful wildlife populations, through the simple process of requiring federal agents to obtain state permits. Next step would be to harvest surpluses in national parks and federal wildlife refuges by means of special hunting licenses issued by state game departments to the public. From this to the opening of the parks and refuges to regular hunting seasons would be an easy step, and this would spell the end of wildlife preservation.

Conservation Departments and Game Managers. Who knows better than we, who love nature and spend a share of our lives in the open, the tragic rate at which wilderness vanishes and the wildlife we knew as youngsters disappears. Each year the list of endangered species grows; yet, oddly, some wild birds and animals not only hold their own but manage to increase. When we analyze this situation, we find most of these are the game species, managed intensively by our wildlife agencies for the benefit of hunters and fishermen.

Where this intensive management does not lead to artificiality in sport so that it has no true recreational value, the game managers deserve credit. Many species that they promote might soon disappear, and some have literally been brought back from near-extinction. Equally important, however, is the job these men do in preserving wild lands, restoring wildlife habitat, and teaching landowners and sportsmen that good land use can mean more of both tame and wild crops.

State organizations devoted to wildlife management generally call themselves conservation departments and their employees game managers. It seems to me that both terms have become outdated. Conservation, if it means anything, means *more* than providing creatures of air, land, and water to be shot or caught by a small segment of the recreation-loving public. And *game* takes in only a tiny portion of the wildlife that inhabits our woods, fields, and streams. Moreover, these agencies, although largely financed by license money, already do a bigger job than this. Aside from promoting game and its habitat, which creates homes for many nongame species that we do not reduce to possession with rod or gun, the wildlife agencies are interested in forestry, watersheds, clean streams, good land use, and teaching adult and youngster to appreciate and enjoy the outdoors.

The real difficulty today has to do with the complexity of modern life and the whole recreational scene. Right now if frogs and songbirds happen to benefit from good land and water management, it is pretty much an accident. If birdwatchers happen to enjoy the flight of waterfowl before or after the shooting season, this also is incidental.

The thing we see happening, then, is this. As pressures on the land increase, so do pressures on all of our wildlife—especially on those forms for which we are making no specific effort. Yet these may be just as valuable in the ecosystem, and of interest to more people than are the so-called game species. The same is true of forest lands, marshes, and prairie remnants—each supporting its myriad life forms that are part of the total natural resource.

Having always been an enthusiastic fisherman, and a hunter whose bag grew more modest as the years passed, I will always support all conservation departments. But the time has come to broaden their effort and field of interest to include the whole spectrum of nature. Instead of the old-line conservation department, devoted to raising things to catch and kill, we'd like to see more states with a department of natural resources with a responsibility to all citizens instead of just to hunters and fishermen—and with a recognition of other outdoor values besides fish and game. The shorebirds and warblers and kingfishers—the forest trees and wildflowers of prairie and roadside—the chipmunk and chipping sparrow—these are as vital to the biotic community as wild turkey and deer. Here in Missouri our Conservation Department already knows this fact.

Some Wildlife Issues

There are many issues that have come to the public eye in the last several years that have to do with the preservation of wildlife. Some have stirred a great deal of compassion among the general population. Some victories have been won on the side of wildlife by conservationists, ecologists, and others concerned with its welfare. Other problems remain.

Steel-Jawed Trapping. In 1973 our Missouri Conservation Department once again declared open season on Missouri wildlife by means of the inhumane steel-jawed leg-hold trap. One commissioner even suggested our game experts cannot allow moral issues to cloud their decisions. And once again as a humanitarian and as a former director of the Humane Society of the United States, Defenders of Wildlife, and the Animal Protective Association, we state our opposition to the steel trap open season and our abhorrence of this form of cruelty to animals.

From long experience we knew we would hear from the trapping fraternity. Yet for the first time, without even having expressed ourselves on this decision by the Conservation Department, the volume of mail asking for help to end the use of the steel-jawed trap exceeded what we generally get from the pro-trappers.

Interesting in the protrapping mail was the repeated assertion that trapped animals do not suffer. But have you ever watched an animal, wild or tame, trying to escape from a leg-hold trap? The sight is both sickening and pathetic as the animal bites, pulls, and twists frantically at the torn or broken leg, trying to free itself. Consider that this is not a matter of moments or even hours, but oftener of days of torture until death comes slowly from infection or hunger or, most mercifully, from the club of the trapper. Each year 6 million animals, many not even preda-tors or furbearers, are trapped in America for sport or profit.

You may be interested in some of the letters that came to us. One says, "Dear Mr. Hall. Often I've been tempted to write but have hated to add to your burden of correspondence. Now I must appeal to you as a conservationist and humanitarian, to once again try to do something to help end the steel-trapping of animals. I congratulate you on your stand against this senseless cruelty and am thankful for your personal stand in this grim business.

"Once again we ask that you express your sane and merciful views against this indefensible torture of defenseless creatures. Perhaps you can appeal to Christian kindness—'blessed are the merciful, for they shall obtain mercy' or other teaching of Jesus. Perhaps an appeal to intelligence—but can any user of steel traps claim intelligence? Or shame the trapper by describing once more the unspeakable torture he causes countless helpless animals.

"One can only say to these people: 'Please—in the name of God, in the name of decency and your own self-respect—spare our animals this torture of slow death! And to you, Mr. Hall, thanks for your effort."

Another writer says: "Is there any way an individual can reach through to those in authority to urge legislation to protect animal life from the torture and inhumanity of the steel trap? Do legislators ever listen to what plain people feel in this mat-ter? How can we believe that any but sadists or those few who care about nothing whatever can be for this protrapping legislation. Let's join the civilized states who have outlawed the steel-jawed trap—or does our Conservation Department listen only to those who kill for pleasure and profit?"

In a recent statement the Humane Society of the United States says, "The steel jaw trap is one of the cruelest devices ever invented by man. As its pain becomes unbearable, many animals twist or chew off their own legs to free themselves."

There is a way we can all help. We feel there is no justification for taking wild animals in traps for sport or to satisfy fashion. We know there are traps that can painlessly capture or immediately kill their victims. We can, first, join organizations that oppose the steel-jawed trap. And we can express ourselves to our governments, to the heads of our conservation departments and their commissioners, to our senators and congressmen in Washington. This is one of the ways in which we make democracy work.

Baby Seals. Every year in February and March for many centuries, the great seal herds of the North Atlantic have "hauled ashore" on the drift ice of this bitter coast, to whelp and raise their pups and to breed for next season's crop of young. And each season for the past one hundred and fifty years, fishermen have come from far-off Norway and from Quebec, Newfoundland, and the Maritime Provinces of Canada to harvest the seals, for this is a large share of their livelihood.

It would be difficult to find a harder or more dangerous mode of life than that of the sealer—and it was far worse in years past. Life in sealing ships was filthy and comfortless and subsistence was as bad. No winter passed without ships being crushed in the ice and sunk with all hands. Men died of exposure on the ice when fog rolled in. Despite radio, weather reports, icebreakers to free trapped ships, and helicopters to rescue marooned sealers, ships have often been lost in the ice on the sealing grounds.

There are two primary Atlantic seal herds. One is the harp seal herd of the Gulf of St. Lawrence, which comes ashore on Magdalen and Prince Edward islands, the west coast of Newfoundland Island, and the coast of Quebec. The other, ranging as far as Greenland, includes the larger hood seals and uses the

Labrador coast and outer islands called "The Front." This distribution of an aquatic species makes management extremely difficult.

Back in the early nineteenth century the annual kill of adult and baby seals in this whole area totaled more than one million animals of which a half-million were baby seals. This kill was probably more than the total of animals alive in both herds today, and it shows how man greedily and inevitably destroys every natural resource not protected by law. Since this kill on the outer islands continues today with no regulation except a theoretical season, it shows why the controversy surrounding baby seal killing may soon become academic. At today's rate of kill, the harp and hood seals can soon be as dead as the dodo. Canada's fifty thousand limit on baby harp seals in the Gulf of St. Lawrence is now reached in three days, and the sealers then move out to "The Front" where killing continues unchecked.

North Atlantic seals are "hair seals" without the fur undercoat that makes the Alaska seal so valuable. However, baby harp seals are born with a dense, fine, almost pure-white fur that is shed after the first week of life. Killed during this week, the pelts have a considerable value, and it is this that makes the season on baby harp seals a veritable madhouse of butchery. The civilized mind can hardly conceive it, until we remember Dachau. The Canadian director of wildlife conservation has called it "an outdoor slaughterhouse."

Several points must be made. First, the killing of the baby seals is inhumane to an unimaginable degree. Second, in criticizing our Canadian neighbors, we must consider that we killed the three-year-old bachelor Alaska fur seals in exactly the same way—by bashing in their skulls with clubs, although under better supervision. Third, we know that the butchery of baby seals results in the killing or maiming of countless adult females as they hopelessly attempt to protect their young. Fourth, there is the total willingness of American and other women to pay high prices for baby seal furs, which is largely responsible for the kill. Finally is the danger of wiping out the species—a matter as important as the slaughter and cruelty involved.

If humane Americans want to stop this butchery, and in our opinion it has continued far too long and is both degrading and savage, the campaign to the Canadian government must be waged before the baby seal killing season starts. They need time to work out compensatory measures for the low-income sealers involved. Moreover, a campaign begun in March merely guarantees a hundred thousand more dead baby seals, which are forgotten ere the next season rolls around.

Coyotes. A family of coyotes, universally though mistakenly called wolves through the Ozarks, denned and raised its young in a wooded ravine not far from our farm boundary. Both coyote parents care for the young, and once or twice while the pups were small, we glimpsed an adult loping across a nearby field in daylight. By midsummer, however, the pups were old enough to learn to hunt and the coyote family was doing their wood rat, mouse, and rabbit hunting by night.

Now and then, along about two or a bit later, Maggie will set up a tempest of barking on the back terrace where she sleeps. If I go out to quiet her, I'll hear every dog in the valley barking, and from far over against the mountain will come the wild and somehow thrilling music of the running coyote pack. It is a

A family of coyotes, mistakenly called wolves in the Ozarks, denned and raised its young in a wooded ravine not far from our farm boundary.

high-pitched series of "yip yips," rising in volume and ending in a long howl. The sound was once common at night in our hill country but is now rarely heard except by the night hunters. Most likely, as do the true wolves, coyotes "sing" for pleasure as well as for communication.

We have long found it strange how far from actual fact are many beliefs of country folk about wildlife, including the coyote. Tales about size, habits, ferociousness, and ability to kill livestock are as tall, and as far from fact, as tales told about candidates in political campaigns. The wonder is that any coyotes survive, considering that they can be hunted or trapped year round, that our Conservation Department gives them no protection, and that our legislature stupidly votes an annual bounty on them, year after year.

We are slowly starting to learn, in these days of shortages of wildlife, land, energy, and even good red meat, that man lives in an ecosystem made up of countless related plant and animal forms. We must also learn that most of these play their necessary parts in the healthy functioning of the ecosystem that insures our survival. Thus we spray with poisons that persist in the environment and start chain reactions of disaster. In like manner we eliminate all so-called predators in a given environment with resulting explosions of animal, insect, or plant populations more harmful to our interests than the predators.

Consider our surviving coyotes. Their diet is mainly of animal food and their hunting is probably 85 percent beneficial to man. This diet consists largely of wood rats, moles, mice, rabbits, and other wild animal food—alive or dead. They thus serve to keep rodent populations in check and they are also scavengers. They eat the old, the weak, the sick and injured, as well as dead animals. If chickens roost outdoors, poultry may provide 5 percent of the coyote diet. Domestic livestock, including the injured, sick, or dead, may total 8 percent of the total food, although most livestock losses in our country are caused by free-running or feral dogs.

Now and then coyotes do become livestock killers. Missouri has an excellent plan for elimination of such predators through an on-the-farm training program for trapping individual animals causing damage. Aside from this, since the coyote is not an endangered species and most coyote killing is done in the name of sport, we should class them as game animals to be protected except during a specified hunting season.

We believe that everyone who enjoys the outdoors should become something of an environmentalist, whether we hunt or not. We should learn the value of birds of prey and of so-called predators like the coyote, in the healthy functioning of their ecosystems. Instead of this, in the case of our coyote family here in the valley, we have every hunter and alleged sportsman waiting eagerly for the day when the pups are big enough to warrant the bounty payment. Then the coyote family will be wiped out in the name of sport.

Beavers. There are certain sounds in nature that never fail to give us a thrill. Among these are the melody of the first wood thrush of the season, the spring song of the garden toad, the wild call of the pileated woodpecker as he wings across our valley, the ventriloquil chorus of a coyote family out on the hunt, or the loud report of the beaver's tail as he heads upstream toward his den with a willow branch for his larder. This last sound was missing at Possum Trot for several years, until we discovered two new beaver dams as we explored Saline Creek.

We are glad to see these interesting animals fairly well established again as a Missouri wildlife species. Prior to the Civil War they were common on all of America's major watersheds, with a continental population estimated at 60 million animals. Trapping and land-use methods that destroyed their habitat, however, cut their numbers until by the beginning of this century only a few colonies remained in the northwestern part of our state.

In the late 1920s our Conservation Department secured a half-dozen pairs of beavers from farther north and released them along the upper Missouri River. Much of today's population has resulted from this planting. Meanwhile a few of the river colonies grew and migrated up and down the Missouri, while a few colonies apparently moved into the Ozarks from the west. By 1939 the Conservation Department had started a regular program of livetrapping the animals in the heavily populated areas and releasing them in other suitable localities.

Unlike the big beaver colonies of the marshlands and sluggish

Beaver dams have been built along Saline Creek in recent years. Bark is the staple of the beaver's diet.

streams, our beavers live in bank burrows along even our swift, clear creeks. But the colonies are small, limited by the available food supply, and thus the big houses that we associate with beaver colonies are both impractical and unnecessary. One of the first successful stream plantings was made back in the 1940s by our good friend Buck Hornkohl, now retired from the U.S. Forest Service. This was made on Spring Creek in the Carman Spring Wildlife Refuge in the Mark Twain National Forest.

The problem here was to get the newly planted animals to settle down, instead of scattering along the stream and failing to establish a colony, and this is the plan Buck developed. A sizable trench was dug back from the bank, with the mouth of the trench underwater. A good supply of willow branches and other beaver food was stored in the trench, which was then

There may be places within the continental range of beavers where their dams can cause damage through flooding. On the whole, however, bank-dwelling beavers in Missouri probably do more good than harm.

roofed over with earth and branches to make a tunnel. The beavers were then released in the trench and sealed in.

The animals stayed until their food supply was eaten up, after which they burrowed out into the creek; and by this time the burrow seemed like home. Their next step was to build a dam at the lower end of the pool, which soon deepened so that the beavers had a place to store their winter food supply. This happened to be primarily willow, with perhaps a bit of cottonwood, these being two of their favorites.

We found this process already taking place above our two small dams on Saline Creek. Some green saplings were being towed in and stored at the burrow mouth. Bark being the staple of the beaver's diet, when the branches had been stripped, they were floated down to reinforce the small dam that is a combination of rocks, gravel, and small tree trunks and branches. Incidentally, some of the food material may be brought in by land, and we found well-established paths into the woods from the edge of the creek.

There may be places within the continental range of the beavers where their dams can cause water problems such as the flooding of valuable hay and grazing lands. Even here in Missouri an occasional bank may be cut to start erosion. On the whole, however, our bank-dwelling beavers probably do more good than harm by creating pools that help slow down the streams during periods of high water.

Peregrine Falcon. For several years Tom Cade of the Cornell Laboratory of Ornithology and his assistants have been working to save the magnificent peregrine falcon, or duck hawk. This bird has been brought close to extinction throughout its range in the United States by the pesticide DDT, which makes the eggs infertile and the shells too soft to endure until hatching and renders the male birds incapable of mating.

Work done by the scientists is supported by The Peregrine Fund, which, from a small start, has grown to $175,000 per year with facilities at Cornell and Ft. Collins. Now in its seventh year, the fund has enabled the scientists to raise a total of 229 young peregrines and to introduce 133 of these birds into the wild. This is no easy task, since in most cases new eyries must be built and the young birds made accustomed to the new quarters.

As might be expected, losses of the young birds are still heavy. Every effort is made to determine the causes, and the two most serious are predation by great horned owls and shooting. The most curious case is probably that of a New Jersey pigeon hunter who shot a young falcon that carried both Fish and Wildlife and Cornell leg bands and also a tail-mounted radio transmitter. The hunter kept the bird in his freezer for a year, then had it mounted complete with decorations. The case was reported, and New Jersey eventually collected a two-thousand-dollar fine, which was given to The Peregrine Fund.

Appreciating Wildlife

Country is most enjoyed in our maturity, we believe, by those who have had some background of childhood experience. In my case it was Grandpa Hall's farm outside Potosi, and the wisdom he imparted on outdoor and agricultural matters when, as a youngster, I rode behind him on his old saddle mare as he made the rounds of his country patients. As for Ginnie, it was the country place just outside St. Louis that provided an orchard, a vineyard, and a vegetable garden—never forgotten during the years of her career in New York.

My own education in conservation and wildlife matters began a good deal longer ago than those we talk of today. Back in the Dust Bowl years we came to know Hugh Bennett, who made America's first soil erosion survey, organized the Soil Conservation Service, and with it saved the farm and grazing lands of the Great Plains. Along about that same time we explored the Irish Wilderness with Chief U.S. Forester Lyle Watts.

Two Missourians we came to know especially well during those days were soil scientist William Albrecht and ecologist Rudolf Bennitt, who headed the Wildlife Unit at the University of Missouri. At an early North American Wildlife Conference where we spoke, we first made friends with Aldo Leopold, Clarence Cottam, and Ira Gabrielson—giants in the fields of ecology and wildlife management. Then at an early conservation conference down in Springfield, we spent four hours on the train back home forming a fast friendship with the great cartoonist "Ding" Darling, who was then head of our Biological Survey, which preceded the Fish and Wildlife Service.

There was a day along about then when I came in from plowing to find Durward Allen of Purdue University at the kitchen table having coffee with Ginnie. Durward directed early research in predator-prey relationships and none was more famous or valuable than that of the wolf-moose study on Isle Royale National Park. It was in those same years that an organization called Friends of the Land gained national recognition and importance and brought us the lasting friendship of Louis Bromfield.

There were other friends of those years: Chester Davis, the conservationist-president of our St. Louis Federal Reserve Bank;

ecologist Paul Sears of Yale, who wrote *Deserts on the March*; William O. Douglas, who had lately become a Supreme Court justice; Jesse Stuart of the Kentucky mountains; Missouri ecologist Alfred Etter; and Russell Lord, whose editorship of *The Land* made it America's leading conservation voice.

This experience was actually a conservation college, without campus or formal degrees but with a faculty it might be impossible to muster today. It taught us that the decades ahead would surely see revolutionary developments in the whole area of land use and wildlife preservation.

Somehow our proximity to our wildlife, when we come in from the day's work, sets us thinking whether a word of thankfulness and appreciation for our birds and animals, both wild and tame, might not be appropriate as the year draws to a close. Certainly these have added much to the pleasure of living and no less because we have lived with them while doing them no harm.

Our Western culture has always had a mixed-up attitude toward animals, carrying a belief that our mission is to conquer the earth and all things that live thereon. Perhaps it would be well to turn for a touch of humility to scripture, and we read in Ecclesiastes: "For that which befalleth the sons of men befalleth beasts; even one thing befalleth them: as the one dieth, so dieth the other. Yea, they have all one breath; so that a man hath no preeminence above a beast; for all *is* vanity."

Epilogue

Our book opened a dozen chapters ago with the harvest moon of autumn. Now the countryside is green again—and in our fields and woods we find the first bluets, bloodroot, and bluebells. The martins circle their houses with cheerful chatter, and all day long we hear the song of meadowlarks and mating notes of black-capped chickadees as they explore their nesting boxes.

Because we are basically farmers, it is fitting that we should have chosen our title from the Roman agriculturalist Vergil, whose "Georgics" was perhaps the greatest country poem of antiquity. Yet we must add a word for old Hesiod, whose "Works and Days" is the true dirt farmer's poem. Written twenty-seven centuries ago in far-off Boeotia, it is filled with enough toil to make your bones ache.

It seems remarkable to us that farming has produced a continuous and worthwhile literature through all the centuries—from Horace and his Sabine Farm a few miles from Rome, to Thoreau and his field in Walden wood not far from Concord. There his garden, if we may believe him, measured seven miles of bean rows.

Yet Walden was as far from old Hesiod's labor as it was from those elegant English country houses, from one of which, in the summer of 1750, Horace Walpole wrote to a friend: "I beg of you, write often. This will be my only entertainment since I neither plant, hunt, brew, drink or reap."

But the country has compensations that were never better put than by Aldo Leopold in his *A Sand County Almanac*. He said, "There are some who can live without wild things, and some who cannot. . . . Now we face the question whether a still higher 'standard of living' is worth its cost in things natural, wild, and free. For us of the minority, the opportunity to see geese is more important than television, and the chance to find a pasque-flower is a right as inalienable as free speech."

Somehow through the years it has been our aim to put all these values together. There has been the labor of a working farm, the care of our livestock, the building of the life-carrying capacity of our few acres. But there has also been appreciation of the beauty of the country scene, of wildflowers and wildlife—and the effort to achieve something of Thoreau's cheerful philosophy.

Perhaps most important of all has been absorbing Leopold's belief in man's ethical relationship to land—which leads to love and respect and a high regard for its value in a philosophical, rather than an economic, sense.

So we have written of country life and farm labor and our domestic animals—but also of the value of nights under canvas and of wildflowers and of wilderness and all the wild things that inhabit it. It is all these things together that have created the "Earth's Song" of our title.

Index